CROSS-BORDER NETWORKS IN WRITING STUDIES

INKSHED PUBLICATIONS

Inkshed is an imprint for works of Canadian scholarship about writing, reading, and learning. More information about Inkshed Publications can be found at the Inkshed blog, http://www.inkshed.ca/blog/inkshed-publications/.

INKSHED BOOKS

Cross-Border Networks in Writing Studies by Derek Mueller, Andrea Williams, Louise Wetherbee Phelps, and Jennifer Clary-Lemon (2017).
Genre Studies around the Globe: Beyond the Three Tradition, edited by. Natasha Artemeva and Aviva Freedman (2015).
Writing in a Community of Practice: Composing Membership in Inkshed by Miriam Horne (2012).
Rhetorical Genre Studies and Beyond, edited by Natasha Artemeva and Aviva Freedman (2006).
Writing Centres, Writing Seminars, Writing Culture: Writing Instruction in Anglo-Canadian Universities, edited by Roger Graves and Heather Graves (2006).
Critical Moments in the Rhetoric of Kenneth Burke: Implications for Composition by Martin Behr (1996).
Integrating Visual and Verbal Literacies, by W. F. Garrett-Petts and Donald Lawrence (1996).
Writing Instruction in Canadian Universities by Roger Graves (1994).
Two Sides to a Story: Gender Difference in Student Narrative by Jaqueline McLeod Rogers (1994).
Contextual Literacy: Writing Across the Curriculum, edited by Catherine F. Schryer and Laurence Steven Jaqueline McLeod Rogers (1994).

CROSS-BORDER NETWORKS IN WRITING STUDIES

Derek Mueller, Andrea Williams,
Louise Wetherbee Phelps, and Jennifer Clary-Lemon

Afterword by Andrea Lunsford

Inkshed
Edmonton, Alberta
http://www.inkshed.ca/blog/

Parlor Press
Anderson, South Carolina
www.parlorpress.com

Parlor Press LLC, Anderson, South Carolina, USA
© 2017 by Inkshed.
All rights reserved.
Printed in the United States of America on acid-free paper.

SAN: 254-8879

Library of Congress Cataloging-in-Publication Data on File

1 2 3 4 5

978-1-60235-922-2 (paperback)
978-1-60235-923-9 (hardcover)
978-1-60235-924-6 (PDF)
978-1-60235-925-3 (ePub)

Copyeditor: Jared Jameson.
Cover design by Derek Mueller.

Parlor Press, LLC is an independent publisher of scholarly and trade titles in print and multimedia formats. This book is available in paper, cloth and eBook formats from Parlor Press on the World Wide Web at http://www.parlorpress.com or through online and brick-and-mortar bookstores. For submission information or to find out about Parlor Press publications, write to Parlor Press, 3015 Brackenberry Drive, Anderson, South Carolina, 29621, or email editor@parlorpress.com.

Contents

Acknowledgments   *vii*

1 Becoming Networked, Cross-Border Scholars:
   Sources and Development of the Project   *1*
   *Derek Mueller, Andrea Williams, Louise Wetherbee
   Phelps, and Jennifer Clary-Lemon*

2 Emplaced Disciplinary Networks from Middle Altitude   *20*
   Derek Mueller

3 Voicing Scholars' Networked Identities through Interviews   *46*
   Andrea Williams

4 Four Scholars, Four Genres: Networked Trajectories   *81*
   Louise Wetherbee Phelps

5 A Case-Study Approach to Examining Cross-Border Networks   *123*
   Jennifer Clary-Lemon

6 Conclusion   *148*
   *Derek Mueller, Andrea Williams, Louise Wetherbee
   Phelps, and Jennifer Clary-Lemon*

7 Afterword   *179*
   Andrea A. Lunsford

Index   *185*

About the Authors   *195*

Acknowledgments

This book is a collaborative work beyond having four co-authors. Surveys and interviews generated much of our data, so we would like to thank the many people who completed the surveys and participated in the interviews. The following scholars generously shared their time, stories, and insights in interviews: Natasha Artemeva, Doug Brent, Rick Coe, Jay Dolmage, Aviva Freedman, Roger Graves, Dale Jacobs, Lorelei Lingard, Anthony Paré, Margaret Procter, Dan Richards, Cathy Schryer, Ron Sheese, and Graham Smart. We thank Aviva Freedman, Jim Reither, Sharon Hamilton, and Cathy Schryer for graciously providing biographical materials and responding to questions. We also appreciate Ian Pringle's and Janice Lauer's help with research: Ian searched his garage for conference materials and shared memories of his collaborations with Aviva Freedman, while Janice provided information on Canadian participation in the Purdue Seminar. We are grateful to scholars at the University of Rhode Island willing to share their work and materials, as well as those at the University of Winnipeg who shared their memories of the birth of the program.

We are also grateful to Andrea Lunsford for her invaluable contribution to the early development of Canadian writing studies and for writing the response.

We owe thanks to Roger Graves for suggesting at the Writing Research Across Borders Conference 2014 conference that we publish our research as a book. We would also like to thank the Inkshed editorial board, along with David Blakesley, who has given this book a wider audience by co-publishing it with Parlor Press.

We would like to acknowledge the University of Winnipeg and Eastern Michigan University for contributing funds for the editing and indexing of this book. We thank Jared Jameson for his meticulous copyediting and Jo-Anne Pelissier for her indexing.

1 Becoming Networked, Cross-Border Scholars: Sources and Development of the Project

Derek Mueller, Andrea Williams, Louise Wetherbee Phelps, and Jennifer Clary-Lemon

It's always a bit arbitrary to pinpoint the origin of a project or piece of writing, but our cross-border collaboration began with Jennifer Clary-Lemon's initiative to bring Louise Wetherbee Phelps from the US to the University of Winnipeg as a Fulbright Specialist Scholar in the spring of 2011, to consult and collaborate with the Department of Rhetoric, Writing, and Communications on a vision for its future development. Winnipeg's anomalous history in Canada as a longstanding independent writing department with an American-style first-year program and a major in rhetoric and communications made this cross-border consultation especially appropriate. Based on Louise's work on the Visibility Project seeking recognition for rhetoric and composition as a research field in American higher education (Phelps and Ackerman, 2010), Jennifer's proposal envisioned that the project could not only inform the department's own strategic planning but also promote greater visibility and agency for writing studies as a discipline in the Canadian academy. Jennifer, herself a dual citizen with an American doctorate, emphasized the potential for cross-border conversations to use complementary strengths and develop the field both nationally and internationally.

> "The project's outcome will be . . . one of the only existing attempts at co-constructing knowledge about a North American (rather than simply American) concept of writing studies, drawing on the strength and history of the development of the field in the United States, and the innovation and initiative of fledgling programs in Canada." (Clary-Lemon, Fulbright proposal)

1

To further these goals, part of Louise's commission was to research various contexts for understanding the department's history, character, and potential future: a local perspective, situating it in the university, the city of Winnipeg, and the region; a comparative perspective, placing its curriculum in the landscape of Canadian instructional programs in writing and rhetoric and, contrastively, undergraduate and graduate programs in the US; and a field perspective, examining the department in the context of discourse and writing studies as a still-emerging scholarly field in the Canadian academy, interlinked with US rhetoric and composition and contributing to international writing studies. To fulfill this charge, Louise read widely in Canadian scholarship on writing and rhetoric, including publications by faculty at Winnipeg; studied websites and writings on Canadian programs; and interviewed several Canadian scholars at other institutions by phone and Skype. She was particularly informed by Jennifer's own inventory of Canadian scholarship (Clary-Lemon, 2009), the first to survey Canadian research and publication in writing studies as distinct from instructional programs. This article examined how the Canadian field is historically rooted in the themes of location and national culture, expressing a tension between Canadian independence and dependence on the US field, with more recent research such as the new genre theory exemplifying a more hybridized North American scholarship rather than one defined in opposition to "rhetoric and composition" in the US.

> *"Canadian scholarship has shown itself as loyal to its historical themes of location and national culture . . . ; yet at the same time, there are, and must be, hybrid systems that blend the best research and practice of North America, as dual citizens and Canadians with American rhet/comp PhD specializations enter the picture."* (Clary-Lemon, 2009, p. 105)

After Louise completed her report (Phelps, 2011), it was taken up by the Department of Writing, Rhetoric, and Communications as a starting point for curricular revision at Winnipeg (discussed in chapter 4). The following spring Jennifer, Louise, and other Winnipeg faculty (Judith Kearns, Jaqueline McLeod Rogers, and Tracy Whalen) presented a roundtable at the Conference on College Composition and Communication ("4Cs") on the Fulbright collaboration (March, 2012). Their session, "Cross-Border Collaboration in Charting a Department's Future: Toward a North-American Conception of Rhetoric and Writing Studies," placed the project's cross-border conversations in the context of an "evolving, convergent, (inter)disciplinarity in North American rhetoric and writing studies," which in turn was being integrated into an increasingly interdisciplinary and internationalized field of writing studies (4Cs roundtable proposal, 2011).

Shortly before meeting at 4Cs that year, Louise and Jennifer exchanged emails about building on this work to develop a proposal for the 2014 Writing Research across Borders (WRAB) international conference in Paris. Louise also contacted American scholar Derek Mueller about joining the group, suggesting that they could use his methodological skills to study Canadian scholarly networks. She was inspired by a 4Cs presentation on the Writing Studies Tree, a visual, crowd-sourced map of the genealogy of American scholars that was being built by some City University of New York (CUNY) graduate students. Wondering how the Tree might be extended or emulated to map Canadian scholars, Louise thought immediately of Derek, a former student at Syracuse University who had been pursuing his interests in "distant" methods, mapping, and visualization of data since graduate school. Derek and Louise contacted the CUNY team about working together on this project, but despite strong interest from graduate student Ben Miller and the faculty leader of the project, Sondra Perl, plans for combining forces and developing correlated proposals for WRAB in Paris didn't work out. Instead Derek went forward with his own mapping project, using survey data (see chapter 2). However, as we worked toward our own plans and methods for exploring scholarly networks, we remained inspired by the CUNY team's pioneering project to look at scholarly networks, in part, through the lenses foregrounded in the Tree: person-to-person relations (genealogical/mentoring; collegial/co-location); and person-to-institution relations (educational; workplace).

Meanwhile, at the invitation of Canadian scholar Doug Brent, Louise was preparing a keynote talk for the Canadian Association for the Study of Discourse and Writing (CASDW) conference in May, 2012 in Waterloo, Ontario. At his request, she drew together lessons from her Winnipeg studies to compare the struggles for disciplinary recognition in the United States for rhetoric and composition to those in Canada for discourse and writing. Responding to Canadian writing scholars' ambivalence about their "pushme-pullyou conflict with American sites and conceptions of rhetoric and writing" (Clary-Lemon, 2009, p. 97), Louise suggested deconstructing and reconstructing this historical binary between dependence and independence so that "the Canadian discipline need not think of itself any more as defined either by imitation or opposition" to US writing studies (Phelps, 2014, p. 17). This movement toward a conception of Canadian-US interdependence, foreshadowed by Jennifer in her article and the Fulbright proposal, echoed in the Winnipeg roundtable at 4CS, and taken up by Louise in this address, shaped our ongoing planning for the research project we would propose for the WRAB conference in Paris.

> "We sort of zeroed in on the idea of focusing on the interdependence of American (US) and Canadian writing studies—mutual influence, partnerships, cross-fertilization through graduate education—within a framework of difference. It seemed that we are playing with a set of polarities: independence/interdependence, disciplinarity vs. academic identity, disciplinarity vs. diffuse interdisciplinarity, plus methodologies at different scales." (Email from Louise to Derek and Jennifer on planning the proposal)

Louise's reading for her CASDW talk included Randall Collins's *The Sociology of Philosophies* (2000), which offers a global theory of how intellectual networks operate to develop, debate, and circulate ideas, emphasizing the synchrony of thought and social relationships. His essential insight, that intellectual activity is a flow of ideas among people energized and informed by their engagement with one another, reinforced the interest we shared in exploring scholarly networks, especially genealogical ones, as a way of understanding how disciplines form, develop, and sustain themselves.

These experiences, meetings, readings, and interchanges all fed into our proposal for the 2014 WRAB conference in Paris as we began putting it together in February, 2013, now including Andrea Williams, a Canadian scholar and writing program administrator who had met Louise at the CASDW conference. Andrea would add an interview-based qualitative study to what we were now thinking of as a multi-methodological study of "interdependencies and cross-pollination between Canadian and U.S. writing studies" (proposal for WRAB 2014). Our methods would use different scales of description, ranging from "distant to close," to describe the role of transnational networks in shaping and sustaining writing studies in both countries. Collectively, we would gather data through surveys and interviews of Canadian scholars that all of us could draw on; individually, we would employ methods including data visualization, digital mapping, qualitative analysis of interviews, case study, and historical and textual inquiry.

After working on these research goals interactively over the next year, we came away from the Paris conference with a plan for co-authoring this book, which in many respects fulfills our original goals but has also evolved in ways we couldn't have foreseen.

You may wonder why we have told this story of how we got together, planned this project, and came to put our work together in this collaborative book. It's not special in any way—most co-authors or co-editors of books in our field have had similar experiences. They seldom detail the process for readers, wonder what makes it possible, or examine how it works. It's taken for granted, along with all the features of disciplinarity (for example, conferences) that we recognize as "professional" but seldom study to find out how they actually afford intellectual activity. In fact, making all that visible is one point of our study. In tracing this history, we see the kinds of affordances for, and examples of, the very intersection of intellectual and social relations that we set out to identify and study in this project:

> *"In this symposium a team of two Canadian and two U.S. researchers will combine methodologies at different scales of description to demonstrate the vital role of transnational networks in shaping and sustaining writing studies in both Canada and the United States. These studies, challenging the common trope of Canadian writing studies developing in opposition to its U.S. counterpart, explore an array of reciprocal relationships: genealogy, partnership, adaptation of model, mentorship, mutual presence."* (Proposal for WRAB 2014)

- co-location of scholars in the same place (graduate school, a consultancy)
- mentorship, beginning with genealogical relations (senior to junior) and then evolving to mutual mentorship in the context of collegial relations and collaboration
- collaborating on research, on publication, on curricular review and revision
- connecting one another to other scholars in extended scholarly networks (for example, the process by which we identified Canadian scholars to survey and interview)
- reading one another's published writing
- connecting through common organizations
- attending (cross-border) conferences: meeting to discuss projects, hearing one another's presentations, presenting together
- referring each other to scholarly ideas and texts

- using technologies like Skype, email, and Google Docs to work together and keep in contact.

In other words, this history introduces us as networked, cross-border scholars, a microcosm of what we are studying. We are Canadians and Americans, insiders and outsiders to one another's scholarly communities and cultures, different generations, from different institutions. We brought to this project different but overlapping inspirations, histories, knowledge bases, methods, and home contexts. The book in its final form reflects the evolution of both goals and methods through the reciprocal influence of our different roles and contributions to the project. Most importantly, we have increasingly knitted them together into blended, coordinated, and complementary—"networked"—methods for understanding the development of disciplines, ideas, and scholars in terms of scholarly networks.

A Networked Methodological Approach

Our study of Canada-US writing studies interdependencies enacts what we identify as a "networked methodological approach." We consider this approach novel because it applies network logics to the design and execution of a collaborative, mixed methods research project. This "networked methodological approach" is influenced by disparate theoretical insights from network studies. Generally, network studies provide theoretical perspectives useful for attending to fluid structures of activity and relationships that may be articulated through links and nodes or simple, granular models of complex phenomena. Counter to isolating phenomena at too narrow or bounded a scope or, on the other hand, relinquishing a tightly-delineated scope to comparably baggy and inclusive references such as *community* or *field*, our use of *networks* for this research circumscribes the work with principles of delineated but flexible interconnection (i.e., locating connections that operate between and among differing methodological distances) and discernible granularity at scale (i.e., forms of evidence appropriate to a suite of methodologies, operating in concert).

Our reference to *networks* in this approach acknowledges a well-established, extensive tradition involving considerable topical and methodological variation where interconnected, complex phenomena are concerned. Social Network Analysis (SNA) has been widely adopted in quantitative sociology for more than three decades, offering greater technical precision in both *modeling* and *measuring relationships* among links and nodes (Wasserman & Faust, 1994). By contrast and with a far greater emphasis on tracing non-obvious connections using field *observation* and descriptive *accounts*, Actor-Network Theory (ANT) has influenced numerous studies that draw upon network vocabulary as researchers seek to follow human and non-human actors, from science and technology studies (see Latour, 1996) and interdisciplinary field studies in forest ecology (see Latour, 1999) to political philosophy (see Latour, 2004) and urban infrastructure (Winner, 1986; Woolgar & Cooper, 1999). Still other research on networks has framed them as a way to *explain* material and organismic phase transitions, or shifts at a moment of criticality from seeming chaos to pattern or order (Strogatz, 2004; Barabási & Frangos, 2002; Buchanan, 2003). Yet more network studies research has been used to *theorize* tensions between a rising technocracy and educational reform (Taylor, 2003) and to examine contemporary sociocultural power relations (Castells, 2009; Benkler, 2007; Galloway & Thacker, 2007). Although this is by no means a comprehensive gloss, it sufficiently locates a rich backdrop of network-oriented adaptations for inquiry and scholarly research, pointing toward the ways in which network logic encourages a methodological range of modeling, measuring, observation, analysis, narrativizing, and theorizing.

> "Network studies generally have established that phenomena observable at one scale of activity are not necessarily observable or structurally equivalent at another scale. For instance, patterns of cross-border activity in which Canadian scholars complete BAs and MAs in Canada are demonstrable only on a local, anecdotal level, unless we ask the question . . . using a large-scale survey and distant readings methods to visualize the cross-border pattern of activity. Such a large scale and distant study, however, proves insufficient for helping us grasp the micro-level influence of a brief consultation visit from a U.S. scholar to a Canadian university." (Book prospectus)

Recently and more proximate to the domain of writing studies, Swarts's entry in *Keywords in Writing Studies* (2015) differentiates network as a noun from network as a verb, noting that networks emerge as "settings in which new kinds of literate information gathering, processing, and composing practices emerge" (p. 121). It is in this sense of co-location and connection that our carrying out of related, coordinated methodologies manifests, as an interdependent, orchestrated—and thus "networked"—series of operations. That is, each methodology, highlighted chapter by chapter, is tied to and intertwined with each other's methodology. To ground our thinking about these ties and intertwining, Gochenour's "Nodalism" (2011) has been helpful for its articulation of networks as a structural metaphor that keys on nuanced structural attunement. This attunement is most apparent in cooperative modeling, in which part and whole function more smoothly together because of their being doubly constituted as nodes and as elements in an integrated system (para. 23–24).

The most apt synthesis of networks relevant to our methodological approach stems from Spinuzzi's *Network* (2008), which through its focus on workplace studies offers a definitional orientation to networks and simultaneously recognizes their methodological promise at the intersection of activity theory and Actor-Network Theory, a "synchretism" (p. 197) of grounded description and pragmatic, problem-solution exploration. Spinuzzi argues that networks share four characteristics: they are heterogeneous, multiply linked, transformative, and black-boxed. We find these principles harmonious with our interdependencies research in the following ways:

1. Networks are *heterogeneous*, Spinuzzi explains, because they are "constituted through relationships or associations among elements" (p. 198). For Spinuzzi as for us, these relationships are dynamic, only ever achieving relative, temporary stability. In the context of our studying Canada-US interdependencies for writing studies, this might refer to the relocation of a survey respondent from one location to another; the network of associations fluctuates accordingly, and this type of change is constant.

2. Networks are *multiply linked*, and this is achieved through what Spinuzzi terms weaving and splicing (p. 198). Weaving refers to the development of relatively stable parts of a network over time, whereas splicing refers to branching that converges as new interaction. For this study of Canada-US interdependencies, this has been realized methodologically as weaving in our coordinated efforts to have, for example, the survey results inform the interview questions, and, in turn, to have outreach for interviews cycle back into new survey results. In terms of splicing, a networked methodological approach operates as multiply linked in the discovery of unplanned convergence, such as when an interview informs

a closer-up perspective on a smaller selection of maps developed from the survey's geolocative data.

3. Networks are *transformative*. Spinuzzi discusses this quality in terms of circulating representations, that a network "must represent and reprepresent phenomena in various ways, often conflicting ways" (p. 199). Representations and re-representations are constituted among the people, texts, narratives, identifications, institutions, and locations detailed in the study. The mélange of representations coheres around questions of interdependence, yet the assortment of evidence answers to interdependency with considerable variation. The network transforms as these representations and re-representations circulate, and our work has, as it evolved, participated in that transformative endeavour.

4. Networks yield "*black boxes*", which means they subsume and eventually obscure constitutive qualities that would be too complex to revisit with description or examination. That is, black boxes reduce complexity by replacing complex qualities with satisfactory stand-ins. This is represented in our work by survey and interview questions that center on nation-based identification. As Spinuzzi attests, black boxes "emerge from historically developing activities" (p. 199)—in this case, citizenship activities that asked respondents to identify themselves along a contained and historicized North-American boundary. Yet Spinnuzi also notes that these boxes "take a lot of work to achieve and maintain" (p. 199), and these complexities came to light as scholars discussed their nation-based identification in greater and more varied detail in the interviews.

In addition to these principles introduced by Spinuzzi, what we frame here as a "networked methodological approach" adds a fifth principle: networks afford and also therefore obligate researchers to *multi-scale and multi-scopic consideration* of the assemblage. This resembles Spinuzzi's point about transformation insofar as it considers materially circulating representations; however, this additional principle introduces deliberate, purposeful considerations of scale (distance versus close) and aperture (wide versus narrow). Much like Johanek's (2000) argument that we must systematize inquiry in order to contextualize research in the service of both flexibility and multidisciplinarity (p. 207), we suggest that one focus of research—here, the historic development and movement of Canadian and US writing studies scholars across the North American border that frame *interdependence*—may be better understood with "network sense" (Mueller, 2012) developed by mixed methods. Our individual chapters embrace different scales and different lenses in studying interdependence as both node *and* element, part *and* whole.

> "The methods drawn together in this study are themselves interwoven, connecting across the multiple scales to 'bring networks out of hiding' (Latour, 1993) across different scales of activity. . . . The methods themselves form a systematic inquiry, operating as interdependently as the Canada-U.S. influences the study brings to light as a whole." (Book prospectus)

Chapter 2, "Emplaced Disciplinary Networks from Middle Altitude," written by Derek Mueller, posits its approach at the greatest distance, inquiring into relationships among survey respondents and the geographic locations they identify with. This chapter emphasizes the notion of network heterogeneity in terms of a *person-geolocation* nodal connection. The chapter's use of interactive maps assumes a broad scale and wide scope to attend to patterned movement, particularly for the critical mass of Canada-based writing studies scholars who have taken up doctoral programs of study in the US before returning to Canadian universities. In tandem with the maps, the chapter presents summary findings from a survey concerned with geolocation and professional identification. These low-touch, distant methods work together to engage non-obvious phenomena in an attempt to get at the big picture of cross-border interdependencies, and provide a broad back-drop to the research featured in other chapters.

Andrea Williams's chapter 3, ""Voicing Scholars' Networked Identities through Interviews," shifts to a slightly closer-up scale and narrower aperture in its interview-based methodology. In focusing in on *person-to-person* nodal connections in a network frame, the methodological emphasis here is on showing the multiply linked, relational aspects of a network, as well as the narrative representation and re-representation of conflicting perceptions of intellectual communities, such as the varied interpretation of organizations and conferences like the 4Cs, Inkshed/CASSL, and CATTW in creating and maintaining professional identities. In addition to tracing shifts in individual scholars' identities, this chapter explores the different kinds of institutional hubs where Canadian scholars have clustered and their relation to the discipline in Canada and internationally. The interview-based methodology and thematic narrativizing of insights from the interviews both complements and intersects with the methodologies featured in the other chapters.

Chapter 4, "Four Scholars, Four Genres: Networked Trajectories," by Louise Wetherbee Phelps, focuses even more tightly than chapter 3 on the networked individual, profiling the careers of four Canadian scholars to illuminate their participation in social networks over time and space. But it introduces a new element to our concept of networks by pairing each scholar with a genre, using their writings in these genres to trace their overlapping interpersonal and intertextual trajectories through multiple contexts. Beginning with the nodal connection of *person-to-text* (often already *person-to-person* through co-authorship or co-editing), chapter 4 expands the aperture to encompass layers of historical and contemporaneous connections among persons, places, institutions, organizations, events, texts, and documents, emphasizing the multiply linked and transformative notions of the network. By including genres whose functions in mediating disciplinarity have been overlooked, chapter 4 examines relationships among genre, transnational scholarly identity, and presence that can't be explained by indices and citation analysis, with a view to challenging traditional disciplinary accounts and histories.

In chapter 5, "A Case-Study Approach to Examining Cross-Border Networks," Jennifer Clary-Lemon adopts the most localized of the methodologies featured in the study. In examining the University of Winnipeg's movement from intrinsic to instrumental case study, chapter 5 focuses in on a *person-locale* nodal connection. Clary-Lemon explores interdependencies from an institutional locale, comparing centrifugal and centripetal influences in the circulation of disciplinary influence into and out of a single institution. This chapter also highlights the transformative element of a networked approach by attending to the ways one networked locale illustrates the concept of interdependency over time and in conflicting ways.

In the conclusion to this volume, chapter 6, we draw together the insights gleaned by examining the concept of Canadian-American interdependencies in writing studies from the multiple scales and perspectives taken up in our individual chapters. Here, we collectively examine what kinds of "black-box" knowledge the survey, interview, and case-study data, taken together, provide in allowing researchers to manage, filter, and make sense of the complexity presented by doing multi-scopic work. In acknowledging nodal links among people, geolocations, documents, and locales, this chapter enacts the balancing work of interdependency as a black box: on one hand, stabilizing the interface of what we know about transnational scholarship; on the other, recognizing that that stability is always partial and temporary.

Taken together, we see the coordinated studies in our book as constituting a new methodological approach to multi-scopic forms of inquiry into one subject, serving our purpose of examining the contemporary and historical networks of Canadian writing studies as they have emerged in the last half-century.

The Role of Cross-Border Scholarly Networks: Canadian Writing Studies as a Case Study

According to Clary-Lemon's 2009 study of Canadian writing research, "disciplinarity—its representation in terms of research publication, graduate programs, professional organizations, and field expertise—was a late arrival in Canada" compared to the field's development in the US, where professionalization accelerated in the 1980s (p. 99). Two reasons often cited for this delay are the nationalist rejection of an American model of composition by Canadian departments of English and the absence of a universal first-year writing course. As a result, the field was—and is—still struggling to emerge in Canada, as reflected in the limited number of publication venues and professional organizations, and, especially, the dearth of PhD programs to educate new scholars. Despite strengths in particular areas of research, the field in Canada has lacked a "central organization, convention, or conference that unites the interests" of writing studies scholars and had trouble achieving a common sense of identity (p. 96). Although undergraduate programs have grown slowly, without an institutional base like that provided by the American first-year writing requirement, Canadian writing studies programs have developed as "ad hoc structures, contingently funded and located," making their faculty and programs vulnerable to shifting conditions (Phelps, 2014, p. 6). Phelps describes the dilemma facing the Canadian discipline thus: "It is difficult to compose a nationally viable identity [for writing studies] around practices of instruction that are so decentered and disparate, lacking common pedagogical philosophies, habits, formats, or students" (p. 7).

The lack of visibility of writing studies in Canada is also tied to funding and disciplinary structures, which in turn influence hiring practices, all of which inform academic identity. In Canada, most university research is funded at the federal level where it is administered by three major agencies: the Social Sciences and Humanities Research Council, the Natural Sciences and Engineering Council of Canada, and the Canadian Institutes for Health Research. Although some provinces and private foundations also fund university research, such funding varies hugely by region and discipline and is far less common than federal funding. In fact, when new faculty are hired at research institutions in Canada, not only are they expected to apply for federal research grants, but their ability to secure such funding usually plays an important role in promotion and tenure decisions. However, the federal granting agency where faculty researching writing and rhetoric apply, the Social Sciences and Humanities Research Council, does not yet have a category for writing studies, which poses a considerable impediment to researchers in the field, including graduate students. (In the US, between 2004 and 2010 scholars successfully lobbied to add categories for rhetoric and composition/writing studies to several higher education databases used by government and private agencies for multiple purposes, including grant eligibility [Phelps and Ackerman, 2010]).

In addition to funding barriers to research, hiring practices are another way that writing studies scholars are marginalized in Canada. Many writing specialists, if they are fortunate enough to secure permanent positions, are hired into the growing number of teaching-intensive appointments, where they lack the status of their colleagues in the research-stream (Vajoczki, Fenton, Menard, & Pollon, 2011) and are either discouraged or prohibited outright from applying for research grants or unable to do so because of their heavy teaching loads. Yet scholars in such teaching-focused appointments are generally more visible than the writing specialists who work in writing centres, who are increasingly hired into less secure staff (rather than faculty) appointments where they are seldom supported or given credit for research and are vulnerable to administrative whims. The vulnerability of Canadian writing scholars who work in writing instruction outside of academic areas is taken up by MacDonald, Procter, and Williams (2016) and was the focus of a session at the 2015 Conference of the Canadian Association for the Study of Discourse and Writing, one of the field's emerging central organizations in Canada.

Clary-Lemon's focus on themes of location and national culture in her (2009) taxonomy of Canadian writing research points to a distinctive preoccupation with geography and space/place, both literal and metaphorical, in what she calls its "scholarship of definition." All the cultural factors cited so far have contributed to the decentralization of writing studies in Canada, in the scattered, isolated, and often transitory location of its heterogeneous sites for instruction and, even more, in its rare assemblages of writing scholars. But geography has played a principal role, both in the decentralization of writing studies and in the crucial role of cross-border relations in developing Canadian scholars and an intellectual community around writing studies. Canada's enormous landmass and relatively small population (thirty-five million), which is concentrated along the US border (at almost nine thousand kilometers it is the longest international border in the world), means that for many Canadian scholars their closest colleagues at other universities are in the US rather than Canada. Another divisive factor is language, for although the nation is officially bilingual, Canada's French and English populations are starkly segregated geographically, with most parts of the country either predominantly francophone (such as Quebec and parts of New Brunswick, Ontario, and Manitoba) or anglophone (like most of Western Canada) rather than the languages co-existing in the same regions. Clary-Lemon shows how these institutional and geographical factors have prompted many Anglo-Canadian scholars to do doctoral studies and to professionalize in the US rather than in Canada. This strong north-south rather than east-west orientation, which Clary-Lemon traces, has important implications for cross-border scholarly networks, as we recognized in designing our study.

> *"Canada's unique geography, conflated by its largest cities' and universities' close proximity to the US border, contributes to a fractured professional identity both aligned and in tension with that of the United States." (Clary-Lemon, 2009, p. 97)*

In her CASDW address in 2012, Phelps (2014) analyzed the situation of the Anglo-Canadian field of discourse and writing in terms of the role played by social networks in forming and sustaining a discipline as a productive locus of intellectual activity, which she distinguished from academic identity, "an intellectual network in its public persona, as it is projected, legitimated, and treated by others as disciplinary" (p. 9). Like Clary-Lemon, she emphasized location and culture in shaping both disciplinarity and the ability to gain recognition for an emergent field within a national academy.

A networked understanding of disciplinarity draws attention to how historical, geographical, institutional, and linguistic conditions can facilitate or hinder networks, informing how scholars understand and conceive of both their individual academic identity and the intellectual communities to which they belong. For example, the fact that Anglo-Canadian scholars share a common language with their US-counterparts provides an additional incentive for networks to develop along a north-south rather than an east-west axis that would connect Anglo-Canadian and French-Canadian writing instruction and studies.

Phelps (2014) uses the notions of *territoire*, place "in and of the academy," and *terroir*, "the way all the elements of a particular environment combine to make a product like wine unique to its place," to analyze the historical formation of Canadian writing studies (p. 14). Such an ecological understanding of place is useful in accounting for the influence of local conditions on institutional nodes for scholarship and instruction, which she did in her contextual study of the University of Winnipeg:

> "A discipline is an ad hoc, opportunistic accomplishment, an assemblage rather than an intentional construction, no matter how many scholars try to define and determine it. Disciplines are open networks, self-organizing and constantly on the edge of chaos. Intellectual communities, because of the way they work through competition and argumentation, tend to be internally diverse and fractured and to move through cycles of division and merger. Networks are constantly in the process of being assembled, disassembled, and reassembled at different scales, for different purposes, and on different principles of commonality."
> (Phelps, 2014, p.10)

> The way it grows in a particular place [is] a unique expression of the totality of how its local network interacts with and responds to that environment—its geography and demography, financial resources, the university's mission, ethos, and themes, institutional structures and sites for its work, other disciplines it works with, and so on (p. 14).

But a networked framework for our project helps us examine how intellectual activity and scholarly identities can transcend the purely local *territoire*, by linking individuals and their small networks in layered ways into larger ones. After all, although scholars are rooted in their local contexts, they often derive their intellectual energy and identities from their networked connections to people, texts, institutions, organizations, and events that may be far from their home *territoire*.

As we will show here, the connections between different *territoires*, both within and across national borders, are both spatial and temporal, for as scholars relocate geographically they nonetheless maintain connections to people they have known and to places they have previously inhabited. The multiple methods used in this book trace these complex interactions among place, identity, and community (whether rooted in a local *territoire* or a more symbolic one such as a disciplinary organization).

> "It is important to understand the complex ways that individuals, in becoming enculturated into a discipline, form their own professional identities through their participation not only in intellectual communities of practice—often more than one—but also in multiple other activity systems. I am particularly interested in the emotional investments people make when they identify with intellectual networks as disciplinary and draw emotional energy for creative work from their interactions." (Phelps, 2014, p. 10).

It is in this respect that we believe Canadian writing studies can serve as a case study that exemplifies the kinds of factors—cultural, economic, geographic, and linguistic, for example, or the organizational structure of a national academy—that inform whether and how such networks arise and successfully establish writing studies in particular countries and regions at particular historical moments and periods. Despite its own distinctive history and geography, we suspect that the field of Canadian writing studies shares many conditions with other countries, such as its distributed and fractured institutional location in a hierarchically structured academy that excludes and renders both writing and writing studies invisible, and the consequent challenges of securing tenure-track positions and research funding.

By offering Canada as a case of how local conditions and cross-border relations can both facilitate and hinder the development of disciplinarity and academic identity, we hope that our coordinated studies will provide insights for understanding parallel processes, obstacles, constraints, and enabling factors in other countries. We are interested in the affordances of border crossing for disciplinarity, particularly in the case of disciplines that are still struggling to achieve academic identity, as in the case of Canadian writing studies, and how such efforts can be supported by transnational networks. Canada's shared border and common language with the US (at least for Anglo-Canadians), along with its relatively similar cultural traditions to the US, invites consideration of how such collaboration might work across borders that are both more and less geographically removed as well as culturally and linguistically porous. At the same time, we believe that by looking at the histories of writing studies in Canada and the US as intertwined, rather than discrete, our study will prompt revisionist historical studies that "complicate and challenge the conclusions drawn by more general earlier histories" (Gold, 2012, p. 16).

In the spirit of transnational disciplinary inquiry, then, we hope that both the data and the mode of inquiry offered here will be useful to a wide range of scholars doing disciplinary invention, historiography, and program development in writing studies not only in Canada and the US but also in their own national and cultural contexts. As Bazerman, et al. (2010) showed, there is rich work going on worldwide in writing studies that engages a wide variety of approaches, emphases, communities, and perspectives. What the work of international writing studies researchers have in common, however, is that each international context must necessarily respond to its local and specific circumstances—and we hope that the Canadian case that we showcase here offers a useful glimpse into the complexities of building and professionalizing a discipline. For as Phelps (2014) argued, although disciplines may be international, academic identity, because it is rooted in funding and institutional structures, is national, and can be strengthened by cross-border connections.

> "While 'the academy' is now globalized, it still matters for intellectual networks, if they are to operate practically as communities, that they have a primary base and identity in their own country's educational system, its national academy" (Phelps, 2014, p. 9).

Finally, although this project studies networks not for their own sake but because disciplines are formed and sustained by means of the connections among scholars, we hope that the design of this study will interest writing studies scholars working with mixed method approaches to research, as well as those working collaboratively with multi-scaled or multiscopic data. Our purpose here is to both engage in and model what Fleckenstein, Spinuzzi, Papper, and Rickly (2008) term an ecological orientation to research projects that embrace "research diversity: multiple sites of immersion, multiple perspectives, and multiple methodologies within a particular discipline and research project" (p. 401) and that honour the boundaries of traditional methods while learning to re-invent and blur such boundaries in response to rhetorical constraints (see also Rickly, 2012). Thus we believe our work here offers a model and a view of the kinds of research called for in twenty-first century writing studies by scholars such as Gesa Kirsch (1992), Anne DiPardo and Melanie Sperling (2004), and John Law (2008), who speak to pluralistic and rhetorically rigorous—but "messy"—methods of research design and data collection.

References

Barabasi, A., & Frangos, J. (2002). *Linked: The new science of networks*. Cambridge, MA: Perseus Books Group.

Bazerman, C., Krut, R., Lunsford, K., McLeod, S., Null, S., Rogers, P., & Stansell, A. (2010). *Traditions of writing research*. New York, NY: Routledge.

Benkler, Y. (2007). *The wealth of networks: How social production transforms markets and freedom*. New Haven, CT: Yale University Press.

Buchanan, M. (2003). *Nexus: Small worlds and the groundbreaking science of networks* (Reprinted ed.). New York, NY: W. W. Norton & Company.

Castells, M. (2009). *The rise of the network society: The information age: Economy, society, and culture volume I* (2nd ed.). Chichester, West Sussex; Malden, MA: Wiley-Blackwell.

Collins, R. (1998). *The sociology of philosophies: A global theory of intellectual change*. Cambridge, MA: Belknap.

Clary-Lemon, J. (2009). Shifting tradition: Writing research in Canada. *American Review of Canadian Studies, 39*(2), 94–111.

DiPardo, A., & Sperling, M. (2004). Editors' introduction: Toward complementarity. *RTE, 38*(3), 245–247.

Fleckenstein, K., Spinuzzi, C., Rickly, R., & Papper, C. (2008). The importance of harmony: An ecological metaphor for writing research. *CCC, 60*(2), 388–419.

Galloway, A. R., & Thacker, E. (2007). *The exploit: A theory of networks*. Minneapolis, MN: University of Minnesota Press.

Gochenour, P. H. (2011). Nodalism. *Digital Humanities Quarterly, 5*(3). Retrieved from http://digitalhumanities.org/dhq/vol/5/3/000105/000105.html

Gold, D. (2012). Remapping revisionist history. *CCC, 64*(1), 115–34.

Johanek, C. (2000). *Composing research: A contextualist paradigm for rhetoric and composition*. Logan, UT: Utah State University Press.

Kirsch, G. (1992). Methodological pluralism: Epistemological issues. In G. Kirsch and P. Sullivan (Eds.), *Methods and methodology in composition research* (pp. 247–269). Carbondale, IL: Southern Illinois University Press.

Latour, B. (1996). *Aramis, or the love of technology*. Cambridge, MA: Harvard University Press.

Latour, B. (1999). *Pandora's hope: Essays on the reality of science studies*. Cambridge, MA: Harvard University Press.

Latour, B. (2004). *Politics of nature: How to bring the sciences into democracy*. (C. Porter, Trans.). Cambridge, MA: Harvard University Press.

Law, J. (2004). *After method: Mess in social science research*. New York, NY: Routledge.

MacDonald, B., Procter, M., & Williams, A.L. (2016). Integrating writing into the disciplines: Risks and rewards of an alternative independent writing program. In J. Everett and C. Hanganu-Bresch (Eds.), *A Minefield of dreams: Triumphs and travails of independent writing programs*, Fort Collins, CO: The WAC Clearinghouse. http://wac.colostate.edu/books/minefield/chapter5.pdf

Mueller, D. (2012). Views from a distance: A nephological model of the CCCC chairs' addresses, 1977–2011. *Kairos: A Journal of Rhetoric, Technology, and Pedagogy, 16*(2). Retrieved from http://kairos.technorhetoric.net/16.2/topoi/mueller/index.html

Phelps, L. W. (2011). *Liminal practice in a maturing writing department*. (Unpublished Fulbright Project Report).

Phelps, L. W. (2014). The historical formation of academic identities: Rhetoric and composition, discourse and writing. Keynote address, Canadian Association for the Study of Discourse and Writing, Waterloo, ON. (2012). *Canadian Journal for Studies in Discourse and Writing, 25*(1), 3–23. Retrieved from http://journals.sfu.ca/cjsdw/index.php/cjsdw/article/view/37/22

Phelps, L.W., & Ackerman, J. (2010). Making the case for disciplinarity in rhetoric, composition, and writing studies: The visibility project. *CCC, 62*(1), 180–215.

Rickly, R. (2012). Making sense of making knowledge. *CCC, 64*(1), 224–237.

Spinuzzi, C. (2008). *Network: Theorizing knowledge work in telecommunications*. Cambridge, MA: Cambridge University Press.

Strogatz, S. H. (2004). *Sync: How order emerges from chaos in the universe, nature, and daily life*. New York, NY: Hachette Books.

Swarts, J. (2015). Network. In Heilker, P., & Vandenberg, P. (Eds.), *Keywords in writing studies* (pp. 120–124). Logan, UT: Utah State University Press.

Taylor, M. C. (2003). *The moment of complexity: Emerging network culture*. Chicago, IL: University of Chicago Press.

Vajoczki, S., Fenton, N., Menard, K., & Pollon, D. (2011). *Teaching-stream appointments in Ontario universities*. Higher Education Quality Council of Ontario. Retrieved from http://www.heqco.ca/SiteCollectionDocuments/Teaching-stream%20Faculty%20in%20Ontario%20Universities.pdf

Wasserman, S., & Faust, K. (1994). *Social network analysis: Methods and applications*. New York, NY and Cambridge, ENG: Cambridge University Press.

Winner, L. (1989). *The whale and the reactor: A search for limits in an age of high technology*. Chicago, IL: University Of Chicago Press.

Woolgar, S., & Cooper, G. (1999). Do artefacts have ambivalence? Moses' bridges, winner's bridges and other urban legends in S&TS. *Social Studies of Science, 29*(3), 433–449.

2 Emplaced Disciplinary Networks from Middle Altitude

Derek Mueller

> *Can a person visit a country yet never set foot upon it? Does an airplane journey across a territory entitle the traveler to claim that "he has been there"?*
>
> —William I. Fox, *Aereality: On the World from Above*

The following chapter advances contributions positioned methodologically as the most distant among the four approaches featured in this book. This portion of the broader study relies on low-touch research methods, such as data visualization and digital cartography, to gain initial perspective on matters of transnational interdependencies in writing studies. Generally, such methods are suited to gaining perspective on aggregate activity that would not otherwise be observable because the activity is scattered or dispersed unevenly or too broadly in space or time. Distant methods are applied extensively in other fields to bring to the surface non-obvious phenomena, and thus they may adapt well to disciplinary research questions about the continuing growth and maturation of writing studies. The as-distant-as-possible opening inquiry that follows *surveys* Canadian writing studies in two distinct but complementary senses: first, as a means of collecting responses to a uniform set of questions circulated among Canadian writing studies scholars (i.e., inviting responses to a survey) and second, as a systematic process of plotting scholarly activity as it occurs across a vast terrain (i.e., mapping both as attendant to physical geography and, figuratively, as concerns a varied epistemological landscape). Before delving into the chapter's twin applications of surveying, however, a brief accounting for Canada's physical geography is warranted because it establishes an orienting backdrop for understanding conditions underpinning the country's still-evolving disciplinary geography. Following this geographic sketch and situating distant methods as an important first step for defining, or lending shape to, disciplinarity, the chapter turns in its second section to an annotated synopsis of results from a survey of 111 Canadian writing studies scholars, followed by a more refined, granular exploration of patterns in the career paths of the 55 respondents to the survey. That is, the third section of the chapter plots onto a series of three maps the geolocations of career activity as a way to investigate cross-border patterns and related mentorship networks. I refer to this definitional treatment involving maps and geolocations using the phrase *indexical aereality* because, while on the one hand its purpose is to seek out a unique perspective available from middle altitude (i.e., a *high-flying* bird's-eye view), it is also among the limited number of cases in which disciplinary geographies have been plotted onto scalable, interactive digital maps. *Indexical aereality* approximates a fly-over logic, ways of thinly getting acquainted with basic qualities of disciplinary activity in Canada. Finally, based on the exploratory maps of career activity, the concluding portion of the study extends two different approaches taken with the career-path maps to theorize about value—as a model of disciplinary formation—in conceiving of a scholarly career as simultaneously emplaced and distributed. This final turn focuses on Dale Jacobs from the University of Windsor as its illustrative case while also demonstrating the significance of modest adjustments in scale for research that begins at the most distant, zoomed out perspective available.

Physical Geography, Disciplinary Terrain

Human and cultural geographers have since the 1970s theorized, studied, and demonstrated in case upon case the intricate relationship between physical and social geography (Harvey, 2001; Wood, 1992; Wood, 2010; Soja, 2011; MacEachren, 2004). Mindful of the well-documented intersections between space, place, and cultural activity, several accounts of Canadian writing studies provide context for the country's disciplinary footprint, likewise acknowledging a linkage between the country's massive, out-stretched landscape, the population centres and the universities they host, and the consequences of being separated by hundreds of kilometres from other scholars who identify disciplinarily (Graves & Graves, 2006; Coe, 1988). For example, Roger Graves's (1993) account of composition in Canadian universities notes a total of 87 universities operating across the country; among 61 of the institutions surveyed in that study, more than three-quarters of them were located in the 6 easternmost provinces (Ontario, Quebec, Newfoundland and Labrador, Prince Edward Island, New Brunswick, and Nova Scotia), a measurable Atlantic-coast-leaning that corresponds to the population distribution reflected in the 2011 census (Government of Canada, n.d.). Approximately 23 million of Canada's 33.5 million people reside in these same provinces. Across all 10 provinces (i.e., territories notwithstanding), Canada's population density (persons per square km) averages 8.8, whereas the population density in the United States was 33.8 as of 2010 (Mackun & Wilson, 2011). For the expansive Canadian landscape and the scholars who work there, modern telecommunications platforms have established relatively new means for connecting with colleagues at a distance, as the survey responses reflect later, though the point of this brief sketch is that Canada's vast physical geography has bearing on disciplinary formation and the methodologies best for initial inquiries into such widely distributed activity. The inquiry that follows begins with distant methods because they provide an aperture adequate for initial inquiry into such an immense terrain.

Defining Disciplinary Activity: Essences, Differentiation, and Shape-Finding

Over the past two decades, traditional accounts of research by writing studies scholars have documented, and thereby lent visibility to, disciplinary activity in and across Canada. In "Shifting Tradition: Writing Research in Canada," Jennifer Clary-Lemon (2009) retraces several such studies and characterizes one cluster of them as fitting with "scholarship of definition," which "seeks to name and define a Canadian context of teaching, writing, and research" so as to "carve out a space uniquely [Canadian] in in a landscape dominated by American practices" (p. 99). According to Clary-Lemon's review of numerous books and articles, these studies reflect distinct, varied circumferences, from highly localized characterizations of curricula, programs, and institutions (Turner & Kearns, 2002 and 2012; Graves & Graves, 2012) to comparably broad-based, encompassing narratives about regional or multi-institution activity, often around an issue such as writing across the curriculum and writing centres; professional writing, technical writing, and workplace writing; or genre studies. Scholarship of definition is, as Clary-Lemon explains, necessary for establishing ways of understanding distinctly Canadian factors affecting disciplinary emergence and maturation. And while the graphs and maps that follow qualify as scholarship of definition, I am interested in their operating differently than has been common in previous definitional scholarship. To put a finer point on this difference, consider definitional scholarship as dividing into three predominant pursuits: fixed essences, contrastive differentiation, and shape-finding.

Definition toward fixed essences seeks to settle what something is unto itself (e.g., Canadian writing studies is x); definition toward contrastive differentiation, which is likewise useful for apprehending disciplinary knowledge, marks out qualities by comparison (e.g., Canadian writing studies is x relative to writing studies elsewhere). The twin applications of surveying featured in this chapter, however, offer definition a third, more exploratory sense: definition toward shape-finding. My objective has been to create a series of graphs and maps that not only add to definitional scholarship but also complicate definition pursuant to essences or differentiation because disciplinary formation is continuing, yet-emerging. The shapes and patterns will continue to shift, change. The data visualizations and digital maps featured in this chapter offer telescopic perspectives on Canada-US writing studies interdependencies that stand in service of shape-finding, or inquiry that should continue to be revisited, updated, or inquired into yet again. As the design of this book and the broader study it conveys presumes, no one scale or method of inquiry is singularly adequate for grasping such a complex, distributed phenomena as a disciplinary network, much less even this modest slice of an emerging network that spans several decades, several thousand kilometres, and more than two countries. Inquiring into patterned activity at any one scale can tell us something that is not evident at any other scale. Through the deliberate alteration of scale, this opening segment of the project seeks to define Canadian-American writing studies interdependency from perspectives that are yet uncommon; it seeks to introduce a viewshed for graphical, distant, and aerial treatments of disciplinary activity that may contribute to a definition concerned less with fixed essences or contrastive differentiation than noticing time-sensitive patterns and emerging shapes.

Survey of Canadian Scholars

The study opened with an eleven-question survey designed to inquire into three general classes of information related to transnational interdependencies between Canada and the United States. Questions 1–4 addressed locations associated with professional activity. Questions 5–8 considered involvement with organizations, conferences, listservs, and publishing. And questions 9–10 provided limited-option responses on the geographic reach of publishing and self-identification. Lastly, the survey invited respondents to provide a CV as an attachment, if one was available. The survey's design took into account Roger Graves's (1994) study of the ways writing instruction is organized in Canadian universities, yet the overlap is limited, and as such we consider this instrument to feature an original, unique set of questions that have not been circulated in any other disciplinary survey to date.

SURVEY QUESTIONS

1. Where are you from?
City, Province or City, State

2. From what institutions did you obtain the following degrees (as applies)?
BA or BS
MA or MS
PhD
Other
Please specify degree.

3. Where do you currently live and how long have you been there?
City, Province or City, State; x years, x months

4. What is your current (or most recent) academic teaching, research, or administrative appointment?
Please include the name of the institution.

5. What professional organizations do you belong to?
List up to five.

6. What conferences do you attend most frequently?

7. What professional/disciplinary listservs do you subscribe to?

8. Which journals and presses (including both print and online) have you published in and do you consider the most amenable to your scholarship?

9. Please indicate the geographic circulation/reach of the journals and presses you identified in the previous question.
Primarily Canada
Primarily U.S.
North America
International

10. Do you see yourself primarily as a Canadian scholar, an American one, something in between, or something else?
Canadian scholar
American scholar
Something in between
Something else
Please briefly explain your response to question 10.

CV UPLOAD

11. Would you be willing to provide your CV? If so, please attach the document.

Our team distributed the survey to a list of scholars that the four of us compiled together—scholars who work at Canadian universities; who studied at both Canadian and American institutions; and who, based on scholarship, citations, or informal connections, we believed to identify professionally with writing studies, rhetoric and composition, or professional and technical communication. To begin, the original roster consisted of 112 scholars. We were unable to locate email addresses for 11 prospective respondents, and, working with the best collection of addresses available, 6 more emails were returned as undeliverable after we circulated the survey the first time. Four prospective respondents replied to ask that they be removed from the distribution list, citing disidentification with the disciplinary frame or apprehensions about the survey's identifying respondents by name (see the maps in the following section). Thus, after smoothing the roster, 91 scholars were invited to complete the survey. Holding the survey open for approximately 10 weeks, from November 20 to December 18, 2013, and May 1 to June 12, 2014, we received 55 responses. The 60.44% response rate this survey received is markedly higher than the benchmark of between 20–30% typical for surveys initiated via email.

The following discussion of the survey responses proceeds from the last question to the first because the initial questions about locations associated with professional activity are directly applicable to the maps presented in the following section. Across the questions and responses, a portrait of the fifty-five scholars gradually becomes clearer, such that the responses confirm complex Canada-US interdependencies interwoven in myriad ways throughout professional, scholarly activity and identifications.

Questions 9–10: Geographic Reach of Publishing and Self-Identification

Question 9 inquired into the geographic reach of publishing activity. Nearly half of the respondents (25, or 45.5%) selected North America, and just over a quarter (15; 27.2%) answered International, which was the most encompassing among the four choices. Identifications primarily with Canada (5; 9.1%) and the US (8; 14.5%) were significantly fewer, which suggests a recognition that the circulation of scholarship exceeds national boundaries and that a clear majority of respondents think of their scholarship as operating more broadly than either Canada or the US, alone.

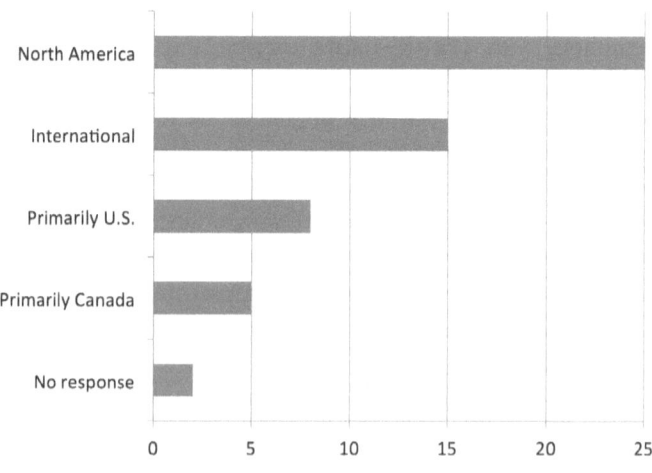

Figure 1. A horizontal bar graph presenting compiled survey responses for the geographic reach/circulation of journals and presses.

North America: 25 / 45.5%
International: 15 /27.2%
Primarily US: 8 / 14.5%
Primarily Canada: 5 / 9.1%
No answer: 2 / 3.6%

Question 10 asked about how participants regarded themselves, as a Canadian scholar, an American one, something in between, or something else. A close plurality of respondents selected Something in between (22; 40%) or Canadian (20; 36.6), with Something else (10; 18.8%) and American (2; 3.6%) receiving fewer selections. This indicates a mixed but balanced quality among the ways the respondents identify as emplaced scholars, and the tension elicited here shows up in other questions, too, which suggests a complex, transnational self-understanding among Canadian writing studies scholars.

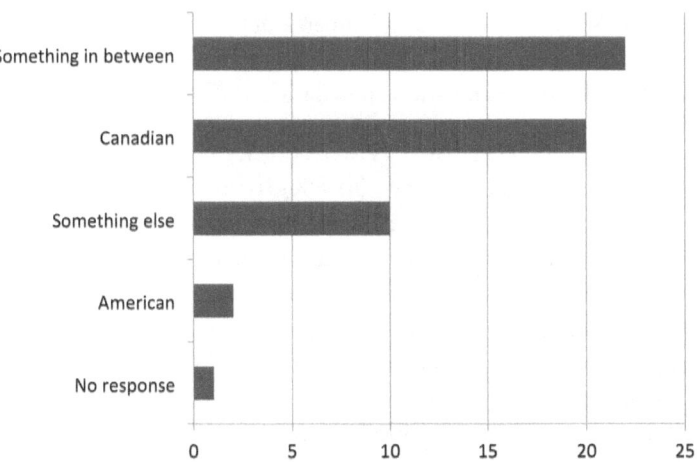

Figure 2. A horizontal bar graph presenting compiled survey responses for identification as a Canadian scholar, an American one, something in between, or something else.

Something in between: 22 / 40%
Canadian: 20 / 36.6%
Something else: 10 / 18.8%
American: 2 / 3.6%
No answer: 1 / 1.8%

Questions 5–8: Involvement with Organizations, Conferences, Listservs, and Publishing

Question 5 invited open-ended answers about memberships in disciplinary organizations. Collectively, respondents referred to 67 organizations, with twelve receiving mention by at least four respondents:

Canadian Association for the Study of Discourse and Writing (CASDW): 25
National Council of Teachers of English (NCTE): 25
Conference on College Composition and Communication (CCCC): 21
Rhetoric Society of America (RSA): 12
Canadian Association for the Study of Language and Learning (CASLL): 10
Canadian Writing Centres Association (CWCA): 7
Canadian Society for the Study of Rhetoric (CSSR): 6
Modern Language Association (MLA): 6
Inkshed (also known as CASLL): 4
Council of Writing Program Administrators (CWPA): 4
Association of the Rhetoric of Science & Technology (ARST): 4
The National Communication Association (NCA): 4

In addition to those listed here, responses noted 55 more organizations. Twenty-three respondents (41.8%) listed organizations appearing *only* among the 12 shown above. Twenty-three more respondents (41.8%) mentioned either one or two organizations in addition to the ones listed above. Six respondents did not mention any organization among those listed. This points to a relatively high density in the open-ended responses; a locus of leading organizations, with 5 of the 12 (41.6%) based in Canada, recurred with high frequency in the responses. Notably, responses to this question also hint at a problem of anachronism in organizational naming practices related to the timespan of careers. Inkshed was rebranded as CASLL, and respondents identified the organization both ways, a likely indicator of both names resonating depending on one's relationship to the organization and the timeframe corresponding to that relationship.

Question 6 attended to conferences, and answers included several acronyms appearing in question 5, as well, which is to be expected considering how common it is for scholarly organizations to sponsor annual conferences.

Conference on College Composition and Communication (CCCC): 24
Canadian Association for the Study of Discourse and Writing (CASDW): 20
Rhetoric Society of America (RSA): 10
Inkshed: 6
Canadian Congress: 5
Computers and Writing (CW): 4
International Writing Across the Curriculum Conference (IWAC): 3
Canadian Society for the Study of Rhetoric (CSSR): 3
Society for Teaching and Learning in Higher Education (STLHE): 3
Association of the Rhetoric of Science & Technology (ARST): 3
Canadian Writing Centres Association (CWCA): 3

Beyond the 11 leading conferences, respondents noted 42 additional conferences, each receiving 1–2 references. Twenty-one respondents answered with conferences showing up entirely in the 11 listed here. Forty-eight responses had at least one reference to a conference in the top 11; seven respondents had none. Canada's geographic expansiveness bears mentioning again in the context of this question considering that half of the top mention-getting conferences, CCCC, RSA, and Computers and Writing, have never been hosted in Canada.

Compared to organizations and conferences, the focus of question 7, listservs, has a far lower threshold for participation. Respondents noted 75 listservs, with the following 10 receiving three or more mentions:

CASDW-L: 23
CASLL-L: 13
WPA-L: 10
H-Rhetor: 8
CWCA: 7
WAC-L: 4
Techrhet: 4
CSSR: 4
ATTW: 3
wcenter (IWCA): 3

Similar to questions 5 and 6, 23 respondents referred to listservs appearing exclusively in the list above, whereas 28 respondents noted one or more listservs beyond those listed. Four respondents answered "none" or declined to answer. While one might speculate about the important function of electronic communication fostered by listservs to be an impactful presence in boosting a sense of connection among Canadian writing studies scholars, the survey does not substantiate this speculation. Responses support the conclusion that a clear majority of respondents subscribe to disciplinary listservs, many of which are affiliated with Canadian organizations, and yet one respondent's noting parenthetically "I hardly read any of them" offers an important caveat, reminding us that subscribing to listservs does not necessarily equate to participating actively as a reader or writer. Nevertheless, although the conferences' respondents mentioned are predominantly American, the prominence of listservs oriented toward Canada and Canadian organizations appears to be a distinctive counterpart for sustaining professional and disciplinary interactions across distances.

Question 8, on publishing activity, elicited the most varied set of responses because the question asked both about journals and presses, and about actual and prospective publishing activity. Total responses included 239 items. The coding schema sifted the responses into 97 unique journals, 27 unique presses, two newsletters, and one conference proceeding. The following lists indicate journals mentioned by at least three respondents and presses mentioned by at least two respondents.

Journals

College Composition and Communication (CCC): 16
Written Communication (WC): 13
Rhetoric Society Quarterly (RSQ): 7
College English (CE): 6
Journal of Business and Technical Communication (JBTC): 6
Canadian Journal for Studies in Discourse and Writing (CJSDW): 5
Rhetoric Review: 5
Technical Communication Quarterly (TCQ): 5
Composition Studies (CS): 4
Present Tense (PT): 4
Enculturation (ENCULT): 3
JAC (JAC): 3
Kairos: 3
Technostyle (now CJSDW): 3

Presses and Publishers

Parlor Press: 5
Inkshed: 4

Routledge: 4
WAC Clearinghouse: 3
Boynton Cook: 2
Lawrence Earlbaum: 2
NCTE Press: 2
Sage: 2
Taylor and Francis: 2
Utah State UP: 2

A distinctive American orientation in both lists further contextualizes the prevalence of North American identification with publishing activity from Question Nine. Each list includes just one Canada-based publishing venue, *CJSDW/Technostyle* among the journals, and Inkshed among the presses. Online journals (*Present Tense* and *Kairos*) reflect a receptiveness to contemporary delivery formats, and the comparably high number of mentions for Parlor Press, WAC Clearinghouse, and Inkshed indicates, as well, that open access publishing is as prevalent as proprietary and paper-based publishing. *Present Tense*, which was inaugurated in 2009 as an online journal for medium-form scholarship, is the newest of the journals and publishers mentioned.

Questions 1–4, 11: Locations associated with professional activity

The first three geography-oriented questions confirmed that over 70% of the respondents are from Canada, completed a BA or BS in Canada, an MA or MS in Canada, and live and work in Canada now. However, just 23 (41.8%) of the respondents completed a PhD in Canada; whereas 29 (52.7%) undertook doctoral studies in the United States. In an otherwise Canadian-oriented set of geographical identifiers, doctoral studies are the anomalous class, signaling cross-border activity through which a majority of Canadian writing studies scholars surveyed went to the United States for a PhD and returned to work in Canadian universities. Although this does not account for those who did not return in the future, or who might not, within this data-set, responses to this question offer a limited, distant report on patterned interdependency. The survey results provided sufficient warrant for exploring this cross-border pattern more carefully—a pursuit that will be focal in the following section.

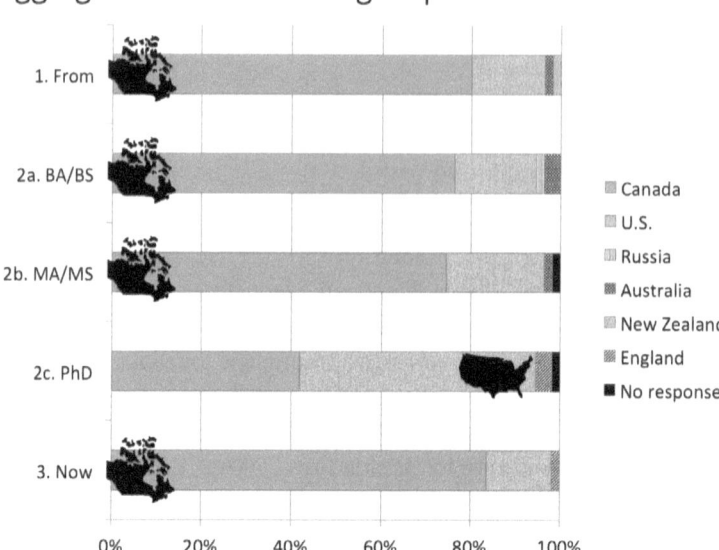

Figure 3. An information graphic presenting compiled survey responses for the aggregate locations among respondents.

Table 1. Survey tabulation of the geographic locations among respondents as relate to where they are from, where they took up undergraduate and graduate programs of study, and where they are now.

Toponym Distribution									
	CA	US	RU	AU	NZ	UK	N/A	% Canadian	n
FROM	44	9	0	1	1	0	0	80.0%	55
BA	42	10	1	2	0	0	0	76.4%	55
MA	41	12	0	1	0	0	1	74.5%	55
PHD	23	29	0	0	0	2	1	41.8%	55
NOW	46	8	0	0	0	1	0	83.6%	55

Finally, Question 11 invited respondents to include a curriculum vitae as an attachment. With CVs from 49 of the 55 respondents, more precise details became available, such as other locations where respondents had worked and the years in which they completed their PhDs. In a few cases, when attached CVs did not provide sufficient detail, supplemental queries on Google or in databases, such as ProQuest's Dissertations & Theses Global, supplied further information to develop Figure 4, a block histogram showing the years in which respondents completed PhDs and whether the PhDs were from Canadian universities. While this figure provides yet another perspective on the data presented in Figure 3, it also acknowledges a reasonably balanced rate of participation from late career, middle career, and early career scholars.

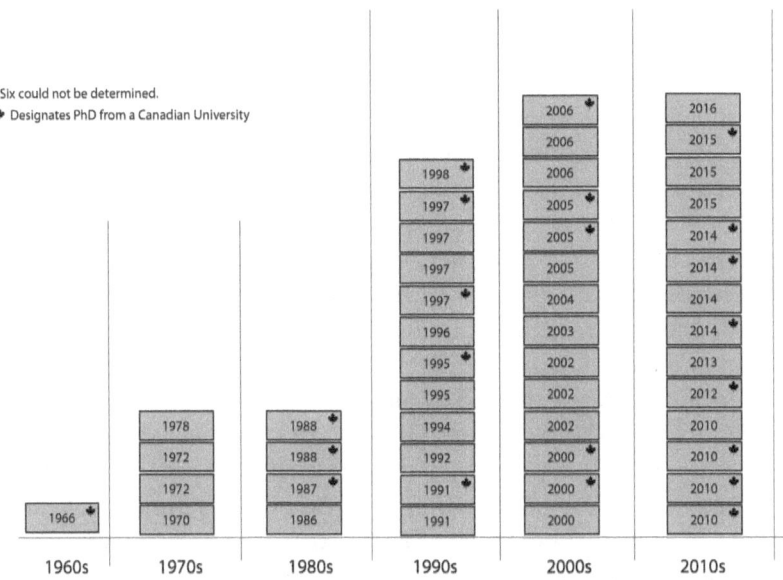

Figure 4. Block histogram presenting compiled survey responses for the year of PhD completion. Doctorates completed at Canadian universities are annotated with a maple leaf in the upper right-hand corner of the rectangular block.

As a preliminary, distant instrument for inquiring into cross-border interdependencies in writing studies, the survey confirmed numerous instances of blending, hybridity, and transnational thinking on the part of participants. Yet the survey also primed new questions—harder questions, I would say—about the methods best suited to tracing transnational disciplinary interdependencies at the broadest, most encompassing scales. In addition to this survey, my initial explorations of how best to trace interdependency were keyed to geographic locations, on the affinities that coalesce and cascade from one location to the next along emplaced, distributed career pathways. In the following section, as a way to further consider patterned interdependency based on geographic locations identified in the survey results, a series of interactive, digital maps reaffirm with slightly more refined granularity the ways interdependency operates both in specific career paths and in the aggregate career paths of the 55 respondents.

From the survey's specific place names to an encompassing North American viewshed for getting to know data indicative of interdependencies, the exploratory digital maps featured in this section contribute a distant, preliminary intervention in the broader study. Grouped as they are, the maps constitute an inquiry atlas, the points marked in them only after geocoding more than 300 locations referenced in the survey responses and curriculum vitae. Methodologically, we should think of this process as a pursuit of *indexical aereality*—the plotting of geographic coordinates onto map projections such that we can read the maps for otherwise non-obvious patterns and shapes. Indexical aereality names the process of translating a geolocative data-set and plotting it cartographically, so viewers can explore an emerging definition shape as one report on some disciplinary domain of activity. There have in recent years been similar efforts to map disciplinarily relevant, geographic data-sets, such as Jim Ridolfo's rhetmap, which documents job ads by geographic location (n.d.); Christopher Thais and Tara Porter's mapping of WAC/WID programs (2010); Jeremy Tirrell's (2012) study of the geographical history of online journals, and maps by the Doctoral Consortium in Rhetoric and Composition (Phelps & Ackerman, 2010) and Master's Consortium of Writing Studies Specialists (n.d.) to show membership locations. Yet, a full realization of disciplinary cartography is early in its development, and many geographies of writing have by-passed cartographic representations altogether, instead focusing on narrative and descriptive accounts.

The mapping process began with a simple line map developed using R, a programming language for visualizing statistical data. The detailed technical steps exceed the scope of this chapter, but the basic process required creating a file with the toponyms already geocoded, or assigned accurate latitude and longitude coordinates (geocoding is the translation of a place name into these numerical coordinates; I used the GPS Visualizer website and an API key from Bing Maps, which, in tandem, yielded a comma separated format that imported easily into other applications for sorting, analyzing, and plotting). The R console could process and overlay these geocoded data on a stock map projection from one of the available R libraries. The result from an early iteration of the project appears here.

Figure 5. A map projection of geolocative survey data rendered in R.

The rudimentary line map positions a marker where a scholar is currently located and adds radiating lines to all of the locations where that scholar has studied or worked. This approach to mapping career activity is synchronic (see Figure 6); the visual representation suggests the cumulative presence of every past position is bundled together, emanating from a locus situated in the here and now. I consider this a *career footprint*; it resembles a starburst or hub and spoke pattern. As a function of representing networks visually, it is understood to be a reductive, limited scope representation of merely one slice of professional activity, though it is nevertheless an invaluable way of grasping complex cross-border activity at the outset. In terms of interdependencies, this projection reflects numerous cross-border traversals. And yet the visual output from R was not quite *satisficient* (Simon, 1991). The map data in this early draft was neither satisfyingly navigable nor sufficiently selectable.

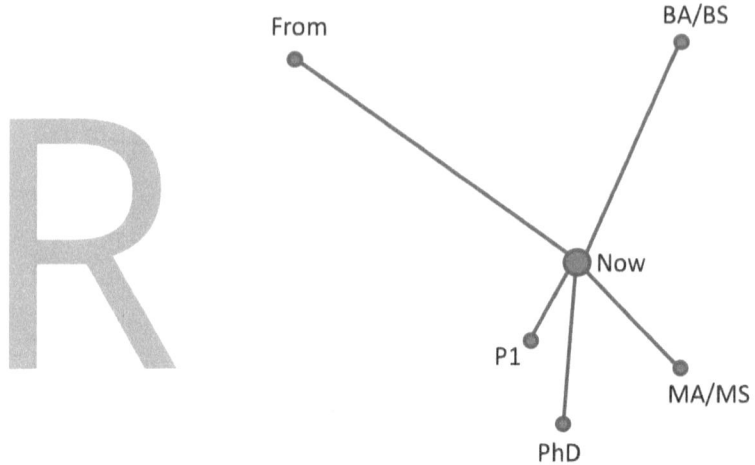

Figure 6. A simple visual model depicting *synchronic* career paths. The respondent's current geographic location is positioned as a hub from which all other geolocations emanate as radial edges or links. The model's logic was derived from R's plotting schema.

Desiring better maps and a better platform for exploring these data and connections among them, the next iteration of the maps required learning about geoJSON, a coding specification suited to the challenge of plotting points and lines, which can then be easily imported and overlaid on a more dynamic and interactive map projection. GeoJSON turned out to be a more powerful and flexible alternative to R, but its role in the development of the maps was far more than technical. Exploring geoJSON introduced a second, slightly different logic for plotting career activity.

geoJSON

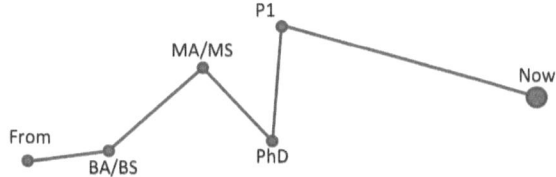

diachronic

Figure 7. A simple visual model depicting *diachronic* career paths. The respondent's from identification is designated beginning point, with subsequent geolocations plotted sequentially, ending with the respondents current location. The model's logic was derived from the Mapbox plotting schema involving geoJSON.

Compared to the starburst or hub and spoke in the examples using R, the default presentation of geolocative series in the geoJSON template I adapted appeared like an angling line segment, or a daisy chain. The string of coordinates were entered and subsequently output linearly, which introduced as a counterpart model a different perspective on career activity that, although it still reflected cross-border traversals, showed careers to be more path-like and sequential. Though neither pattern is inherent or prefigured in the programming code, the pairing of R and geoJSON signaled two distinct logics for plotting career activity as relates to geographic coordinates: the synchronic, starburst pattern, and a diachronic, pathway pattern. The pairing of these two coding specifications, moreover, presented variations that changed up the cartographic representation of cross-border activity, but that also deepened the maps' roles in rethinking cross-border influence in the context of mentorship as it has manifested for many of the scholars who responded to the survey.

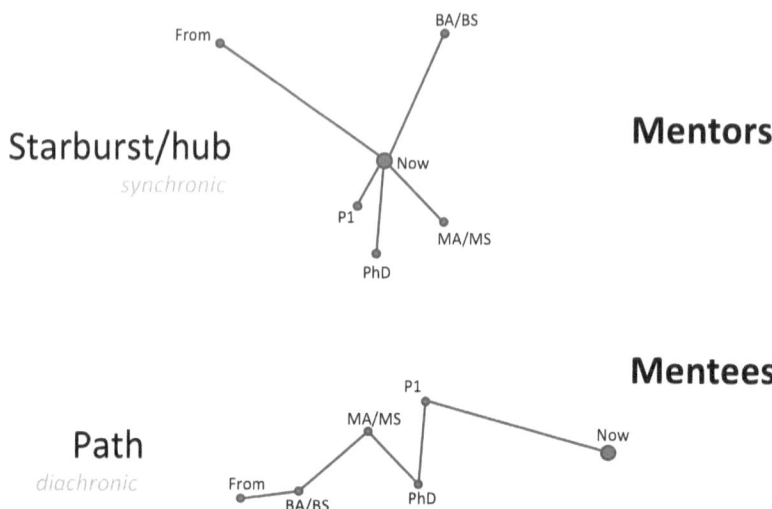

Figure 8. Two logics for plotting career activity. Side by side, the synchronic and diachronic models set up as a pair of complementary heuristics for inquiring into the dual nature of career activity as simultaneously distributed and emplaced.

Thus, the experimental map making led to new, fortuitous questions for examining disciplinary activity at a distant scale: Which representation is most telling when tracing networks suggestive of transnational interdependencies?

With these two simple models in mind (and sight) for thinking about how careers unfold, temporally and spatially, I scrapped the flat maps rendered by R and developed two new maps from all of the geographic data collected in the survey using geoJSON only. Complete, interactive versions of both maps are available for reference online, and accessing them directly (via a web browser) is preferable because their interactive affordances offer much more to explore than do the two dimensional screen-based or off-print versions. The maps are online at http://lab.earthwidemoth.com/lines.html (permanent: http://bit.ly/2i2IyIdlines) and http://lab.earthwidemoth.com/path.html (permanent: http://bit.ly/2iUiWSjpath).

Emplaced Disciplinary Networks from Middle Altitude 39

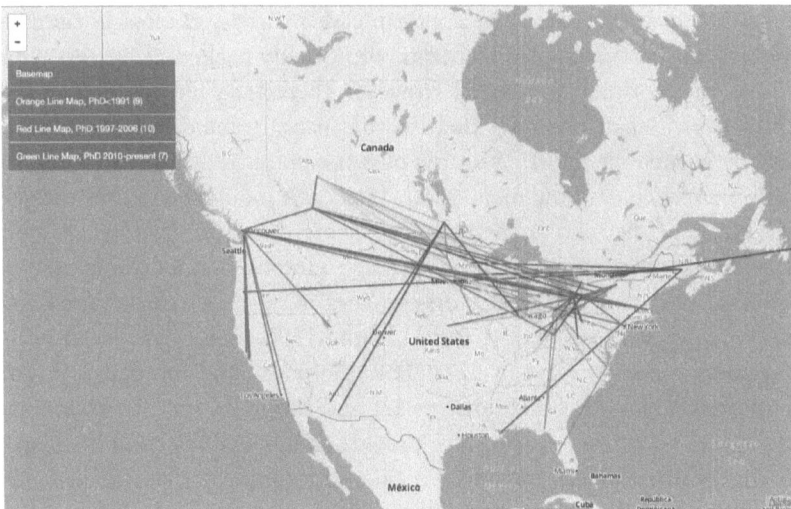

Figure 9. A screenshot of the interactive map available at http://lab.earthwidemoth.com/lines.html (permanent: http://bit.ly/2i2IyIdlines), which has been overlaid with geolocative survey data following the synchronic model.

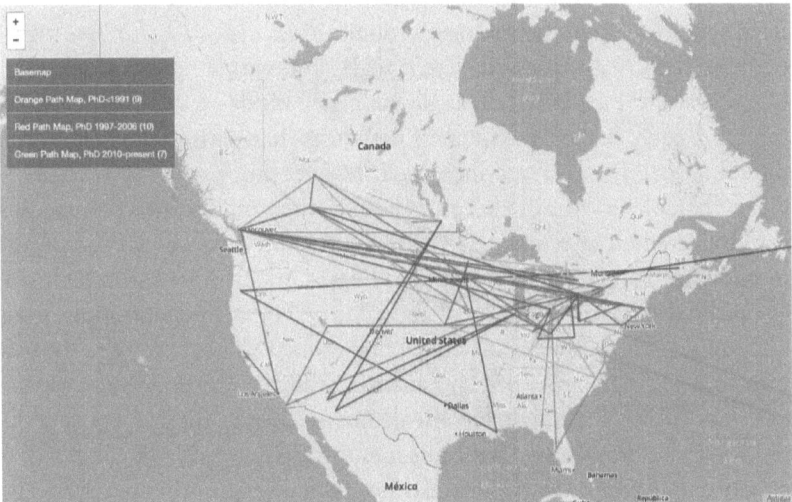

Figure 10. A screenshot of the interactive map available at http://lab.earthwidemoth.com/path.html (permanent: http://bit.ly/2iUiWSjpath), which has been overlaid with geolocative survey data following the diachronic model.

At the default scale, both maps (one based on each career model) look like a skein of densely entangled lines, and although they corroborate the cross-hatching of Canadian-American career activity evident in the survey responses, the maps project data too thickly packed to process with visual ease at the default scale. However, there are a few features in the online versions of the maps that may aid users in making sense of each tightly packed viewport. With the plus symbol, it is possible to zoom in and thereby change the map's scale. Users can mouseover a line and see the name of the scholar the line documents. Also, the layer selector on the left allows the singling out of smaller samples of data differentiated by stage of career. Lines with orange hues show career paths for survey respondents who completed a PhD before 1996. Red lines are for mid-career scholars. And green lines show the paths and footprints in the respective maps for doctoral students and junior faculty. In effect, although the colour-coding doesn't provide complete relief from the map's overcrowding, it does introduce a time series quality that allows us to look for distinct patterns for each group.

While these two exploratory maps figure significantly into the distant approaches attempted in this chapter, and while both provide compelling interactive reports on the aggregate place-to-place career activity of our survey respondents, the separation of diachronic representations from synchronic representations is too limiting, especially for investigating how such maps can at different scales and with a narrower selection of geographic locations tell us about other kinds of networks operating here, such as tacit mentorship networks that play a vital role in the discipline's ability to reproduce itself. Mentorship networks are notoriously difficult to visualize because, even though mentoring relationships are common, their referential basis is extremely irregular and difficult to confirm. In fact, most disciplinary accounts of mentorship circulate as personal narratives and local accounts of key influences, sponsoring and inviting figures who welcomed a newcomer to the field (viz. Andrea Lunsford's "The Nature of Composition Studies," 1991). Mentorship oftentimes surfaces through specific geographic locations and the institutions at their coordinates, but these mentorship relays do not come across clearly enough in one map or the other because mentoring faculty operate from a synchronic position, having themselves already accumulated myriad, distributed affinities whereas students tend to operate more from a diachronic position, in the sense that they are stopping through programs before moving to another location. The point here is that a combination of the two visual models along with compound criteria for defining mentoring relationships offers a unique handle on these emplaced disciplinary networks that span across generations and distances.

To explore this more fully, I created one final map.

Clearing away many lines from the comprehensive maps, the final map combines the diachronic and synchronic models to focus on Dale Jacobs, Associate Professor at the University of Windsor, and eight respondents to the survey who he worked with when they were master's students at Windsor between 2000 and 2013. Jacobs's career footprint is represented by a pink line, consistent with his stage of career as coded in the previous maps. This map is accessible online at http://lab.earthwidemoth.com/network.html (permanent: http://bit.ly/2i14Oaqnetwork)

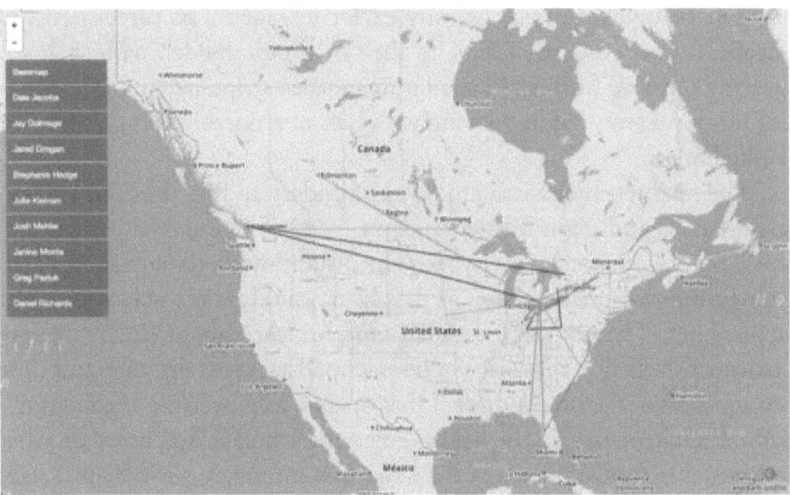

Figure 11. Screenshot of the interactive map available at http://lab.earthwidemoth.com/network.html (permanent: http://bit.ly/2i14Oaqnetwork), which has been overlaid with geolocative survey data focused specifically on Dale Jacobs and respondents he has mentored at the University of Windsor.

Notice how the synchronic model reflects that Jacobs in his current position is simultaneously influenced by radii connecting him with Edmonton, where he took his BA and MA, to the University of Nebraska, where he completed his PhD, to East Carolina University, where he held his first tenure-track appointment, and finally to the University of Windsor, where, over the past fifteen years, he has worked with ten MA students who have gone on to PhD programs in the US. Although the visualized links and nodes remain a shallow description of the influence that resonates for Jacobs with each of these moments in his career, representing his career path in this way underscores that academic careers accrete with layers of influence and experience, much of which amalgamates in direct relation to programs of study, employing institutions, and the people inhabiting each of these at coincident times. Returning to the map, the eight survey respondents (former students) Jacobs mentored appear with hues corresponding to the stages of their respective careers, so Jay Dolmage, Jacobs's first student at Windsor is in red, and Julie Kiernan; Jared Grogan; Janine Morris; Greg Paziuk; and also Stephanie Hedge, Daniel Richards, and Josh Mehler—a recent cohort who Jacobs referred to as "The Rhetorical Three" when I interviewed him in early December of 2013—are cast here in green hues corresponding to their being categorized as early career scholars. The career paths of Jacobs' former students adhere to the synchronic model, with each appearing to move from one location to another, stopping through Windsor in most cases, before moving yet again to a doctoral program in the United States.

The map sets up a distinctive way of understanding these nine scholars—Jacobs and eight former students—as belonging to a compound, cross-border mentorship network. The distant methods stop short of investigating this phenomenon as deeply as would be possible with other approaches. That is, there is much more to learn about the qualitative nature of these ties, the forms of interaction that cross distance and time sustain senses of connection and that operate as powerful, ongoing invitations to participate in the field as emerging scholars. Yet, based on what is knowable from the survey data and one interview with Jacobs, such a mentorship network might also serve as a model for scholars working in relative institutional isolation who seek to sponsor the disciplinary interests of master's students and thereby welcome newcomers to the field, much in the same way Lunsford (1991) described in her definitional account of composition studies.

The most significant takeaway from the survey data and inquiry atlas presented in his chapter is the way that visualizing mentorship networks across Canada and the United States, but also more generally, gains much from the use of compound reference points, one set geographic, in this case, and the second set drawn from explicitly articulated mentoring relationships. Combining the synchronic hub-mentor—Jacobs—and the diachronic through-passing-mentees—Dolmage, Kiernan, Grogan, Morriss, Paziuk, Hedge, Richards, and Mehler—suggests how one type of transnational influence manifests—that there is a strengthened sense in which Jacobs's influence has conducted along these lines—to Waterloo (Dolmage), Michigan State University (Kiernan), Wayne State University (Grogan), University of Cincinnati (Morriss), University of Windsor (Paziuk), SUNY-Potsdam (Hedge), Old Dominion (Richards), and Florida State University (Mehler). At another degree removed, we can begin to understand how the influences of Joy Ritchie, Kate Ronald, and Robert Brooke, professors at Nebraska who Dale Jacobs identified as mentors, are similarly implicated in and constitutive of this disciplinary network. Jacobs isn't at Waterloo, and yet he is. He isn't at Old Dominion, but he is. He isn't at SUNY-Potsdam, Michigan State, Florida State, Wayne State, or Cincinnati, but he is. Digital cartography is useful for seeing the emerging definitional shape of this network—for grasping an image of Dale Jacobs as simultaneously emplaced and distributed. Distant methods, such as the two types of surveying enacted here, may prime a variety of related investigations into writing studies, rhetoric and composition, and professional and technical communication as hosting numerous comparable networks, many of them proving powerfully impactful for the continuing growth and maturation of the field. These emplaced, distributed disciplinary networks are comparable to the field's invisible colleges (Crane, 1972), and yet far more work is due if we are going to begin conceiving of them in this way, increasing their visibility, and realizing more completely our agency both in bringing them about and participating in them.

There remains, of course, much more to explore in the three maps featured here. Such is the nature of an inquiry atlas—it is a pursuit designed to balance, on one hand, an *indexical aereality* in service of definitional shape-finding, and on the other, an open-ended and flexible resource useful for further exploration and for cross-referencing the gradually closer methodological approaches to disciplinary interdependence in the emphases on interviews, genre profiles, and cases presented in the following chapters.

References

Clary-Lemon, J. (2009). Shifting tradition: Writing research in Canada. *American Review of Canadian Studies, 39*(2), 94–111. doi:10.1080/02722010902848128

Coe, R. M. (1988). Anglo-Canadian Rhetoric and Identity: A Preface. *College English, 50*(8), 849–860. doi:10.2307/377981

Crane, D. (1972). Invisible colleges. *Diffusion of knowledge in scientific communities*. Chicago and London: The University of Chicago Press.

Fox, W. L. (2009). *Aereality: On the world from above*. Berkeley: Counterpoint.

Government of Canada, S. C. (n.d.). Population and dwelling counts, for Canada, provinces and territories, 2011 and 2006 censuses. Retrieved December 10, 2014, from http://www12.statcan.gc.ca/census-recensement/2011/dp-pd/hlt-fst/pd-pl/Table-Tableau.cfm?LANG=Eng&T=101&SR=1&S=3&O=D

Graves, R. (1993). Composition in Canadian universities. *Written Communication*, *10*(1), 72–105. doi:10.1177/0741088393010001003

Graves, R. (1994). *Writing instruction in Canadian universities*. Winnipeg, Manitoba: Inkshed Publications.

Graves, R., & Graves, H. (2006). Introduction. In R. Graves & H. Graves (Eds.), *Writing centres, writing seminars, writing culture: Writing in Anglo-Canadian universities*. Winnipeg, Manitoba: Inkshed Publications.

Graves, R., & Graves, H. (2012). Writing programs worldwide: One Canadian perspective. In C. Thaiss, G. Bräuer, P. Carlino, L. Ganobcsik-Williams, & A. Sinha (Eds.), *Writing programs worldwide: Profiles of academic writing in many places* (pp. 117–127). Fort Collins, CO: WAC Clearinghouse and Parlor Press. Retrieved from http://wac.colostate.edu/books/wpww/chapter10.pdf

Harvey, D. (2001). *Spaces of capital: Towards a critical geography*. New York: Routledge.

Kearns, J., & Turner, B. (1997). Negotiated independence: How a Canadian writing program became a centre. *WPA*, *21*(1), 31–43.

Lunsford, A. (1991). The nature of composition studies. In E. Lindemann & G. Tate, *An introduction to composition studies*. New York: Oxford.

Mackun, P., & Wilson, S. (2011). *Population distribution and change: 2000 to 2010* (2010 Census Brief) (p. 12). US Census Buerea. Retrieved from http://www.census.gov/prod/cen2010/briefs/c2010br-01.pdf

McEachern, A. (2004). *How maps work: Representation, visualization, and design*. New York: The Guilford Press.

Master's Degree Consortium of Writing Studies Specialists. (n.d.). [Geolocations of institutions overlaying an interactive digital map]. Map. Retrieved December 12, 2014, from http://www.mdcwss.com/map/

Phelps, L. W., & Ackerman, J. M. (2010). Making the case for disciplinarity in rhetoric, composition, and writing studies: The visibility project. *College Composition and Communication*, *62*(1), 180–215.

Rhetmap. (2012–present). [Geolocations of institutions hiring each year overlaying an interactive digital map]. Rhet Map: Mapping Rhetoric and Composition. Retrieved December 12, 2014 from http://rhetmap.org/

Soja, E. W. (2011). *Postmodern geographies: The reassertion of space in critical social theory* (2nd edition). London; New York: Verso.

Simon, H. A. (1996). *The sciences of the artificial* (3rd edition). Cambridge, Mass: The MIT Press.

Thaiss, C., & Porter, T. (2010). The state of WAC/WID in 2010: Methods and results of the U.S. survey of the international WAC/WID mapping project. *College Composition and Communication, 61*(3), 534–570.

Tirrell, J. (2012, May 15). A geographical history of online rhetoric and composition journals [Text]. *Kairos,* 16(3). Retrieved December 12, 2014, from http://kairos.technorhetoric.net/16.3/topoi/tirrell/

Turner, B., & Kearns, J. (2012). Department of rhetoric, writing, and communications at the University of Winnipeg. In C. Thaiss, G. Bräuer, P. Carlino, L. Ganobcsik-Williams, & A. Sinha (Eds.), *Writing programs worldwide: Profiles of academic writing in many places* (pp. 129–138). Fort Collins, CO: WAC Clearinghouse and Parlor Press. Retrieved November 10, 2014, from http://wac.colostate.edu/books/wpww/chapter10.pdf

Wood, D. (2010). *Rethinking the Power of Maps.* New York: The Guilford Press.

Wood, D. (1992). *The Power of Maps.* New York: The Guilford Press.

3 Voicing Scholars' Networked Identities through Interviews

Andrea Williams

INTRODUCTION

Whereas the previous chapter visualized the scholarly networks that comprise writing studies in Canada, including Canadian-American interdependencies, this chapter gives voice to the networked locations and identities of fourteen scholars through interviews that probe these scholars' perceptions of their disciplinary locations and identities and how these have been shaped by their relationships with other people (such as teachers, mentors, and collaborators), institutions, professional organizations, and events such as conferences. The scholars interviewed for this chapter include Natasha Artemeva, Doug Brent, Rick Coe, Jay Dolmage, Aviva Freedman, Roger Graves, Dale Jacobs, Lorelei Lingard, Anthony Paré, Margaret Procter, Dan Richards, Cathy Schryer, Ron Sheese, and Graham Smart. As Mueller (2012) has argued, distant methodologies can help "corroborate" the "local, tacitly felt impressions about changing disciplinary conditions," which are examined here (p. 196). This analysis of individual scholars' accounts of their introduction to the discipline and subsequent career trajectory foregrounds both the deliberate and serendipitous encounters—with texts, people, events, and organizations—that shape scholarly careers and that comprise larger disciplinary activity. In exploring the interpersonal ties that have connected these scholars to classmates, teachers, mentors, colleagues, collaborators, and friends as well as institutions and professional organizations, this chapter provides an alternative way to represent scholarly networks than the maps presented in the previous one. Phelps and Ackerman (2010) examined the importance of disciplinary identity to sustaining "the working identities of practitioners, scholars, and teachers across the US" (p. 181) in writing studies. In giving voice to these scholars' evolving identities and networks, this project contributes to efforts to strengthen the disciplinary identity of writing studies in Canada.

I approach this study of cross-border scholarly networks as someone whose own involvement in writing studies has crossed national borders: a dual Canadian-American citizen born and raised in Canada, I completed my first two degrees in Canada, my doctoral studies in the United States, and have worked in both countries in various institutional roles and locations. Like many of the scholars interviewed for this study, I first encountered writing studies (or rhetoric and composition as it was and still is called by many) by chance[1] and have ever since been interested in its disciplinary history and status in Canada, particularly its close connection to the American field and more recent connections to the international field. One of the issues this chapter explores is how, given the situation of these Canadian scholars, the discipline as a whole has taken root in marginal soil, i.e., in the absence of a traditional institutional home in the way that first-year composition in the United States has given composition and rhetoric an identity and institutional place, despite its often subterranean location (Miller, 1991). For if composition scholars in the United States have often been relegated to the basement, writing studies scholars in Canada have, as I will show, often had to couch surf—i.e., find institutional places for themselves and their work by collaborating with or joining other disciplines.

In examining the networked presences of these fourteen Canadian scholars,[2] I first discuss the role of conferences such as the Conference on College Composition and Communication (known as "4C's"), Inkshed, and the Canadian Association for the Study of Discourse and Writing (CASDW) in introducing newer scholars to the field and providing communities that support more advanced scholars. As the previous chapter demonstrates, the field in Canada is characterized by widely distributed activity, yet there are also more concentrated areas or institutional hubs of disciplinary activity, three of which I analyze here: the Carleton University group, the University of Windsor, and the University of Toronto (a fourth hub, the University of Winnipeg, is also discussed in chapter 5). From the inception of writing studies in Canada, the movement of scholars between Canada and the United States has followed a largely bi-directional pattern with many Canadian graduate students going to the

United States for graduate studies and faculty appointments and many American scholars, particularly in the early days of the field, accepting roles at Canadian universities. Through interviews with individual scholars, I have sought to understand how they saw their intellectual and disciplinary development and their relationship to scholarly networks. In doing so, I aim to contribute to our understanding of the interchange of ideas, texts, and events such as conferences that comprise disciplinary networks in Canadian writing studies.

The data analyzed here were generated from semi-structured interviews, which provide a useful mode of inquiry for understanding the meaning people make of their experience (Seidman, 2006). Interviews were conducted with a cross-section of scholars to evoke participants' rich, complex, and varied accounts of their own evolving scholarly identities and networks, an approach to scholarly networks that complements the others presented in this book. We interviewed fourteen Canadian scholars from thirteen different institutions across Canada and the United States, choosing participants to represent the major strands of Canadian writing studies as identified by Clary-Lemon (2009): rhetorical genre studies, writing across the curriculum, and professional and technical communication. In addition to choosing a cross-section of scholars by research area, we[3] also interviewed scholars at different stages in their career (early, middle, and later) and included scholars who had studied, worked, or continue to work and live in Canada and the United States. "Snowball sampling" was also used to select participants, a method whereby interviewees recommend additional participants, a particularly appropriate technique for a study of scholarly networks.

We asked participants about their heroines and heroes, mentors, mentees, or former students; how they locate (and have located) themselves (whether by institution, region, nation, discipline, research field, and/or other groups); the disciplinary or interdisciplinary fields and research specializations they have identified with; and whether, how, and why these identifications have changed over time. To learn about their affiliations, we asked participants about their memberships in professional and mentoring networks, collaborators and co-investigators, and about their roles in scholarly and professional organizations. (Appendix A has a complete list of our questions.) Interviews ranged from thirty-five minutes to over an hour and were conducted and recorded over Skype except for the interview with Dale Jacobs, which was done in person. Three of us (Mueller, Phelps, and Williams) conducted the interviews and I transcribed all but one myself, which helped familiarize me with the data.

Rapley (2001) has argued that interviews are a form of "artful social interaction" (p. 309) in which both interviewer and interviewee perform particular selves, which has implications for how interviews should be analyzed: if interview data are not windows onto a neutral reality outside the interview but are instead collaboratively produced and context-specific interactions, then interviewers' talk should be included along with that of interviewees. I followed this practice in transcribing the audio recordings, a process that reminded me that participants' discourse is always shaped not only by what questions are asked, but also by whom and how they are asked. Although space constraints permit me to quote only selectively and therefore include only the interviewees' responses, acknowledging the partiality of any one source of data reinforces the value of using different methodological approaches together as we have done in our coordinated studies of scholarly networks in Canadian writing studies. Since interviews are themselves a form of social interaction, my method echoes our object of study: the social nature of scholarly networks that originate in face-to-face relationships and are forged in particular geographical and historical contexts.

The analysis presented in this chapter, like those throughout this book, is both synchronic and diachronic: synchronic because the interviews captured different scholars' views and recollections of particular people, places, texts, themes, issues, and events at a particular moment in time and diachronic because scholars' answers to our questions retraced the routes they have travelled over time that have connected them to (and also separated them from) classmates, colleagues, collaborators, mentors, mentees, texts, institutions, conferences, organizations, and disciplines. One of the biggest challenges methodologically in analyzing interview data from multiple participants is to tease out common themes that link the interviews while recognizing and respecting that each interviewee is a particular case. One way of doing this is to group scholars according to institution and mentoring hubs, which I have done here.

Although this chapter in a sense voices these scholars' changing disciplinary identities and network affiliations by reporting data from their interviews, I of course bring my own perspective as researcher to this as I select from and interpret the interview data. Like the approach used to transcribe our interviews, my data analysis was rhetorical-hermeneutic, that is, informed by the assumptions that any interpretation (including my own) is partial and only one of the many that are possible (Patton, 2002, p. 114) since meaning is always negotiated (Silverman, 2005). My perspective is emic (that of an insider): as a writing studies scholar based in Canada I know or knew of almost all of the scholars before interviewing them, whether through reading their work or through common institutional affiliations, conferences, or organizations. The coding scheme used here emerged from not only the interview transcripts but also from my ongoing conversations (like the interviews, conducted over Skype) with coauthor, Louise Phelps, who brought a different perspective as an American scholar. These discussions were an important way to corroborate my analysis and avoid both overlooking and overstating particular themes and issues. The interviews themselves served as a form of triangulation as scholars' stories of their own experiences of the discipline often corroborated each other's perspectives. However, where scholars have presented contradictory or conflicting perspectives, I've included these to present the rich and diverse lived experience that comprises social phenomena, including scholarly networks.

Conferences as Disciplinary Gateways and Hubs: The 4Cs, Inkshed/CASSL, and CATTW

Because many scholars in Canada work in departments or programs and sometimes entire institutions where they are the sole writing specialist, the social rituals afforded by conferences, whether in the United States, in Canada, or elsewhere, have been vital for introducing newer scholars to the field and for providing more experienced scholars with colleagues and intellectual communities. This section examines the role of three key annual conferences and their sponsoring organizations in forming scholars' identities: the American-based Conference on College Composition and Communication (the conference it sponsors is known as "4Cs" and the organization itself is abbreviated as the CCCC) and the Canadian organizations Inkshed/CASLL (the Canadian Association for the Study of Language and Learning), and CASDW. (Chapter 4 discusses the equally important conferences organized by Aviva Freedman of Carleton University in Ottawa, which were international in scope and included prominent scholars from both the United Kingdom and the United States and were important sites of networking for Canadian scholars.) One of the earliest hubs for scholarly networks in Canadian writing studies was the CCCC, which all but one of the fourteen scholars interviewed mentioned and most of whom identified as a key locus for their introduction to the discipline and for fostering collegial and mentoring relationships. As I will show, the CCCC has played a crucial role in facilitating the emergence of writing studies in Canada, not only by supporting American scholars who emigrated to Canada, but also by supporting Canadian scholars who emigrated to the United States.

Richard (Rick) Coe, Professor Emeritus at Simon Fraser University, was born and raised in the Bronx, New York, but has spent more than half his life in Vancouver, British Columbia. Coe entered the field as it was forming and when there were no PhD programs in rhetoric and composition, so conferences were even more vital places for networking and peer mentoring. After winning a contest judged by Edward P.J. Corbett, Coe participated in a pre-conference seminar at 4Cs, which connected him with other junior scholars who would go on to make significant contributions to the field. Coe, downplaying his own considerable influence in the area of genre theory, described the peer mentoring that these early conferences fostered and how the personal connections forged there were important in shaping the emerging field in the United States:

> I was thrown together with a bunch of people who ended up doing maybe more than I did: Susan Miller, Ellen Nold, David Bartholomae, there were eight or ten of us who hung out together and influenced each other. The profession was at a place where it was ready to make changes and we could influence that. The idea of process was already in play but the focus had been on creativity. More complex, rhetorical, notions of process were not quite there yet. So I guess I was influenced by and part of a group of Young Turks. We influenced and helped each other and invited each other places (R. Coe, interview, June 9, 2014).

Although Coe was discussing here the key role of the 4Cs early in his career, he remained active in the organization for many years, long after moving to Vancouver, Canada, to accept a newly created faculty position in composition and rhetoric at the University of British Columbia (UBC) in 1976, the first of its kind in rhetoric at a Canadian university since the nineteenth century. For part of his time at the University of British Columbia, Coe was joined by fellow American, Andrea Lunsford. (After Coe moved across town to accept a similar faculty position at Simon Fraser University, Lunsford was joined at UBC by another American scholar, Nan Johnson.) Unlike Coe, Lunsford and Johnson eventually returned to the United States, but during their time in Canada and after leaving for the Ohio State University both continued to teach and mentor Canadian writing studies scholars, including Doug Brent, Judy Segal, Roger Graves, Tania Smith, and others.

The CCCC was not only an important organization for American scholars like Coe who would spend most of their careers in Canada, but also for Canadian scholars before there were such organizations in Canada. For example, when Anthony Paré, now Head of the Department of Language and Literacy Education at the University of British Columbia, was doing his PhD at McGill University in Montreal in the early 1980s (before there were any doctoral programs in writing studies in Canada), he relied heavily on American seminars and conferences not only to learn about the field but also for mentoring. At 4Cs, Paré met Linda Flower, who despite having no official role on his committee, gave him crucial support as he wrote his dissertation in what was then a completely unrecognized discipline in Canada:

> I was doing my dissertation and was in some considerable conflict with my supervisor who was not really in the composition and rhetoric tradition at all and who could not really grasp the kinds of things that I was on about. I sent my proposal, after he gave me a great deal of grief about it . . . to Linda Flower who I knew a bit because I'd done that conference at Carnegie-Mellon, that workshop. And I'd bumped into her at conferences, 4Cs. I sent it to Linda and to get her kind of approval of it, to make sure I hadn't lost touch with the kinds of intellectual issues and concerns. Linda phoned me, I don't know how she got a hold of my phone number. I think it was not Christmas Eve but the 23rd of December and I said, "hang up, I'll call you back" and she said, "No, it's been too long. I delayed responding to you, it's been too long so I want to pay for this." We probably talked for an hour and a half and I saw that kind of generosity in a lot of Linda's work (A. Paré, interview, November 27, 2013).

This is just one of many examples from the interviews that suggested the importance of cross-border mentoring for junior scholars, particularly in the context of a discipline still in formation.

In addition to enabling such cross-border mentorship, the CCCC has been and remains an important launching pad for scholars new to the discipline, both American and Canadian-based. Doug Brent, Professor

Emeritus at the University of Calgary, learned about the CCCC while teaching remedial writing and being frustrated by the approaches offered by textbooks: "Something just felt wrong to me. I kind of stumbled onto a reference to CCCC and some of the journals and thought, 'Holy cow!' There's a whole organization devoted to this!" Attending his first 4Cs was a watershed moment for Brent as he found his scholarly community:

> I went to my first 4Cs in the very early 80s, maybe 1980, and was absolutely flabbergasted: here I was in a building with about 3000 other people, most of whom were doing the things and asking the same questions that I was and sometimes coming up with much better answers. That was a pivotal moment where I saw, "Hey, there's a community here!" (D. Brent, interview, December 12, 2013)

Most participants described their first 4Cs as a transformative experience where what they had believed was their own (or their mentor's) unique or idiosyncratic interest in writing proved to be one shared by thousands of other people. Despite the overwhelming size and scope of the 4Cs, it has been an important point of entry into the field for many junior scholars from both the United States and Canada where they have made connections with other scholars.

For several new scholars, attending the 4Cs not only provided a recognizable scholarly community, but also conferred a legitimacy on the discipline. A generation after Doug Brent discovered the 4Cs in the early 1980s, for Canadian scholar, Daniel (Dan) Richards, who is now an assistant professor at Old Dominion University in Virginia, it wasn't until he attended 4Cs as a graduate student that he recognized writing studies as a discipline: "I didn't really get the sense I was entering something distinct until later on in my Master's . . . when I found out that there was a conference on it and that people went to these things and they did this for a living" (D. Richards, interview, May 28, 2014). It is striking that over twenty-five years after Canadian scholars like Anthony Paré and Doug Brent first found a community and a discipline at the 4Cs, Richards had the same key moment of recognition.

The 4Cs has remained an important cross-border disciplinary gateway for many Canadian scholars by influencing their decisions about where to do doctoral studies. Jay Dolmage, Associate Professor in the Department of English at the University of Waterloo, did his BA and MA in Canada, but it was at 4Cs where he met his future dissertation director Cynthia Lewiecki-Wilson. Meeting Lewiecki-Wilson at 4Cs made Dolmage realize that he could combine his interests in composition and disability studies and influenced his decision to do his PhD at Miami University in Ohio. As it was for Coe, Brent, and Richards, attending 4Cs early in Dolmage's career was a formative experience:

> Going to 4Cs as a Canadian Master's student and looking around and seeing, like "Wow! There is a huge discipline here!" Seeing that there was a huge group of people who care about the same things that I care about was gigantic (J. Dolmage, interview, October 15, 2014).

The impact of Dolmage's first 4Cs experience is understandable in view of the isolated context in which he and Dan Richards did their Master's degrees at the University of Windsor where their teacher and mentor, Dale Jacobs, is the sole scholar of composition and rhetoric. Although both Dolmage and Richards emphasized how well Jacobs had prepared them for doctoral studies, what no teacher can give students single-handedly is a sense of membership in a larger disciplinary community, which 4Cs was able to do. For Dolmage, the initial importance of 4Cs in providing him with a scholarly community has continued well past his initial disciplinary acculturation. In describing his ongoing involvement in 4Cs, particularly in the group committee on disability issues, Dolmage explained the close link between scholarly community and identity, "If I didn't have all those folks I can't imagine what my academic identity would be like. They're also such an important support network for me" (J. Dolmage, interview, October 15, 2014). Dolmage allowed that he might have found a similar network of disability studies colleagues in Canada, but that the "diffuse" nature of the composition and rhetoric community in Canada (a perception supported by the findings in the previous chapter) was not as cohesive as the one he found in 4Cs (J. Dolmage, interview, October 15, 2014).

Although most of the scholars interviewed emphasized the importance of 4Cs early in their careers, unlike for Dolmage, many scholars' involvement with the conference and sponsoring organization declined as their research interests shifted. Even junior scholars like Richards described a gradual move away from 4Cs to narrower and more immediately relevant disciplinary subgroups, in his case the Association for Teachers of Technical Writing (ATTW). Richards described the shift this way:

> I always thought that 4Cs was my network of people, however overwhelming that was for me at times. That's where I like to meet people. That's where the panels where I sought to make connections were . . . But attending ATTW this last year I realized I made more connections in that one single Wednesday in Indianapolis—more single ideas for publication and long term relationships with people in that one day—than I had at the previous 4Cs that I had attended (D. Richards, interview, May 28, 2014).

The smaller sub-disciplinary group, ATTW, provided Richards with a more concentrated network than the larger, more diverse 4Cs. This loosening of ties to the 4Cs over the course of scholars' careers was mentioned by most of the fourteen scholars, including those based in Canada, and is likely attributable to both disciplinary and generational shifts. Roger Graves, Associate Professor of English at the University of Alberta, who did his PhD at Ohio State University, explained the shift as a result of a "spinning out" of smaller, more specialized organizations from the larger hub of the 4Cs:

> The 4Cs has changed over time. It has spawned the computers and composition people, the technical writing people ATTW conference, it spawned the WAC conference. . . . but it got too big and those groups had to be spun out . . . what hasn't left is the bulk of its core membership, which is the first-year writing enterprise and that's why it has that character and is dominated by that (R. Graves, interview, November 28, 2013).

This dispersal of scholars' conference activity and membership in professional organizations such as these is supported by both our survey and interview data. Even scholars like Jacobs, who closely identified with composition, admitted that he no longer attends the 4Cs as often as he once did; however, rather than seeing this shift in terms of scholarly interests, he attributed it to generational differences: "It feels like a different conference than when I first started going . . . and some of the people that I used to see have started retiring. That's part of it, it's generational" (D. Jacobs, interview, December 3, 2013). In this way, scholarly networks can be seen to evolve both synchronically, as people's interests change and/or branch out, and diachronically, as new scholars enter the field and older ones pursue other interests or retire.

Despite the trend of scholars seeking increasingly specialized conferences and organizations, 4Cs nonetheless continues to play an important role in providing junior scholars from both the United States and Canada with a scholarly community. As Clary-Lemon (2009) noted, for a variety of reasons many Canadian scholars still professionalize either locally or in the US. In fact, until the early to mid-1980s, the networks and educational forums for Canadian writing studies were located exclusively in the US where Canadian scholars participated in conferences such as 4Cs, the ATTW (the Canadian Association for Teachers of Technical Writing was established in 1982), and the Wyoming Conference, popular with Canadians; and programs like the Summer Rhetoric Seminar organized by Janice Lauer and Ross Winterowd (Lauer, 1998) and the Carnegie Mellon seminar on research methods. Paré described how the impetus for forming a Canadian organization in 1984 came about from 4Cs' Canadian Special Interest Group (SIG):

> We kept bumping into each other at conferences in the States and decided, "It's time, there's enough of us, there's a critical mass developing," for us to begin meeting in Canada. The first Inkshed conference was in Fredericton in 1984, which I think was hugely influential in establishing, not just that one year but obviously out of that the beginning of that network establishing a Canadian writing studies community, which I think has been a remarkably productive and influential community (A. Paré interview, November 27, 2013).

That one of the key organizations for writing studies in Canada, Inkshed/CASLL, emerged from the Canadian Caucus of the 4Cs (which no longer exists although many of the Canadians who attend usually have a lunch or dinner together) speaks to the importance of American rhetoric and composition to Canadian writing studies. Not only was the idea for Inkshed seeded at conferences in the United States, two of its co-founders, Russell Hunt and James Reither, along with many early members were from the US, including Rick Coe, Stan Straw, Andrea Lunsford, and Nan Johnson. The annual Inkshed conferences, which have been studied by Smith (2000) and Horne (2012), are distinctive for their remote locations, talent nights, and practice of "Inkshedding." Smith (2000) has argued that one of the key purposes of the organization (later renamed the Canadian Society for Language and Learning or CASLL) was to create a community for scholars and teachers of writing who saw language and learning in similar ways, an exigence which grew out of the lack of local communities and institutional homes for writing scholars in Canada. Many of these scholars met at US conferences and Inkshed actively encouraged its members to attend conferences and events in the United States, which were advertised and reported on in the Inkshed newsletter as explained in chapter 4. According to Paré, the Inskshed or CASLL community coalesced around issues related to writing in specifically Canadian contexts, which were distinct from those of the United States and the United Kingdom; in other words, it was the institutional location of writing in Canada rather than the scholars themselves that distinguished the Canadian discipline:

> There were all these people in Canada, not all of them were Canadians, working in this odd context: it was *not* freshman comp, it was *not* the American university setting. We were *not* trying to recreate the kind of teaching and research that was happening south of the border because we couldn't. We didn't have it; there was no historical sediment to build on top of. We had something new and it wasn't Britain either, it wasn't at all like Britain although there were some traditions there I suppose . . . it was interesting to discover this group of people who were struggling with some of the same theoretical and institutional issues. That was hugely important for me: to find this group of people who were working across Canada (A. Paré interview, November 27, 2013).

Roger Graves also emphasized the importance of institutional context in shaping the identity of the Canadian discipline, but saw broader cultural differences as playing a role: "There is a Canadian attitude towards writing . . . which is distinct from the American attitude towards writing that comes from where you're working: the conditions and attitudes in that society" (R. Graves, interview, November 28, 2013). Scholars such as Catherine (Cathy) Schryer explained that within some Canadian departments of English there was not only a recognition that Americans approached writing differently, but in some cases an outright hostility towards the field because some faculty viewed it as an unwelcome import from the United States: "There's a really deep suspicion of teaching writing in Canada . . . I've heard it called 'too American'" (C. Schryer, interview, January 3, 2014). If Inkshed/CASLL formed in response to a distinctly Canadian context for writing where it is sometimes viewed with suspicion or invisible, then how have scholars managed to develop professional identities and communities? One way has been the epistemic approach that many Canadian scholars have taken.

According to Coe, the naming of CASLL (The Canadian Society for the Study of Language and Learning) reflected the key belief of its founders that "learning to write and learning other things were part of the same process and should be thought about together. . . . So if you're having a conference of writing teachers, writing should be a part of it, which is how Inkshedding became the defining activity of the group" (R. Coe, interview, January 9, 2014). Such an epistemic approach to writing fits the Canadian institutional contexts where writing instruction is likely to be situated in the disciplines rather than in first-year writing courses (Graves, 1994; Johnson, 2006). As important as 4C's was for many beginning scholars, so Inkshed/CASLL has been an important community for many other influential scholars in Canadian writing studies that were interviewed as part of this study, including Roger Graves, Aviva Freedman, Graham Smart, and Natasha Artemeva, because it addressed the specifically Canadian context in which these scholars have worked. Graves, for example, attended his first Inkshed conference while a doctoral student at the Ohio State University at the urging of his teacher and mentor, Andrea Lunsford, who had joined the Canadian organization during her tenure at the University of British Columbia. Similarly, Artemeva first attended Inkshed while a graduate student at Carleton University at the suggestion of her teacher and mentor, Aviva Freedman. Just as 4Cs was transformative for Coe, Brent, Jacobs, Dolmage, and Richards, so was Artemeva's first Inkshed experience: "I went and met everybody and it changed my life." Artemeva has since sent "dozens" of her own graduate students to Inkshed where several have become regular members (N. Artemeva, interview, November 11, 2014), exemplifying a new generation of Canadian scholars with close ties both within Canada and internationally who are less dependent on American conferences for scholarly community in the way that scholars like Paré and Brent initially were.

For Inkshedders such as Brent, CASLL was not just an annual conference but a close-knit scholarly community: "It was a group of likeminded folks that spent a lot of time chatting with each other in that beer night style of conferencing and collaborating afterwards" (D. Brent, interview, December 12, 2013). Brent emphasized the influence on his scholarship of not only his American teachers such as Andrea Lunsford and Nan Johnson, with whom he studied at UBC, but also scholars like Russ Hunt, whom he got to know through Inkshed. In contrast to the enormous 4Cs, Inkshed's more intimate annual gatherings, held in isolated settings (until 2011 it was held in rural settings) with an informal and interactive format, tended to foster friendships between scholars. Brent recalls the Inkshed conferences sowing the seeds for relationships that continued during the year and across thousands of miles: "Russ Hunt is someone I used to spend quite a bit of time over a beer with whenever we had a chance to get together which was at most once a year but we corresponded by email quite a bit and threw ideas back and forth" (D. Brent, interview, December 12, 2013). Inkshed was similarly important for Paré, who recalled the generosity of Inkshed's cofounders, Jim Reither and Russ Hunt who played important roles as mentors to other scholars:

> They were always so generous with their time. At every Inkshed conference we would spend as much time as you wanted talking about your work and your research and helping you shape it. . . . . It was a place people could go and get their voices heard (A. Paré, interview, November 27, 2013).

Whereas Inkshed has been an important scholarly community for many in Canada, other scholars have found their home not in Inkshed/CASLL, but in the Canadian Association for Teachers of Technical Writing (CATTW) (later CASDW).

Founded in 1982 as CATTW with a fairly narrow focus on professional and technical communication, in 2008, under the leadership of Catherine (Cathy) Schryer, the organization expanded its reach when it became the Canadian Association for the Study of Discourse and Writing (CASDW). Schryer credited CASDW for what she sees as the Canadian discipline's distinctive emphasis on research over lore: "it comes out of that organization, real research and not 'here's what I did in my class last week'" (C. Schryer, interview, January 4, 2013). As President of CATTW when it transitioned to CASDW, Schryer fought to make the new organization as inclusive as possible:

> It was very difficult. I included people in writing centres in that organization and it was bitterly opposed by some of the more senior people . . . but it turned out to be extremely useful because without them I think the organization would have died,

it would have become too small (C. Schryer, interview, January 4, 2013).

Despite her own high profile as a researcher, Schryer insisted on including the many writing centre instructors from the University of Toronto, a group which she saw as essential to sustaining the organization because of its large numbers[4]: "I thought not having the University of Toronto involved in an organization in Canada is pretty crazy because they are the largest university in Canada by far" (C. Schryer, interview, January 4, 2013). Schryer's decision was prescient, for CASDW is now larger than Inkshed/CASLL and the two organizations have begun to schedule their conferences together under the Congress of the Humanities and Social Sciences (Canada's federal research funding granting organization) to ensure as many participants as possible and boost Inkshed/CASLL's waning membership.

In short, organizations such as 4Cs, Inkshed, and CATTW/CASDW have been vital in helping both as graduate students new to writing studies and as more senior faculty members overcome their isolated institutional contexts and connect with scholarly communities in Canada and the United States. The next section explores more concentrated sites of scholarly activity at three different Canadian institutions, each of which has its own distinct scholarly community.

Three Canadian Hubs: How Institutional Context (Territoire) Shapes Identity (Terroire)

The previous chapter examined the diffuse quality of Canadian writing studies, in part the result of Canada's low population density and in part a consequence of the lack of defined institutional homes for writing studies. However, half of the fourteen scholars interviewed for this study belonged to one of four institutions with more concentrated networks or hubs for writing studies, whether in the form of departments, programs, or through other kinds of affiliations. The hubs analyzed here are situated in Ontario, the most populated province, which is located in central Canada. The first institutional group analyzed is centered at Carleton University, although this group has also been closely connected to McGill University; the second group is at the University of Windsor, which is situated on the Canada-US border by Detroit; and the third group is located at the University of Toronto. Although not the only institutional hubs for writing studies in Canada[5] (the University of Winnipeg, located in the province of Manitoba, is examined in chapter 5)—the hubs analyzed here suggest the wide range of institutional contexts and identities for writing studies in Canada, which contributes to the diffuse nature of the field in Canada.

The Carleton Group: Creating a Disciplinary Home

Phelps (2014) has argued that doctoral programs are essential for sustaining disciplinary identity since it is through such programs that disciplines are able to reproduce themselves. One of the reasons for the interdependency between Canadian and American writing studies is the dearth of doctoral programs in Canada, which has sent many Canadian graduate students to the United States. One of the few doctoral programs in writing studies in Canada today is Carleton University's PhD in Applied Linguistics and Discourse Studies, which was launched in 2012. The program was spearheaded by several current faculty members at Carleton and was also a legacy of Professor Emeritus Aviva Freedman, who is profiled in the next chapter. Although a separate institution, Carleton's applied linguistics program has had close ties with McGill University in Montreal in terms of scholarly collaboration and sharing of graduate students doing doctoral studies in the field.

Freedman, like many Canadian writing studies scholars, stumbled on the discipline while teaching composition as a literature student in the United States. As was the case for Doug Brent, Freedman's initial encounter with writing studies was spurred by her interest in finding better ways to teach writing than those provided by textbooks. Freedman's career trajectory shows how even a relatively small, intimate creative group or "circle" (Collins, 1998) that is concentrated at one institution can influence a discipline. Freedman's arrival home to Canada from the United States in 1974 was timely: she was asked both to direct a writing centre for literature students and conduct a major research study on teacher training in literacy for the Ontario Ministry of Education. The research project was prompted by a perceived "literacy crisis," similar to that which had been much discussed in the United States and which was the impetus for creating the faculty position at the University of British Columbia, which took Rick Coe to Canada. Leading this literacy study familiarized Freedman with the work of US researchers such as Janet Emig and Donald Graves as well as that of UK scholars James Britton and Andrew Wilkinson, which laid the groundwork for the international writing conferences Freedman later organized as well as Carleton's MA in Applied Language Studies and Discourse. With her colleague, Ian Pringle, Freedman researched both K–12 and post-secondary literacy and later literacy in professional settings where she collaborated closely with another Carleton University colleague, Pete Medway, along with Pat Dias and Anthony Paré of McGill University. Paré described his connection to his teachers and mentors, who included Freedman, (with whom he would later collaborate) at McGill University and Carleton University as serendipitous: "I just lucked out . . . and fell in with a great gang" (Paré, interview, November 27, 2013). Freedman's career footprint is visible in her significant scholarly output as well as through the scholars whom she mentored such as Anthony Paré, Natasha Artemeva, and Graham Smart, all of whom were interviewed for this study and three of whom, Smart, Artemeva, and Janna Fox (who was not interviewed) teach in Carleton's doctoral program.

The work of Freedman, Paré, Artemeva, and Smart is focused on writing in professional and academic settings and uses the frame of rhetorical genre studies. For example, the publications of Artemeva, originally an engineer from Russia, have examined discourse in professional settings, which started with a piece she wrote with Freedman about engineers learning to write: "Aviva and I co-published a piece in *Technostyle*, what used to be the journal for CASDW, which was based on my Master's research" (N. Artemeva, interview, November 11, 2014). Artemeva has in turn published with her own graduate students, mentoring her students as Freedman had mentored her: "I think it's very important to collaborate and co-publish with students because it helps them enter the discipline" (N. Artemeva, interview, November 11, 2014). Mentoring within institutions strengthens programs and confers on members a strong sense of institutional and disciplinary identity: it is no coincidence that much of the Canadian scholarship in writing studies that has gained international influence has drawn on rhetorical genres studies since this approach has had such strong institutional support through the Carleton-McGill group of scholars. In addition to the scholars from the Inkshed community who were important mentors, Artemeva's work has also been influenced by Americans like Carolyn Miller (interview, November 11, 2014), which may explain her sense of location, which extends beyond Canadian borders: "I think my position is within North American writing studies and North American Genre studies" (N. Artemeva, interview, November 11, 2014).

Like Anthony Paré and Natasha Artemeva, Graham Smart was initially mentored by Freedman (along with Paré and Dias and others from McGill University), while doing his MA at Carleton University in Ottawa and his PhD at McGill University in Montreal. Smart also co-authored with Freedman early in his career and like Artemeva, now publishes with his own graduate students at Carleton. Like all members of the Carleton group, Smart's work has focused on writing in professional contexts such as his ethnographic work on the Bank of Canada and his more recent work on climate change, most of which has been published by presses in the United States or the United Kingdom. As well as the strong influence of Canadian mentors on his work, Smart spent several years on the faculty at Purdue University, where colleagues such as James Porter, Johndan Johnson-Eilola, and Gerald Alred influenced his work, in addition to Canadian genre scholars Cathy Schryer of Ryerson University and Janet Giltrow of the University of British Columbia. Smart considered his scholarly identity to be anchored as much in the intellectual community of rhetorical genre studies as in any national community, although his use of rhetorical genres studies comes out of his location at Carleton University.

Paré saw the rhetorical genre studies approach taken by the Carleton University group of scholars as informed by the Canadian context: because college writing in Canada is not given the same institutional place or importance as it is in the United States, scholars lack an institutional home, which has prompted them to attend more to workplace writing. Without the freshman composition tradition that funds many of the tenured positions in the United States, Paré described Canadian writing studies scholars as "holding on by our finger tips," which has required scholars to "find a place where they could be useful" and "spawned a real interest in non-academic and professional writing outside of the English department" (A. Paré interview, November 27, 2013). Paré saw the contributions to rhetorical genre studies by scholars such as Freedman, Artemeva, Smart, and himself who have studied language in a variety of settings as a way to create disciplinary homes outside of English departments. Such a view resonates with what Schryer (2011) has argued is the defining feature and strength of rhetorical genre studies, where "researchers work at the interstices of various disciplines" (p. 31). In short, interviews with key members of the Carleton-McGill writing studies hub suggest the role of local mentoring relationships, provincial government research agendas and funding, institutional support (culminating in the creation of a doctoral program), hosting international conferences, and applying rhetorical genre studies to writing in a variety of professional writing contexts in creating a scholarly hub with strong spokes connecting it to both national and international networks.

Looking South from the Border: the University of Windsor

Whereas the Carleton group's strong identification with rhetorical genre studies closely links it to both Canadian and international writing studies, the University of Windsor hub is exclusively oriented to the American discipline. Moreover, whereas the Carleton-McGill group had from its inception several scholars and has continued to hire new faculty, the University of Windsor's program is centered on a lone scholar, Dale Jacobs. The sole composition scholar (as he identifies himself) in the Department of English at the University of Windsor, Dale Jacobs stumbled on composition while beginning a doctorate in literature (before switching to composition) at the University of Nebraska after completing two degrees at the University of Alberta. Jacobs has single-handedly mentored at least ten MA students since 2000 who have continued on to doctoral programs in the United States, as Windsor has no doctoral program. In discussing Windsor's mentorship network, the previous chapter argued that scholars "can be in two (or more) places at once, simultaneously emplaced and distributed" and that the mentorship network Jacob has established offers a potential model "for scholars working in relative institutional isolation who seek to sponsor the disciplinary interests of masters' students and thereby welcome newcomers to the field." Jacobs has used his institutional location on the Canada-US border to connect his students to the American discipline. More than any scholar discussed so far, Jacobs identified with "composition" (as opposed to the term, "writing studies," which most scholars used), which he saw as an American discipline. Like Graves, who also did his first two degrees in Canada and doctoral studies in the United States, Jacobs has worked in both countries, but his sense of scholarly identity and intellectual community are entirely oriented to the United States. Being situated at a Canadian institution on the American border has given Jacobs what he sees as the best of both worlds—a Canadian address with an American-based disciplinary community and identity: "living in Windsor I think has been kind of perfect because I am in Canada . . . but it's easy to keep my professional attention on the U.S." (D. Jacobs, interview, December 3, 2013). Despite being geographically located in Canada, Jacobs described the writing program he directs at Windsor not as a hybrid program, but as unequivocally "an American-style first-year comp program." He had no connection to Canadian writing studies organizations or their conferences, which held little appeal for him and which he saw as outmoded:

> I don't go to CASDW, the Canadian writing studies conference, for a variety of reasons . . . It just doesn't seem that it's the most productive conference. And the one that preceded it, Inkshed, is essentially just a throwback to expressivism, and it's just nothing I was ever very interested in (D. Jacobs, interview, December 3, 2013).

Jacobs's view of inkshedding as an expressivist practice contradicts published accounts about the Inkshed community and conferences, which have described the activity as more social and dialogic rather than expressivist (Horne, 2012; Smith, 2000). However, Jacobs's view of Inkshed makes sense given his much stronger identification with the American discipline of composition. For Jacobs, working at a Canadian institution after completing his doctorate and working in the United States was not about joining a Canadian discipline, but about using what he had learned from his American mentors to help develop a discipline still in formation: "Coming back to Canada has been about infusing what I learned about the discipline and what I learned about being an ethical professional—and that goes back to who my mentors were . . . and trying to infuse that into this [Canadian] context" (interview, December 3, 2013). His lack of connection to the Canadian discipline and to Canadian scholars is also in part attributable to his being the sole faculty member in composition in his department and at his institution; unlike the Carleton-McGill group, he has no colleagues within his institution with whom to collaborate. Jacobs saw the Canadian discipline as untheorized and hoped that the return to Canada of his former students who had done doctoral work in the United States would contribute to the development of the discipline in Canada: "As positions open up, I hope that . . . we'll start to get a more theoretically informed look at what happens in Canada" (D. Jacobs, interview, December 3, 2013). Jacobs's identifying himself in opposition to the current state of the Canadian discipline reminds us of the Burkean principle of identification and division (1965), whereby to accept one identity requires refuting another, and suggests the importance of *dis*identification in understanding how networks function. On a practical level, because one has limited time and energy, one must choose which organizations and conferences will yield the greatest intellectual and social rewards.

Given Jacobs's status as the sole composition and rhetoric faculty member at Windsor, it is not surprising that his student, Dan Richards, initially thought that what Jacobs was teaching him about writing was just his professor's "own personal interest" and not part of an actual discipline: "I remember thinking the first semester that I wasn't really entering an established field because it was just Dale . . ." (D. Richards, interview, May 28, 2014). Jacobs introduced Richards and his classmates to the field through directed readings and regular meetings over drinks and lunches, forming a tight-knit composition community within the department. Because of Jacobs's American experience of and orientation to the field, Richards came to see the discipline like his teacher and mentor did, as a "distinctly American enterprise" (interview, May 28, 2014). This orientation towards the American field offers a stark contrast to that of the Carleton group, which has regularly acculturated its graduate students into Canadian writing studies organizations like CASDW and Inkshed as well as the international genre studies community.

Richards described Jacobs's influence on him as "foundational," but also emphasized the importance of peers in forming his scholarly identity and choosing his career path. For instance, the peer support Richards received from fellow graduates who shared his interest in teaching composition informed his decision to pursue doctoral studies in composition (as opposed to literature) in the United States: "We kind of coalesced around it and bonded around our apathy towards literature and our desire to be in the classroom and our desire to think about teaching on a level that our colleagues—our fellow graduate students—didn't" (D. Richards, interview, May 28, 2014). Richards emphasized the importance of his ties with his MA classmates from the University of Windsor who had also pursued doctoral studies in the United States and were now faculty members at American institutions. Like his mentor Jacobs, Richards expressed no sense of connection to Canadian writing studies, despite being receptive to the possibility: "That would be something that I would value but I don't locate myself there" (D. Richards, interview, May 28, 2014).

Jacobs's decision to do doctoral studies in the United States is one that has been followed by at least ten of his former MA students, including Dan Richards and Jay Dolmage. Richards's decision to go to the United States to do a PhD in composition and rhetoric was heavily influenced by Jacobs: "Having Dale talk about his experiences doing his PhD in Nebraska and teaching at East Carolina for a while meant I knew that for him to do what he had to do he went state-side" (D. Richards, interview, May 28, 2014). Similarly, Dolmage recalls his decision to go to the United States for doctoral studies as tied to the web of connections he had through Jacobs: "It's all a family tree. I met Dale and then I applied very widely to do a PhD in comp-rhet, which I never would have heard of if I hadn't met Dale. I went to Miami, Ohio, where Dale's mentor, Kate Ronald, was located" (J. Dolmage, interview, October 15, 2014). Jacobs has mentored an impressive number of scholars in composition, some of whom, like Dolmage, have returned to positions in Canada, thereby fulfilling his hope of enriching the Canadian discipline. Nevertheless, it is striking how the University of Windsor hub is completely without spokes to the Canadian scholarly community. Connecting this important yet isolated (from the Canadian perspective) hub would thus be a logical next step in strengthening writing studies networks in Canada.

Institutional Mentorship and Scholarship at the University of Toronto

When Cathy Schryer recounted her efforts to include writing centre instructors in the newly formed Canadian Association for the Study of Discourse and Writing (formerly the Canadian Association for Teachers of Technical Writing) she emphasized the importance of including the University of Toronto, Canada's largest university, which employs permanent writing faculty in most of its fourteen writing centres, despite having no tenured writing specialists in the Department of English on its main campus and offering no graduate courses in writing or rhetoric (Procter, 2006). My interview with Margaret Procter, retired former Writing Coordinator at the University of Toronto, raises issues of the role of institutional mentorship and scholarship in writing studies networks in Canada. By institutional mentorship and scholarship, I refer to that which operates within, but not necessarily beyond a particular local setting. Before retiring in 2012, Procter held numerous teaching and administrative roles at the University of Toronto, including those in writing centres, a writing across the curriculum program, English language learning programs, and professional writing and rhetoric programs. Among Procter's most important legacies at the University of Toronto, however, were eliminating post-admission testing, establishing a writing-across-the-curriculum program in the University's largest faculty (Arts & Science, with twenty-five thousand undergraduate students), and mentoring junior scholars. As one of the few writing specialists at the University of Toronto during the 1980s and 1990s, Procter drew on the expertise of applied linguistics faculty at the Ontario Institute for Studies in Education (a unit that has since merged with the Faculty of Education) to help her frame her ultimately successful campaign against the post-admission writing test.[6] She relied on the support of these same faculty to establish a writing-support unit in the School of Graduate Studies, a form of cross-disciplinary networking that would be essential to enabling a lone writing specialist to influence writing instruction policy and create multiple homes for writing within a large and complex institution. Of course, creating institutional homes requires securing full-time faculty appointments, which Procter did, not only for the English Language and Writing Support in the School of Graduate Studies, but also for many writing centre directors and instructors, along with the writing-across-the-curriculum program she established. Besides helping create such positions, she actively mentored graduate students (mostly but not exclusively from the English department) to help prepare them for these new writing instruction and administration roles within the University. Procter described encouraging a junior colleague to apply for a newly created director role with the School of Graduate Studies (SGS):

> [She] worked in engineering and I was interested in the research she did on engineering students and their attitude towards writing so I kept in touch with her . . . so when the opportunity came to set up the Writing Centre in SGS I talked to [her] and pushed or pulled her through applying and I was happy to see [her] ace the interviews and get that job.

Not only did Procter engage in individual mentoring, she also helped develop a community around writing instruction and scholarship through professional development events, which she began organizing at the University of Toronto in the 1990s for both the many adjunct instructors and the growing number of permanent writing faculty members. Procter recalled how these sessions provided an informal education about the discipline for the University's burgeoning writing studies community: "it was interesting to have five or six meetings a year to read articles and talk about them and start making presentations." These sessions (which continue today) encouraged the institution's new writing studies faculty to read research, attend conferences, and engage in research, which they began presenting at national and international conferences thanks to a budget Procter secured for conference travel. Several of these writing faculty joined the executives of Inkshed/CASLL and CASDW (Procter, 2006).

In addition to the important role Procter played in establishing writing programs and centres and grooming graduate students to assume newly created faculty positions in writing, Procter also published in writing studies. However, she was uncertain about whether she considered herself a scholar, explaining that such activity was secondary to more immediate institutional priorities:

> I needed to do other kinds of things than publish. I located myself within institutions writing reports with others to administrators to show the value of writing centres . . . and bat down some of the silly ideas administrators had about computers and their ability to replace people.

In helping to develop writing centres, a writing across the curriculum program, and an English Language Learning program and attendant faculty appointments, Procter's mentorship and scholarship at the University of Toronto are examples of vital activities that create scholarly communities, but which are seldom included in institutional histories, let alone disciplinary ones. In creating positions for and mentoring writing faculty who have become active in national writing studies organizations and have published in national and international journals, Procter's scholarly activities, while concentrated at the University of Toronto, where she connected writing studies faculty across the three campuses and fourteen writing centres, have also linked this group to broader disciplinary networks.

SHIFTING SCHOLARLY IDENTITIES AND COMMUNITIES

So far we have seen examples of three different kinds of institutional hubs for writing studies scholars in Canada: the Carleton group with its close identification with Inkshed/CASSL as well as rhetorical genres studies and the international genre studies community; the University of Windsor group with its American-linked circle; and the University of Toronto group, composed mostly of writing centre faculty whose recent permanent status has enabled them to start joining disciplinary networks beyond their home institution. It is important to note that while each of the three hubs analyzed represents an important locus of scholarly activity, these are but three of many such writing studies hubs in Canadian universities. But within these various hubs, how do individual scholars form identities and join communities in the context of a discipline that is still largely supplemental or marginal in the Canadian academy?

Phelps and Ackerman's (2010) description of rhetoric and composition in the United States as a "heteroglot" field "whose identity has been imagined as supplemental or derivative" (p. 202) is also an apt description of writing studies in Canada. As shown in the previous chapter, participants identified with a wide range of subfields and have published in a variety of journals, yet as Brent has argued, such interdisciplinarity is hardly unique to writing studies since many scholars from disciplines other than writing studies draw from other scholars and other disciplines: "Everybody picks up bits and pieces from other folks and combines them as they wish" (D. Brent, interview, December 12, 2013). However, if the interdisciplinarity of writing studies is not its unique or sole defining feature, the idea of writing studies as supplemental to other disciplines is potentially a defining feature and was a recurrent theme of the interviews. Paré attributed the marginal status of writing studies both in Canada and the United States to the invisibility of writing to other disciplines:

> North American writing studies folks everywhere exist always in the shadows of the disciplines who seem to be unaware of the fact that they couldn't have disciplines if it weren't for writing, but don't want to acknowledge somehow the rhetorical nature of knowledge making. . . . That has left writing studies scholars on both sides of the border always on the margins, always attempting to justify themselves, always trying to support writing centres and writing research (A. Paré interview, November 27, 2013).

Moreover, without writing courses and programs at many institutions in Canada, scholars have had to build from the ground up rather than merely find homes within institutions. Notably, the many recent permanent positions for writing faculty have been almost exclusively teaching-intensive positions[7] with more limited opportunities for research (including access to funding) than research-intensive roles. As Paré noted, the inhospitable climate for writing studies in Canadian

English departments has forced many scholars to craft professional identities and institutional homes by studying writing in other disciplines. Paré called this the rhetorician-in-residence model, which he saw as "the absolute ideal situation for those of us who are interested in rhetoric," a path that scholars such as Smart, Artemeva, Schryer, and Paré himself have all travelled with success (A. Paré, interview, November 27, 2013). All four have focused their research on language use in professional sites such as the Central Bank of Canada (Smart); engineering and (more recently) mathematics (Artemeva); veterinary medicine, social work, medical education, and optometry (Schryer); and social work and doctoral education (Paré). However, Paré conceded that this rhetorician-in-residence role can make it difficult for scholars to locate themselves within a community:

> It's hard for scholars in writing studies if they aren't focused primarily on writing studies at the service of freshman composition or at the service of education and writing, if they are interested in the study of writing because of what it tells us about human beings. It's hard to find a community because your community often ends up being the people you're studying—the culture or collectivity you're studying to understand more about what's going on there (A. Paré, interview, November 27, 2013).

One such scholar who has joined the community she studies is Lorelei Lingard, Senior Scientist of the Centre for Education Research and Innovation at the Schulich School of Medicine and Dentistry at the University of Western Ontario. Lingard began studying medical discourse as a doctoral student at Simon Fraser University. Her approach to disciplinarity resembles that of her teacher and mentor, Rick Coe, who explained his own scholarly approach thus: "What I love to do is to be multidisciplinary," adding that "a lot of my doctoral students ended up in odd places" rather than in more traditional writing studies positions (R. Coe, interview, January 9, 2014). Despite early misgivings about what she would be able to do with a doctorate in rhetoric—"I initially thought I might have to be forever a sessional who taught writing"—Lingard has had a successful career as a rhetorician in medicine, securing ongoing research funds, heading research teams, supervising doctoral students, and publishing extensively (L. Lingard, interview, October 16, 2014). Tellingly, questions of disciplinary identity and community came up even before I began the scripted part of my interview with Lingard when she asked, "Am I considered in the field or out of the field or one foot in or one foot out?" (L. Lingard, interview, October 16, 2014). In contrast to the many participants who described the serendipitous nature of their career, Lingard emphasized how she had deliberately cultivated membership in medical organizations rather than in writing studies. Forging a path as a rhetorician in medicine, she saw herself as firmly rooted in medicine: "Fifteen years into my career I feel as though I've moved really deeply into the community I live in and the ties that bind me to rhetoric and writing studies are quite delicate at the moment" (L. Lingard, interview, October 16, 2014). Lingard's former teacher, Rick Coe, when asked about his scholarly identity, suggested that the question be framed more rhetorically, in terms of audience: "When I write academic stuff, I am not trying to be a scholar or publish. I am trying to influence others. So I would answer this question in terms of who I am trying to influence" (R. Coe, interview, January 24, 2014). Similarly, Lingard framed her decision to leave one discipline and join another in terms of audience:

> I very quickly made the decision that I couldn't continue in both those communities: I would have to choose. And I made the conscious decision to turn myself towards medical education research and to use that theoretical lens to talk to people in the educational research world and get them to see problems in a new way rather than use it to talk to the rhetoric community. It was a very conscious decision on my part (L. Lingard, interview, October 16, 2014).

Lingard's decision to make medicine not only the object of her inquiry but her intellectual community and institutional home has not surprisingly informed her evolving sense of professional identity and disciplinary ties: "I would refer to myself as a rhetorician, as a scientist of rhetoric, but I never refer to myself as a writing studies scholar anymore" (L. Lingard, interview, October 16, 2014). Lingard also attributes her identification with rhetoric and medicine rather than writing studies to the fact that her research on how health teams communicate has been mostly on spoken rather than written discourse, as well as because time and funding constraints early in her career made it impossible for her to develop research profiles simultaneously in medicine and writing studies. Although she had colleagues and collaborators such as Schryer whose work she admired, in crafting her scholarly identity she felt she had to create a new path for herself as she knew no one who had made such a complete transition into the community they were studying: "There were no rhetorician role models to turn to; I didn't know anyone else who had done that" (L. Lingard, interview, October 16, 2014).

Lingard has tried to make sure her graduate students in medicine, many of whom also come from other disciplines, understand the trade-off involved in crossing disciplinary boundaries: "Unless they're incredibly bright and efficient at some point in the first five years they will need to choose where they are going to build their profile" (L. Lingard, interview, October 16, 2014). Lingard described being very direct with her students about the difficult choices they faced in choosing between their home disciplines and medicine and the trade-off she had to make in her own career:

> I end up having very explicit conversations with them about what it means to effectively give up your identity, your credible identity as a rhetoric and writing studies scholar . . . I would feel as though I would probably be an imposter at those conferences now. I wouldn't be theoretically up to date, and I might not have something to contribute. And I think that that identity of crossing boundaries and making the choice I described about where you're going to build your profile, where you're going to try to be seen as a credible scientist, the underbelly of that is what you give up (L. Lingard, interview, October 16, 2014).

It is a loss for our discipline that scholars such as Lingard no longer perceive themselves as belonging to writing studies, but the discipline-based funding mechanisms and the ongoing forces of specialization within disciplines are key barriers that prevent scholars from maintaining more fluid identities and membership in multiple communities.

Just as Lingard deliberated about choosing medicine over rhetoric as an institutional home and identity, she has carefully crafted her scholarly identity within medicine. Describing the split between how she perceives herself and how others perceive her, she explained that she still sees herself as a rhetorician, which she defined as the study of the social uses of language because "I always read through the lens of language," whereas to colleagues she is "the language person" as well as "the qualitative methods person" (L. Lingard, interview, October 16, 2014). After her initial appointment to a medical education centre and an unsuccessful grant proposal that was aimed more at an audience in writing studies than medicine, she regrouped and focused on achieving recognition within medicine, which meant eliding her identity as educator and cultivating an identity instead as a research scientist:

> I actually worked very hard and eventually successfully to have the word "educator" removed not just from myself but from the whole centre so that everyone who was hired to do research was known as a scientist because . . . I thought it was important that people acknowledge that the kind of research we do is as credible and rigorous as the kind of research [clinicians] do. It was a real stretch for some people because we're talking about cancer researchers, right. I have been crafting the evolution from educator to scientist quite strategically. Now people in roles like mine in Canada will invariably call themselves scientists, which is something that I think is appropriate and I'm proud of it. We don't mean it in a reductive, biomedical kind of experimental use of science, we just mean, this is systematic inquiry too (L. Lingard, interview October 16, 2014).

Lingard's successful transition from a doctoral student in a Rhetoric and Composition program in an English department to a senior scientist in a faculty of medicine shows the considerable rhetorical savvy and flexibility required to relocate so far from one's disciplinary beginnings and craft a new identity that will be credible enough in the particular institutional context to create a lasting institutional home for oneself as a rhetorician in residence.

As it was for Lingard, flexibility has been essential for Roger Graves, whose career has been characterized by disciplinary (or at least sub-disciplinary) and national border crossing between Canada and the United States. He described how he situated himself in the discipline in a particularly fluid way:

> The characterization has oscillated between writing studies, technical writing, WPA/writing administrator, and WAC researcher. I think that's pretty dynamic. It's changed over time and so the communities I've belonged to have also changed to reflect that. Now we're also talking about location, certainly national location here. I keep border hopping. (R. Graves, interview, November 28, 2013).

Graves observed that such a broad range of professional roles and scholarly identities is unique to writing studies: "I keep thinking in the back of my mind of more typical disciplinary colleagues of mine and I know they don't get hired for such a big range [of roles]. I think writing studies people, we have to be a lot more nimble, flexible, and versatile." (R. Graves, interview, November 28, 2013). For Graves, the elastic quality of writing studies has enabled him to pursue a rich and varied career despite the challenge of being one half of an academic couple (he is married to writing studies scholar Heather Brodie Graves): "My career has been defined by trying to find two jobs in one city: the dual career movie." (R. Graves, interview, November 28, 2013). Moreover, like Lingard, he has been able to secure major research grants through one of Canada's federal funding agencies, the Social Science and Humanities Research Council (SSHRC), which he has used not only to further his own research agenda, but also to collaborate with over a dozen scholars at other Canadian institutions, resulting in numerous publications (see André & Graves, 2013 and Graves, Hyland, & Samuels, 2010). Notably, some of these co-investigators would not have been eligible for such research funding on their own because SSHRC grants must be held by researchers in faculty rather than staff positions, which excludes the many writing centre positions in Canada that are staff rather than as faculty positions. Graves has used research funding to mentor and support scholarship by colleagues across Canada and in this way strengthen writing studies networks in Canada and help sustain the discipline.

In addition to Lingard and Graves, the third scholar whose morphing identity and memberships in multiple communities is revealing for what it tells us about the formation of writing studies in Canada is Ron Sheese, one of the founding members of the writing department at York University in Toronto. His lengthy career has straddled psychology and writing studies, where he is now cross-appointed. The development of York's writing program has been recounted elsewhere (Sheese, Spencer, Rehner, Greenwald, and Rozendal, 2006); here I examine Sheese's disciplinary identity and positioning. Like many of the scholars profiled in this book, Sheese became acquainted with writing studies by chance: appointed in psychology, he was asked to do some tutoring in the writing centre where he became interested in teaching writing as a way to study student learning. His colleagues at the time, Marlene Scardamalia and Carl Bereiter, who had offices nearby, introduced him to writing studies, including the work of Flower and Hayes, who continue to influence Sheese's approach to teaching writing. Sheese, like many Canadians, participated in Janet Lauer's Purdue seminar in 1984 where he was able to talk in a small group setting to prominent scholars such as Janet Emig and Walter Ong and become familiar with the discipline.[8] Whereas many writing scholars in the early days of rhetoric and composition came to writing from literature, Sheese was interested in writing as a means of learning more about psychology: "I was a psychologist interested in cognitive psychology and writing seemed a good place to study cognitive psychology" (R. Sheese, interview, June 25, 2015). Like some of the scholars interviewed here, he wasn't even sure he would consider himself a scholar of writing since most of his publications have been in psychology. Sheese's description of his wide-ranging interests and his refusal to pigeonhole his scholarly interests and identity resonates with the approaches espoused by many of the scholars we interviewed, such as Rick Coe's proclivity to be "multidisciplinary" and Doug Brent's perception of writing studies scholars as picking up "bits and pieces" from others and combin[ing] them as they wish" (D. Brent, interview, December 12, 2013). Sheese expressed ambivalence about his hybrid scholarly identity:

> I kind of wander around. Some days I feel like it's a detriment and other times I think of it as an advantage. I'm not a specialist and I don't care for specialists . . . with a little bit of guilt I identify myself as a Jack-of-all-trades. But I often think of that as a real benefit; certainly my students benefit from that . . . (R. Sheese, interview, June 25, 2015).

Sheese has found a unifying force for his multidisciplinary proclivities in the work of John Dewey who has helped him make sense of teaching writing across the curriculum:

> John Dewey has helped me gain a philosophy of education that helps me ground bits and pieces that I'm pulling from other places, for instance the idea that education is only going to work well when the student is working with something they're interested in and committed to—writing instruction works best when students are writing about something they care about. I found this out when working with students on papers that they're doing for their majors (R. Sheese, interview, June 25, 2015).

In addition to this strong textual influence, Sheese continues to draw new ideas from neighbouring colleagues like the recently hired writing studies scholar, Stephanie Bell, along with his collaborations with university librarians on academic literacies, which has connected him to the work of Brian Street and others, which he is using to develop a Learning Commons project that supports students writing research papers. In this way, Sheese exemplifies the morphing disciplinary identity and location of these Canadian writing studies scholars who have been influenced by colleagues situated in close physical proximity to them, including colleagues from different disciplines.

THE ROLE OF SCHOLARLY COMMUNITIES IN SUPPORTING EVOLVING IDENTITIES

These interviews with scholars about their disciplinary identities and affiliations offer several conclusions: first, conferences, both in the United States and in Canada (and in some cases international in scope) have played a vital role in giving both newer and more experienced Canadian scholars intellectual communities, supporting them in their often isolated institutional contexts by introducing them to new ideas and people and offering them a disciplinary identity. Although the conferences these scholars have attended over the years have changed, the importance of conferences as sites of social interaction has persisted. Second, where they exist, institutional hubs have played important roles in supporting individual scholars, but some hubs have contributed more to disciplinary networks than others. Much of the network activity at the University of Toronto has so far been focused on improving writing instruction within the institution, but some members of this circle have extended their activities to Canadian writing studies organizations and conferences. The Carleton University hub, through its scholars' strong research output and its PhD program, has been closely linked not only to the larger Canadian disciplinary network but also to the international rhetorical genre studies community. The second institutional hub examined here, at the University of Windsor, has strong ties to American networks, but is disconnected from the rest of Canada, which has implications for sustaining the discipline in Canada, an issue we address in chapter 6. Third, identity for these scholars has of necessity been highly pluralistic, fluid, and has changed considerably over time and across place, influenced by historical and institutional contexts. Notably, all of these scholars were initially drawn to the discipline to find better ways to understand and to teach writing, whether across the disciplines, in composition courses, in writing centres, or in other professional contexts; and the capacious nature of our discipline has enabled them to pursue a range of professional interests and roles that one would be hard pressed to find in more homogenous and stable disciplines. At the same time, with neither a firm disciplinary tradition of rhetoric (at least in the twentieth century) nor institutional location, these scholars have had to be catholic in their interests and expertise, engage in cross-disciplinary collaborations, and derive intellectual energy and support from people and events that are often geographically remote from their own institutional location or at least reside in different disciplines within their own institution. Lastly, we have seen how these scholars have had to evolve with their institutions and with the field, in some cases moving to different institutions and even countries where they joined new circles or hubs, often crossing sub-disciplinary or disciplinary boundaries to pursue research interests and funding: sometimes, like Schryer, cultivating collaborations with multiple disciplines, other times, like Lingard, joining another discipline entirely. Notably, these Canadian writing scholars show remarkable self-invention in the face of disciplinary marginalization and invisibility, using the lack of disciplinary markers to stake out new intellectual terrain and audiences for their work.

Notes

1. While studying literature at the University of British Columbia, although I had never heard of composition I enrolled in a course on social and feminist theories of composition because I was interested in feminist theory. The professor, Judy Segal, had studied with Andrea Lunsford and Nan Johnson when they were on the faculty at UBC.

2. I've relied on scholars' own identifications to assign national categories rather than any legal definition.

3. I conducted nine of the fourteen interviews. Derek Mueller conducted the interview with Dale Jacobs and Louise Phelps conducted the interviews with Doug Brent, Catherine Schryer, Dan Richards, and Aviva Freedman.

4. Most of the University of Toronto's fourteen writing centres are now headed by full-time faculty directors, many of whom are active in both Inkshed and CASDW (Procter, 2006).

5. The University of Waterloo offers a PhD in English Language and Literature that combines literary study with rhetoric, new media, and discourse analysis and the University of British Columbia has an English doctoral program with a concentration in language that combines linguistics and rhetoric.

6. For a fuller discussion of the institutional history of writing at the University see Procter, 2006.

7. Unlike teaching-focused positions at other institutions, those at the University of Toronto are not teaching-only positions; rather, as of a 2015 agreement, teaching-stream appointments have entrenched faculty members' right to engage in not only pedagogical but also discipline-based research.

8. From 1978–1985 twenty-two Canadians participated in Lauer's seminars. Personal communication, September 25, 2013.

References

André, J. & R. Graves, (2013). Writing requirements across nursing programs in Canada. *Journal of Nursing Education*, 52(2), 91–91.

Burke, K. (1950). *A rhetoric of motives*. Berkeley: University of California Press.

Clary-Lemon, J. (2009). Shifting tradition: Writing research in Canada. *American Review of Canadian Studies*, 39(2), 94–111.

Collins, R. (1998). *The sociology of philosophies: A global theory of intellectual change*. Cambridge, MA: Harvard University Press.

Graves, R. (1994). *Writing instruction in Canadian universities*. Winnipeg, MB: Inkshed.

Graves, R. and Graves, H. (Eds.). (2006). *Writing centres, writing seminars, writing culture: Writing instruction in Anglo-Canadian universities*. Victoria, BC: Inkshed/Trafford.

Graves, R., Hyland, T, & Samuels, B. (2010). Undergraduate writing assignments: An analysis of syllabi at one Canadian college. *Written Communication*, 27(3), 293–347.

Horne, M. E. (2012). *Writing in a community of practice: Composing membership in Inkshed*. Bloomington, IN: Trafford Publishing.

Johnson, N. (2006). Rhetoric and belles lettres in the Canadian academy: An historic analysis. In R. Graves & H. Graves, (Eds.), *Writing centres, writing seminars, writing culture: Writing instruction in Anglo-Canadian universities* (pp. 43–60). Victoria, BC: Inkshed/Trafford.

Lauer, J. (1998). Disciplinary formation: The summer rhetoric seminar. *JAC* 18, 503–508.

Miller, S. (1991) *Textual carnivals: The politics of composition*. Carbondale, IL: Southern Illinois University Press.

Mueller, D. (2012). Grasping rhetoric and composition by its long tail: What graphs can tell us about the field's changing shape. *College Composition and Communication*, 64(1), 195–223.

Patton, M. Q. (2002). *Qualitative research and evaluation methods* (3rd ed.). Sage.

Phelps, L. W. (2014). The historical formation of academic identities: Rhetoric and composition, discourse and writing. Keynote address, Canadian Association for the Study of Discourse and Writing. Waterloo, ON. (2012). *Canadian Journal for Studies in Discourse and Writing*, 25(1) 3–25.

Phelps, L. W., & Ackerman, J. M. (2010). Making the case for disciplinarity in rhetoric, composition, and writing studies. *CCC, 62*(1), 180–215.

Procter, M. (2006). Catching up with ourselves. In R. Graves & H. Graves (Eds.), *Writing centres, writing seminars, writing culture: Writing instruction in Anglo-Canadian universities* (pp. 297–316). Victoria, BC: Inkshed/Trafford.

Rapley, T.J. (2001). The art(fullness) of open-ended interviewing: some considerations on analysing interviews. *Qualitative Research, 1*(3), 303–323.

Schryer, C.F. (2011). Investigating texts in their social contexts: The promise and peril of rhetorical genre studies. In D. Starke-Meyerring, A. Paré, M. Horne, & L. Yousoubova (Eds.), *Writing in knowledge societies* (pp. 31–52). Fort Collins, CO: WAC Clearinghouse and Parlor Press.

Seidman, I. (2006). *Interviewing as qualitative research: A guide for researchers in education and the social sciences.* New York: Teachers College Press.

Sheese, R., Spencer, J., Rehner, J., Greenwald, T., & Rozendal, P. (2006). Independent writing programs at York University. In R. Graves & H. Graves (Eds.), *Writing centres, writing seminars, writing culture: Writing instruction in Anglo-Canadian universities* (255-272). Victoria, BC: Inkshed/Trafford.

Silverman, D. (2005). *Doing qualitative research: A practical handbook.* London: Sage.

Smith, T. Inkshed (2000). What kind of shed are you? A micro-ethnography of the CASLL/Inkshed Listserv and conference. Retrieved from http://people.ucalgary.ca/~smit/Scholarship/InkshedEthnography.htm

4 Four Scholars, Four Genres: Networked Trajectories

Louise Wetherbee Phelps

> *The hope was to achieve a new angle of vision by following [the] thread of a particular destiny. . . and with it the multiplicity of spaces and times, the complex tangle of relations in which that destiny became involved.*
>
> —Jacques Revel
> *Microanalysis and the Construction of the Social*

INTRODUCTION

In chapter 2, Derek Mueller introduced some concepts that reappear in subsequent chapters, where through our methodological modulations of scale, focus, and perspective they are taken up, reinterpreted, and reapplied in connected but different ways. In that chapter, a "career footprint" initially referred to the visual representation of a scholar's career as a relationship between his or her current location (hub) and all the locations where the scholar has studied or worked (spokes). However, Mueller's experiments with different logics for mapping networks led to a deeper understanding of scholars' career footprints as simultaneously emplaced and distributed, through the cross-border paths followed by those they mentor. Chapter 3 personifies this concept in the careers of fourteen Canadian scholars who have put their imprint on writing studies in Canada, the United States, and beyond. Andrea Williams used scholars' own voices to convey the paths and patterns of their careers, evoking the human experiences of learning, working, and participating in emplaced and distributed networks over the span of a career. At the same time, the hub and spoke metaphor symbolizing a single career (and node in a network of scholars) in chapter 2 took on a new meaning in reference to the "disciplinary hubs" of conferences and "institutional hubs" that emerged from the interviews in chapter 3. They are tied together there by the social, intellectual, and emotional meaning these hubs had for our interviewees, as the sites of interaction in a cross-border intellectual network that allowed Canadian writing studies to develop in an inhospitable environment.

The conferences described by Williams in chapter 3 as social rituals, along with the few institutional hubs where Canadian scholars have been able to cluster, are characteristic means by which scholarly networks form and flourish, according to Collins's (1998) theory of intellectual communities as social networks. In Collins's theory, which influenced our approach to this study, systematic intellectual activity (in our terms, disciplinarity) is a function of the structure and dynamics of social networks, expanding outward from small groups of scholars who engage directly with one another to develop and debate ideas. Their interactions and communications, primarily face-to-face, simultaneously facilitate the flow of ideas through the network and create an intellectual community bound by social relationships. As demonstrated in previous chapters, such networks integrate relationships of two kinds: horizontal or synchronic, linking contemporaries in the same location or across space; and vertical or diachronic, linking scholars intergenerationally to extend the network over time (Collins, 1998, p. 65). Our study supports Collins's belief that the interpersonal interactions fostered in hubs are indispensable for networks to form and function as channels for intellectual activity. Conferences are the quintessential example of what Collins calls an "interaction ritual," where the excitement and exchanges of ideas charge the participants with emotional energy and construct new cultural capital (pp. 23–24). The institutional hubs, often anchored initially by one charismatic scholar, have a larger role in making a network viable and sustainable: first, by providing an organizational base for assembling a critical mass of creative scholars; and, second, by educating young scholars, forming interaction chains that will continue and expand the network into the future, as they travel out the spokes and carry ideas to other locations.

This chapter continues our attention to career footprints, narrowing the focus further to profile four scholars in depth, but exploring a broad span of reciprocal influences through horizontal and vertical links. It juxtaposes their experiences, contributions, roles, and relations to other scholars and to hubs, weaving a texture of overlapping participation in social networks through time and space. But, by using scholar-genre pairings to trace these trajectories, this chapter adds a new element to the understanding of networked disciplinarity we are building: the role of writing in creating and sustaining intellectual communities, in a context where many would-be scholars have had little access to hubs of either kind within easy geographical reach.

Evolving Goals and Methods

Originally, I set out in my part of this project to study a hidden current of Canadian scholarship in the discourse of American rhetoric and composition, constituting one strand in the interdependencies that link Canadian and US writing studies.[1] As an American reader, I knew that Canadian writings could be found in the literature of the field from its earliest days, but these texts seldom emphasized or even identified their Canadian authorship. This practice has limited the salience of Canadian scholarship to US scholars because it is simply assimilated to the disciplinary discourse and disappears as a category. But I conjectured that some Canadian work had achieved broad enough currency to establish, collectively, a "quiet presence" for Canadian scholarship in the literature and history of the American discipline. I wanted to trace that presence as a basis for identifying particular scholars, texts, or strands of work for focused critical or historical study. But such tracing was methodologically challenging, requiring multiple strategies and resources to identify Canadian scholars and determine their contributions and reputation in different research communities of American rhetoric, composition, and writing studies.

Using the list of Canadian scholars that our team had constructed collaboratively, I began with a study of indices to discover the number and distribution of "mentions" of these Canadian scholars in an array of works that aim to represent the field (under terms like rhetoric and/or composition, writing studies) in some comprehensive way: encyclopedias, handbooks, histories and disciplinary overviews, broad-based collections, conference volumes, sourcebooks, and so on.[2] Simultaneously, I extended my reading of Canadian histories, organizational documents, and scholarly writings.

The mentions of Canadian scholars and works in these indexed sources did establish that some are well-known to US scholars and that, collectively, they constitute a significant if quiet stream of scholarly contributions to American rhetoric and composition, especially in its formative period. This conclusion, complicating the historical narrative of a North American nexus, was corroborated by the survey and interview data reported in the previous two chapters (see map of publication venues, chapter 2). However, my project underwent a sea-change in goals and methods as I reflected on the findings (and limitations) of my own preliminary study and the information flowing in from our team's interviews and surveys. For one thing, it became evident that studying scholars' rhetorical presence in terms of a bi-directional US-Canadian exchange oversimplifies Canada's role in Anglo-American writing studies and fails to account for more complex mediations and transnational relationships—and identities—in which its scholars participate. As expressed in survey responses (see map of identification, chapter 2) and the interviews analyzed in chapter 3, the notions of "Canadian scholars" or a Canadian scholarly identity proved to be inadequate to our scholars' experiences and self-perceptions, including ambiguous, multiple, and changing identities as scholars and human beings.[3] As we learned more about our scholars' lives and contributions, I came to believe that the concept of "presence" can't be equated with, or measured solely by, publications in conventional forms and sites, of the kind typically represented in indices and citations. This insight awakened my interest in genres that don't fit this mould as a source of appreciating the diverse, often overlooked ways that intellectual work is performed and scholarly communities are formed and sustained.

My discoveries in the preliminary study highlighted the work of certain Canadian scholars, based on their writings in genres that seemed to hold this potential. In the close-grained hermeneutical inquiry reported in this chapter, I examine the work of four such scholars—Aviva Freedman, James Reither, Catherine Schryer, and Sharon Hamilton—through their writings in genres that fall in some respect outside the norms for high-valued academic writing.[4] My focus is neither the scholar nor the genre, but the writings in each genre as revelation of the scholar's contributions, relationships, and contexts. In the spectrum of distant to close perspectives in this book, my method combines a close, intimate focus on a few scholars with an evocation of the emplaced and distributed intellectual networks their lives and writings traverse in time and space.

I conceived this approach, somewhat playfully, as paying homage to the rhetorical genre studies in which Canadian scholars have played a leading role. But the pairings of scholar and genre proved to be an unexpectedly powerful heuristic, not only serving as a metonym for a scholar's career but also yielding rich insights into the traditions and communities of Canadian writing scholarship and their many forms of connection with one another, American scholars, other disciplines and professions, and international communities.

In order to achieve its hermeneutical goals, encompassing understanding and critical appreciation, my study relies on textual, historical, and biographical strategies to trace the trajectory of each scholar and text through various domains and activities.[5] In each case, I will examine an author's text or set of texts by locating it simultaneously in multiple contexts: in the body of the scholar's work, sustained over time; in the collaborations he or she engaged in; in the traditions and communities a scholar represents, studies, and connects; in the genre itself, as part of the repertoire of scholarly genres in a field; and in each scholar's study and practices of border-crossing. As I weave these contexts together around writings by each scholar, I explore their intertextuality and reveal how these Canadian scholars are linked into networks of ideas and communication, sometimes unknowingly, by overlapping experiences and interpersonal relationships.

Introducing Four Scholars and Their Genres

Although some scholars in my study have appeared in earlier chapters through the lenses of surveys and interviews, let me reintroduce all four scholars here as authors whose impactful writing in nontraditional or undervalued genres drew me to them as subjects of this study. The genres represented in these pairings include the co-edited conference volume (Aviva Freedman); the organizational newsletter (James Reither); the collaborative interdisciplinary research article (Catherine Schryer); and the literacy autobiography (Sharon Hamilton). I begin in each case with a brief biography to situate these scholars and their careers in relation to the development of writing studies in Canada.

Aviva Freedman, one of our interviewees, has emerged in our collaborative study as one of the most influential figures in shaping the evolution of Canadian discourse and writing studies, from teachers' discovery of the emerging discipline in the US to the international contributions of today's rhetorical genre scholars in their research on disciplinary and professional discourses. Canadian-born and educated, after teaching composition briefly in the US in the late sixties she spent her career at Carleton University in Ottawa, where she held academic appointments in Applied Linguistics and Discourse Studies and a series of administrative posts at the university until retiring in 2007. One of these—directing a center for Jewish Studies—continued until 2014, when she went to Israel to study "classic Jewish texts, history, archeology (all of which are enriched by a 'genre' perspective)" (A. Freedman, personal communication, February 9, 2014).

Freedman's practical exposure to composition as taught in the US awakened an interest in scholarly perspectives on writing, and when she returned to Canada and to university teaching she began reading widely in the growing composition literature. Multiple discourse traditions influenced her uptake of American composition. Educated in New Critical methods, the long-dominant literary method in Canada (thanks to Northrop Frye), she was also steeped in the Jewish tradition of reading classic texts by comparing interpretive commentaries on them. Freedman notes that in Jewish practice close reading goes beyond the New Critical focus on the text as a formal object to look at "language in use. . . [and] the ways in which language relates to broader epistemological perspectives, theories of the world, understanding of the world you live in" (interview, December 19, 2013). Her thinking about writing was also shaped by exposure to classical rhetoric from a PhD supervisor, giving her "a sense of a tradition that took writing far more seriously, had a sense of occasion . . . of rhetorical situation and . . . a sense of composing involving so much more than the very narrow very limited part of the process that typical handbooks talked about" (interview, December 19, 2013).

She brought this background to the multi-year research project that initiated her long collaborative partnership with linguistics professor Ian Pringle, investigating how Ontario's faculties of education were preparing teachers to teach writing. Their study convinced them that teachers needed more than one year of training for literacy education, through both undergraduate preparation and courses for practicing teachers, and Carleton appointed Freedman to a position in Linguistics to fill this role. She and Pringle followed the first project with studies, reports, and publications on students' writing development in early grades and then in the university, across several disciplines. As Freedman's research focus evolved from literacy in the schools to writing in the disciplines and then professional discourse, she maintained a commitment throughout her career to professional development and in-service education for teachers, offering countless workshops, presentations, and consultancies for practitioners on writing pedagogy.

A productive scholar herself, Freedman played a catalytic role in developing a community of Canadian writing scholars through the conferences she co-organized with Pringle and others, her mentorship of young scholars (Catherine Schryer among them), and her collaborations with colleagues and graduate students in research projects and publications on language, learning, and genre. As documented in chapter 3, she was a key figure in establishing Carleton University as a hub for such collaborative scholarship and intergenerational mentoring. The recently established (2012) PhD program in Applied Linguistics and Discourse at Carleton (one of the few in Canada) is a legacy of her leadership in graduate education.

What attracted me to Freedman initially as a subject for this project was the collections that she co-edited from two major international conferences held at Carleton under her leadership. I knew about the 1979 Ottawa conference on "Learning to Write" (co-chaired with Ian Pringle) from an American perspective as a milestone in the formation and recognition of composition and rhetoric as a discipline; one of the three volumes Freedman co-edited from that conference, *Reinventing the Rhetorical Tradition* (Freedman & Pringle, 1980), is an international classic in the field.[6] Another conference Freedman organized (with Peter Medway), the 1992 Carleton Colloquium on Rethinking Genre, is widely recognized as inaugurating rhetorical genre studies as a Canadian research program (see Freedman & Medway, 1994a). Freedman's conference-based edited collections suggested a promising focus for the kind of hermeneutical investigation I envisioned, which would encompass and connect an individual scholar's work and career with events, traditions, other scholars, and historical developments in writing studies within and beyond Canada. I will examine Freedman's editorial contributions in this underappreciated genre, highlighting her role in a series of landmark international conferences that were pivotal events for development of the field in Canada and worldwide.

James (Jim) Reither was born and educated in the United States, but emigrated to Canada in the late 1960s, where he taught at St. Thomas University in Fredericton for almost thirty years before retiring in

1996. Though his PhD was in literature, he found himself increasingly interested in writing and writing pedagogy; as early as 1971, he was co-organizing, with his colleague Russell Hunt, a Maritime Provinces Conference on Freshman English. In 1979 he attended Freedman and Pringle's "Learning to Write" conference, which he found "enormously exciting and invigorating," realizing "this was a field I could devote myself to." Reither remembers "the Brits" (rather than the Americans) as "firing me up" (personal communication, February 7, 2014). But, along with some Canadian colleagues, Reither began to connect with American scholars who were developing the new discipline, attending conferences like CCCC and the Wyoming Conference on Freshman English; and in 1981–82 he spent the year as a visiting scholar at the University of Texas-Austin studying American composition and rhetoric. That same year his first article on writing appeared in the new American journal *Pre/Text* (Reither, 1981), and he continued throughout his career to publish on subjects from collaborative learning to genre in both American and Canadian journals and presses. He was also active in professional organizations and learned societies on both sides of the border, including committees and leadership roles in the Conference on College Composition and Communication (CCCC); the Canadian Council of Teachers of English (CCTE); and, most significantly (as co-founder), the first Canadian organizations concerned with writing theory and pedagogy—Inkshed and its successor the Canadian Association for the Study of Language and Learning (CASLL).

I was familiar with Reither's contributions to the developing field in the US, including his much cited and reprinted article "Writing and Knowing: Toward Redefining the Writing Process" in *College English* (1985), which argues for immersing student writers in knowledge/discourse communities where they can experience inquiry, reading, and academic writing as inseparably linked "collaborative, social acts, social processes" (p. 625). But it was reading early archives of the Inkshed newsletter that inspired me to choose Reither for this study. The unique Canadian institution called "Inkshed" began in 1981 as a newsletter edited and distributed by Reither and developed into a close-knit scholarly community, anchored by an annual conference. As witnessed in our interviews and surveys, Inkshed became an anchoring identity for many Canadian writing scholars and teachers, playing a vital educational and support role in their struggle to develop discourse and writing studies in Canada (see Horne, 2012; Smith, 2000; chapter 3, this volume). Reither's contributions to the pre-digital Inkshed newsletter as its founding editor (through 1987) place him at the center of early efforts to make that happen. This humble genre, the organizational newsletter, in conjunction with Reither's career as a pioneer writing scholar in Canada, provides a window on the self-education of a Canadian writing studies community and its relations to US-based rhetoric and composition.

Catherine (Cathy) Schryer, another of our interviewees, is one of the leading scholars in rhetorical genre studies, the author of award-winning research articles, chapters, and edited books on her studies of writing in professional contexts. She did her BA and MA degrees in Canada in the 1970s and had almost completed a PhD at the University of Toronto while teaching at the University of Guelph when, dissatisfied with the traditional Canadian approach to teaching writing, she discovered the emerging American field of composition. She educated herself through reading on her own, networking with the Montreal and Carleton research groups, and finding Canadian and American mentors, notably Aviva Freedman at Carleton and Janice Lauer at Purdue, when—like Freedman before her and Hamilton after her—she attended Lauer's Rhetoric Seminar in 1985. Encouraged by Lauer, she abandoned her dissertation in literature and went to the States to earn her doctorate in rhetoric and composition at the University of Louisville in 1990. Since then she has taught at three Canadian universities, including her current position as Professor and Chair of the School of Professional Communication at Ryerson University in Toronto, where she established an accelerated master's program and, in 2013, a four-year bachelor's degree in professional communication.

Schryer was an early contributor to Canadian conceptualization of writing across the curriculum, as co-editor of the conference volume *Contextual Literacy* (Schyrer & Steven, 1994). But the bulk of Schryer's research focuses on advanced literacies in the professions, particularly in healthcare fields, seeking to understand the resources and functions of particular genres, and how they are taught, learned, and used most effectively by practitioners. A key feature of her inquiries, supported by substantial research grants, is that they are conducted with colleagues from other fields who represent a range of professional experience, expertise, and methodologies (see Lingard, Schryer, Spafford, & Campbell, 2007). Many of Schryer's publications have emerged from sustained collaborations, like her partnership with Lorelei Lingard for more than a decade, which produced more than twenty-five multi-disciplinary research articles (C. Schryer, interview, January 4, 2014; CV). (See chapter 3 on the evolution of Lingard's scholarly identity.) Results from the team's multi-year research projects are disseminated in clusters of collaboratively authored publications, each addressed and tailored to particular audiences in the professions—researchers, practitioners, educators—as well as to writing researchers, theorists, methodologists, and teachers. The diverse (disciplinary and transdisciplinary) publication channels selected and the focus of individual articles reflect not only the fields and interests of the research collaborators, but also the dual goals of the project: building theoretical knowledge about genres and discourse competencies in the professions and making that knowledge available to writers, learners, and educators in the professions as well as to genre or rhetoric specialists.

I was intrigued by the genre consequences of Schryer's collaborative research model and the hermeneutical possibilities of examining these texts in the broader landscape of her work as a genre theorist (including single-authored articles and edited books). The collaborative, multidisciplinary research article, while common in the sciences, is relatively rare in writing studies, and seldom taken as far afield as in Schryer's ventures across disciplinary and professional borders. The genre is rhetorically complicated in Schryer's case by the researchers' dual goals and represents the very phenomena—genre dynamism and evolution, professional communication across communities of practice—that they are studying. I will examine a number of examples from Schryer's work since, as we will see, the point of such articles is to build a cumulative text, collaborative not only in its processes of research but also in its participation in a larger research collaborative and its intertext, within and beyond writing studies in Canada.

Sharon J. Hamilton is a Canadian-born scholar and longtime teacher in Canadian schools who, after getting a PhD at the University of London, moved to the United States for her university career. She grew up in Manitoba, Canada, where she survived a traumatic early childhood to lead a life she describes in her autobiography as "salvaged" and "transformed" by literacy in successive moments: from escape into fantasy as a troubled child, to her pursuit of intellectual knowledge through formal education, to—as "author" of her own life (Hamilton, 1995, p. 98)—becoming a person empowered by self-understanding and empathy to help others like herself.

In 1963, with only a year of Teachers College beyond her high school diploma, Hamilton began her teaching career in a one-room schoolhouse for eight grades and taught at different levels in Manitoban schools for seventeen years. During these years, she struggled to continue her education, working nights and summers to earn her BA and BEd, and eventually starting a Masters, while rising in her profession to become an English department chair and president of the Manitoba Association of Teachers of English. In 1980, the year after Reither attended the Ottawa Conference, she too was inspired by "the Brits" to join the community of writing scholars. A serendipitous encounter with James Britton and Harold Rosen at the annual CCTE conference encouraged her to do her doctoral study at the University of London, where she was tutored by Rosen, Tony Burgess, and John Dixon.

After graduating, Hamilton taught elementary English education briefly at the University of Manitoba, her alma mater. But, like many Canadians, she had to look to the US for a faculty appointment in her own field of writing studies. She found one at Indiana University-Purdue University at Indianapolis (IUPUI), where she became professor of English and an innovative administrator. At IUPUI, in a series of leadership roles beginning with the directorship of campus writing, Hamilton broadened her initial disciplinary horizon (writing studies and literacy education) to the scholarship of teaching and learning and its systematic implementation at an institutional level, enabling the university (and Hamilton) to take a pioneering role in national and international conversations about educational reform focused on enhancing and integrating student learning.

As an émigré who spent her post-graduate career in the United States, Hamilton is an unexpected choice for my study. Despite considerable accomplishments in her US career, she is not well-known in Canadian circles and was not a formative influence on the field of discourse and writing in Canada. But, in the course of reading publications written by Canadian scholars who attended the Summer Rhetoric Seminar run by Janice Lauer during the 1970s and 80s,[7] I came across Hamilton's memoir *My Name's Not Susie* (1995), an unflinchingly candid autoethnography of her tormented childhood and gradual liberation through literacy. As soon as I read it I knew I wanted to pair this scholar and genre for my hermeneutical project. Beyond the intrinsic interest of her story, I sensed in this pairing the potential for revelations about the Canadian cultural scene of writing studies beyond what I had yet glimpsed in its scholarly literature.

Aviva Freedman and the (Co)-Edited Collection from a Conference

In 1980, Aviva Freedman and her colleague Ian Pringle published *Reinventing the Rhetorical Tradition*, one of three publications that came out of the international conference they organized in 1979 at Carleton University, called "Learning to Write."[8] The battered condition of my own copy testifies to its constant use in my research and graduate classes since then, as a record of what James Zebroski (2012) recently called one of the founding events of the discipline. He declares that "the discipline of composition and rhetoric begins to coalesce in the late 1970s; the Ottawa Conference of 1979 is one site where the discipline was born" (p. 42). And, through the efforts of Aviva Freedman and her Canadian colleagues, it was born international.

When Freedman and Pringle began collaborating to study teacher education methods in writing instruction, he was a senior professor in linguistics and dean at Carleton (later, first vice president and acting president) while she was a contingent faculty member (what Canadians call a "sessional"), soon to become an assistant professor with his support. Despite these differences in status, during the project they developed a deep respect for one another, based on appreciation of their complementary interests and different domains of knowledge (A. Freedman, personal communication, February 9, 2014; I. Pringle, personal communication, February 17, 2014). As in many collaborations observed in our study, their differences became the source of mutual learning and creativity in many projects together, including their co-leadership of the 1979 conference and production of its three edited volumes. Their relationship set the pattern for Freedman's collaborative methods in future conferences as well as co-edited volumes and grant-supported, large-scale research projects, working with Pringle (for more than a decade), other colleagues, and students.

Freedman's early work with Pringle, including her responsibility for a bibliography of the field, influenced her intellectual trajectory by enhancing her methodological skills and expanding her knowledge base in literacy and literacy education, particularly from a linguistics perspective (A. Freedman, interview, December 19, 2013). Their studies together conceived and researched writing in developmental terms over the entire span of schooling, reflecting British work by James Britton (Britton, Burgess, Martin, McLeod, & Rosen, 1975) and especially Andrew

Wilkinson (A.M. Wilkinson, 1978; A.M. Wilkinson and M.E. Wilkinson, 1978), which emphasized "the whole development of the individual from the cognitive through the affective and the oral as well" (A. Freedman, interview, December 19, 2013).[9] This theme expanded beyond schooling and evolved conceptually as her attention shifted to disciplinary and nonacademic research sites: "The goal of my research program has been to understand growth in discursive competencies (understood initially as development in abilities and more recently as expansion of repertoire in disciplinary and workplace genres) . . . within a socio-cultural rhetorical framework" (A. Freedman, CV).

At the same time, Freedman's review of the literature had uncovered a "wealth of new material which was, in effect a renaissance of rhetorical studies, with researchers and thinkers in a variety of different geographic jurisdictions looking at the act of composing and the development of writing abilities and using a range of different disciplinary lenses. Ian and I began to fantasize about bringing together some of these thinkers and researchers, since many seemed to be just dimly aware of each other's work at that time" (A. Freedman, 1990 interview, in Maguire, 1995, pp. 83–84).

By the time Freedman and Pringle's proposal for an international conference was accepted by the Canadian Council of Teachers of English in December 1977, their learning together had prepared them for an unprecedented task—bringing together a multidisciplinary, global group of scholars to articulate a new discipline of writing. In the summer of 1978 Freedman attended Lauer's Rhetoric Seminar, which she describes as "seminal in opening up a whole range of thinking for me" (interview, December 19, 2013). It also supplied a potential list of speakers for the conference; Freedman invited all of them, and most accepted. She and Pringle recruited other speakers by exploiting their unique Canadian geopolitical position to broker relationships between their American neighbors and their Commonwealth colleagues. According to Freedman, "we approached a number of the real recognized stars in the field and we found that the way to get everyone's agreement initially was we got one really big British star and we got a big American star who'd never met each other" and used them as mutual inducements to participate. As these stars signed on, proposals flooded in from their call for papers. (interview, December 19, 2013). Ultimately, Freedman and Pringle attracted scholars from five continents and put them into conversation, often lively and contentious. In doing so, they provided the catalyst for scholars from many fields, nations, and intellectual traditions to suddenly perceive their work as mutually relevant, as coalescing into an emergent discipline.

In this genre, editors have many available strategies to present the conference content and to control or nuance its rhetorical effects. These include titling, selection of content, organization (categorizing sections in a table of contents, ordering the selections), and the guiding and summarizing materials written by themselves or others. The material written by editors themselves to orient their readers in such a collection can be more or less substantive and rhetorically purposeful; at its best, it can both convey the experience of the conference and advance its aims. The editors can adopt stances toward the selections ranging from a rather neutral, collectors' attitude to strong interpretation, commentary, and advocacy. In the case of a conference that features considerable debate and diversity of views, as this did, the editors' stance toward the authors' ideas is layered on and intertwined with their position and goals regarding the conference itself.

Freedman and Pringle took full advantage of this array of editorial powers to pursue related but different goals and strategies in three conference-based collections. In each case, they used their own editorial writings as a major tool. Of the three books, *Reinventing* has the most scholarly importance in arguing that multinational writing studies have converged into a discipline, rhetorically established by the very co-presence of so many stellar, multidisciplinary scholars at the same conference—and in the book. The preface and epilogue communicate the mood of the conference—"buoyant, exhilarated, confident" (Freedman & Pringle, 1980, p.176); its significance as a founding event; and the intellectual excitement it generated. Freedman later described the process of organizing the conference as a "wonderful experience because, first, we got to invite the people who, from our reading, seemed to be developing brilliant new insights and, second, we got to read through the hundreds of proposals for papers, and then it became clear that something very important was happening across the English-speaking world, in terms of discovering and redefining a new discipline and a new psychic terrain" (interview, 1990, in Maguire, 1995, p. 84). Especially in the extensive epilogue, they staked out a position regarding competing paradigms—the rhetorical tradition and Emig's "tacit tradition" of twentieth century thinkers: laying out points of difference, balancing claims, and aligning themselves with a new intellectual matrix with multiple roots that reinvents rather than resurrects the rhetorical tradition.

In the two other co-edited books produced from the conference, *Teaching, Writing, Learning* (Pringle & Freedman, 1981) and *Learning to Write: First Language/Second Language* (Pringle, Freedman, & Yalden, 1983), Freedman and Pringle used their editorial roles to address other audiences in different terms. The conference had included a stream of pedagogical workshops. As J. Martin O'Hara observed in his preface, *Teaching, Writing, Learning* "attempts to cast these workshops into written form" for those who couldn't attend the conference (Pringle & Freedman, 1981, p. iii). Whereas the first book's editorial material interpreted, historicized, and synthesized the content of the conference for scholars, here Pringle and Freedman educated teachers. For each representation of a workshop event and its practical lessons they wrote an introduction providing theoretical background and a research context for the practice it evokes. In this way they prepared teachers to integrate such theories and research into the recommended and exemplified practices, constantly explaining and emphasizing why teachers should be interested in these new strategies for their own classrooms. The book is structured through cross-reference to function as a textbook for prospective or practicing teachers.[10]

In *Learning to Write*, Janice Yalden, a second-language scholar, joined Freedman and Pringle to address yet another audience and issue: the first and second language scholars and educators at the conference, and the dramatic difference in their views and practices.[11] In doing so, the editors identified an important divide that foreshadows current differences in genre studies between more linguistically oriented approaches and those that emphasize social context—a problem explored recently by Catherine Schryer in a review of genre (2002). In doing so, they were decades ahead of efforts in the United States to integrate first and second language writing instruction (see Matsuda, 1999; Matsuda, Fruit, & Lamm, 2006). In introductions to the four parts of *Learning to Write*, Freedman, Pringle, and Yalden educate readers from each group about the other's work, comparing and evaluating their approaches, and urge a rapprochement between them. This book, published in London in a series on applied linguistics and language study, has a more international flavor and, more fully than *Reinventing*, places writing in a longer developmental span that includes adult learners and their contexts.

In 1986, Freedman co-hosted another high-impact international conference with Pringle and Nazru Deen (the Fourth International Conference on the Teaching of English), focused on "The Issues That Divide Us." This conference deliberately sought to be more inclusive of practitioners and invited speakers from every English-speaking country (Margaret Gill, interview, 1986, in Maguire, 1995, p. 29; I. Pringle, personal communication, February 15, 2014). While it did not produce a book, sources suggest that the 1986 conference made a powerful impression on participants (Maguire, 1995), reflecting the planners' efforts to highlight differences that would spark debate, a tactic modeled on the most electric moments of the first conference (I. Pringle, personal communication, February 15, 2014). In her interview with Mary Maguire in *Dialogue in a Major Key*, Freedman affirmed her commitment to fostering this kind of engagement in argument and her appreciation of the intense debates that took place. Acknowledging her own impulse to seek commonalities and harmonize differences, she said "at the same time I am very comfortable with a set of assumptions guiding the group which say that it's okay to have an argument over issues or ideas," as long as it doesn't target persons (A. Freedman, 1990 interview, in Maguire, 1995, p. 91).

In the 1990s Freedman's work took a new path when she co-hosted another landmark conference, the "Rethinking Genre" Colloquium at Carleton in 1992, which produced two collections co-edited with Peter Medway, *Learning and Teaching Genre* (Freedman & Medway, 1994a) and *Genre in the New Rhetoric* (Freedman & Medway, 1994b). This select colloquium, which brought together an array of scholars to share work on genre, launched rhetorical genre studies as one of Canada's strongest contributions to writing studies.[12] Freedman has described how discovering the concept of genre completely reconfigured her developmental framework for inquiry into writing, illuminating and clarifying longstanding problems, providing an overarching theoretic base and setting new tasks for her research (interview, December 19, 2013; welcome message to conference, "Genre 2012: Rethinking Genre 20 Years Later," Carleton University, June, 2012). In turn, through her genre conferences and subsequent edited collections, she characteristically provided opportunities for others, including many in our study, to develop this generative idea.

Although an excellent researcher in her own right, Freedman's genius, and her special contribution to writing studies in Canada and beyond, was in her ability to serve as a catalyst, an orchestrator of dialogue and debate, a person who creates occasions for bringing people and intellectual projects into productive new relations. In this underrated role, she embodied the kind of "presence" that energizes and extends intellectual networks. As Janet Emig described her, Freedman "appreciates . . . with extraordinary prescience and creativity . . . . And she builds communities, locally, nationally, and internationally" (J. Emig, interview, 1986, in Maguire, 1995, p. 79). To do this requires a generalist's eclectic knowledge of the field, the ability to synthesize it and to sense where the crucial problems and issues are, what the new ones on the horizon will be, and who the key players are that need to be put into conversation. She was, as well, an educator and mentor who inspired many to learn about writing studies and drew teachers into the community of scholars.

JAMES REITHER AND THE EPISTEMIC NEWSLETTER

In September, 1982 a kind of quiet revolution began when a small group of educators in Canada received a duplicated copy of a modest-looking newsletter, composed by Jim Reither, printed on a dot-matrix printer, and mailed out to about seventy potential subscribers.[13] In 1983 the newsletter became *"Inkshed,"* named for a practice called "inkshedding" that became a signature of the group's annual conference.[14] Originally a teaching strategy invented by Reither and Russell Hunt, "inkshedding" is a dialogic practice of writing in response to a common experience, like a reading. In the classic conference version, participants freewrite after a presentation or event, then pass their "inksheds" around to readers, who mark passages they find interesting. Some appointed as editors select and publish marked passages to the conference attendees.

An interesting example of inkshedding links Reither to Catherine Schryer through a 1990 conference on writing across the curriculum, inscribed in her co-edited book *Contextual Literacy*. Reither and Hunt offered the concluding workshop to the conference, the culminating event in their effort to engage participants in a "collaborative investigation" of the conference itself (Hunt & Reither, 1994, p. 136). They published inksheddings from the workshop—the capstone of this inquiry—in the final chapter of Schryer and Steven's collection. This rare glimpse of inkshedding as Reither practiced it reveals how it embodied a principle he argued throughout his scholarship: "In one way or another, all writing and knowing, and all learning about writing and knowing, are processes we undertake not alone but with others. . . . All of us who make meaning through writing and reading—scholars, teachers, students—do so in community with others who share our interests in the knowing and the knowledge making processes that constitute our fields of inquiry. Writing *is* collaboration" (Reither & Vipond, 1989, p. 866).

Although Reither served as editor until 1987, the inaugural newsletter of *Inkshed* was already the product of a collaborative, comprised of Reither's close colleague Russ Hunt and a handful of other Canadians who for some years had been meeting in the US at the Conference on College Composition and Communication (known as "4Cs") and the Wyoming Conference.[15] As Reither reports, these Canadians, who were energized by the "revolution" in writing and reading studies and wanted to join it, had observed the irony that they had to cross international borders to communicate. Eventually they decided they needed "a Canadian print forum that would allow us to exchange information and ideas" (Reither, Newsletter, September, 1982, p. 2). Some of them were among the "provincial correspondents" the newsletter counted on for reports. Hunt's more prominent role is signaled by his name on the masthead, first as "far-flung correspondent," later as "silent partner." He and Reither were a complementary pair, with their interests in reading and writing, respectively, and their shared views of language and knowledge-making as linked social transactions.

Reither was already quite knowledgeable about the new discipline by the time he wrote the first few newsletters. Besides attending American conferences (and the Carleton Conference on "Learning to Write"), as a visiting scholar at the University of Texas-Austin (1981) he had studied with James Kinneavy, Lester Faigley, and Maxine Hairston. He could, as noted in the November issue, "rattle off the titles of a half-a-dozen genuinely useful—'reputable'—journals . . . easily name several important books and a dozen excellent articles . . . and provide the names of fifteen or twenty widely-published, highly-respected scholars, researchers, and theorists. There is, we can say, a discipline out there" (Reither, *W&R/T&P*, November, 1982, p. 2). He was therefore in a position to articulate goals for the newsletter that reflected both the knowledge revolution and the interdisciplinary spirit of the emergent American field. Consider this language from the inaugural newsletter describing topics for readers to learn about:

- Research into language-use processes, especially writing and reading
- Theories of reading and theories of composing, and research into both
- The history, nature, and uses of rhetoric

- Discourse theory, discourse structure, discourse analysis, discourse processes
- Cross-disciplinary approaches to studying the nature, acquisition, and uses of language and language processes—as, e.g., contributions from linguistics, sociolinguistics, psycholinguistics, text linguistics, anthropology, philosophy [as, e.g., Speech Act Theory, Ordinary language philosophy, semiotical], artificial intelligence, developmental psychology, cognitive psychology, and so on and so on
- Theories of, and research into, the processes of reading literature (as, e.g., reader response [affective] criticism and its theoretical underpinnings
- The roles of language in learning and knowing. (Reither, Newsletter, October, 1982, p. 1).

This eclectic list displays comprehensive understanding of what was going on at the cutting edge of the field at the time, and, moreover, an appreciation of the value of multidisciplinary sources and methods of knowledge-making. Even more striking, though, and contrary to some contemporary Canadian perceptions of Inkshed, Reither makes crystal clear in the inaugural issue that, although the study of written language is motivated by teaching practice and will enrich it, it is to be undertaken for its own sake, not as instrumental to pedagogy. He cites his future consulting editors to emphasize the point: the newsletter will treat "writing and reading and literacy as serious subjects of interest in their own right, not just as 'problems' or fodder for testing or objects of administrative technique'" (Chris Bullock, qtd. in Reither, Newsletter, September, 1982, p. 1); readers "will not 'only want to hear pep talks or find out classroom techniques' (Mike Moore, qtd. in Reither, Newsletter, September, 1982, pp. 1–2). The newsletter represents an intellectual project that is pedagogical in a different sense, to enable the self-education of an expanding network of scholars. As he wrote later, "The pages of *Inkshed* should be a stage on which the activities of participating in, constructing, and developing a scholarly . . . community are acted out" (Reither, *Inkshed*, February, 1985, p. 3).

In 1981, Reither, drawing on discussions with his colleagues, already had a firm sense of methods by which the newsletter could accomplish these goals. He explained many of these in the inaugural issue, although they were revised or expanded as the genre evolved. One generic approach was to compile lists: of experts who could act as consultants;

of journals and organizations; of conferences in the United States and Canada; of important books, articles, and studies. The newsletter would publish announcements of new publications, events, and calls for papers. It solicited descriptions of writing and reading programs in Canada and beyond; it invited essays and responses. Later it was to publish listserv exchanges and inksheds from conferences. As the newsletter developed, readers wrote summaries and critical reviews to share and evaluate what they learned in all venues (mostly US-based): articles, books, conferences, seminars, institutes, workshops. They recommended conferences and readings (Inkshed conferences included advance reading lists). Contributors alerted others to upcoming events and recommended those they found accessible, affordable, and useful. Sprinkled throughout the issues were provocative quotations from what Reither or other contributors had been reading, drawn from a remarkable range of disciplinary sources.

The newsletter didn't just announce or present information; it tried to provoke dialogue, debate, and action. Primarily this was accomplished through the conference, although Inkshed did take steps to connect with other organizations like the Canadian Council of Teachers of English. I think Reither understood action primarily as writing, of a kind that would create knowledge in the discipline. In 1986 he wrote to readers, in some frustration about subscription numbers and submissions: "I challenge you to tell us or show who we are or ought to be, *whether* we ought to be, what we ought to be doing. Action—doing something—is what we need. We should not merely *talk* about what to do: we should *do* it. So, if you can, define us by writing something that exemplifies what we are or ought to be, rather than tackling the definition discursively" (*Inkshed*, September, 1986, p. 1). And again, in 1993, he said, "I keep quoting Aviva [Freedman] . . . 'If we want to be recognized, we've got to do good work'" (*Inkshed*, December, 1993, p. 2, reproduced from discussion on CASLL listserv).

Reither reflected many times over the years about the functions of the newsletter as a genre in relation to the project of Canadian writing studies, and his understanding evolved as the newsletter did. In 1984, he said its primary functions "are those of the bulletin board and the podium" (*Inkshed*, March, 1984, p. 5). In 1986 he called it a "parlor" in the Burkean sense, "*not* a journal, privileging text over discourse, monologue over dialogue . . . It's a place for exploration, not domination" (*Inkshed*, December, 1986, p.1). This comment foreshadows his most insightful characterization, in an editorial essay written for *Inkshed* in

1985, titled "Epistemic Newsletter; or, Inkshed as a Mode of Learning." In this essay, Reither explains that Inkshed was not created to serve an existing academic community, but "to develop and promote such a community." There existed no "rigorous scholarly forum for addressing the questions, problems, and issues of concern to us," and we "envied the lively, generative communities of scholars and teachers which nurtured our colleagues in the States and England. We wanted and needed a more hospitable, supportive context in which to work." (*Inkshed*, February, 1985, p.1) Reither makes a subtle shift here from his original aspirations and sense of audience when, after noting that Canadians had not yet achieved a mature community of writing scholars, he suggests that as scholars, we are all obliged to learn, to grow, even if not all at the cutting edge. Many Inkshedders did, and all should, "at least subscribe to the journals, read the articles and books, attend and present at the conferences; think about, criticize, and try to apply the research, scholarship, and theory; and analyze, use, extend, and cite the work of those who are actually at that edge" (p. 2). Only thus can they achieve their primary aim, "to promote research, scholarship, application, and publication in the field, for we cannot function except from within, and with the support of, a robust community of knowledgeable peers" (p. 2).

But, true to his principles, Reither believed that to learn, to know what people near the cutting edge of our discipline are doing, as practitioners or as aspiring researchers, and to create a scholarly discourse community, Canadians must not only read and listen, they must write. "*Inkshed* ought to be publishing, each issue, cohort reports, reviews, commentaries, notices, announcements, descriptions of courses and programs, think-pieces, analyses, criticism. And you must write them" (Reither, *Inkshed*, February, 1985, p. 2). That was the distinctive way that Inkshed tried, under his editorship, to function as an epistemic newsletter, a mode of learning. Interestingly, perhaps the most robust legacy of Reither's injunction to publish is Inkshed Press, which remains vital in publishing and distributing Canadian scholarship in writing studies.

Looking back in his final issue as editor, Reither reflected that, to the extent Inkshed as newsletter and conference had helped Canadians communicate across the continent, "the whole process has worked wonderfully, magically" (*Inkshed*, March & May, 1987, p.1). And there *is* something magical about watching people educate themselves and form a community that has nurtured most of the important scholars in Canadian writing studies. Many believe that without Inkshed there would be no composition community in Canada, and Jim Reither—and his partner Russ Hunt—were quiet, generous mentors to aspiring scholars in the early days of Canadian writing studies (see chapter 3).

At the same time, the paradox of Inkshed's success is that its dialogic, exploratory ethos, which Reither and Hunt infused in the early newsletter and embodied in the annual conference, ultimately prevented it from serving certain other functions to advance the discipline in the Canadian academy and to embed it within larger, international networks. For one thing, despite its eclectic international sources and the cross-border traveling documented in the newsletter, by its very definition and aims Inkshed is ineluctably Canadian and must remain so.

In a micro-ethnography of the CASLL/Inkshed listserv and conference, Tania Smith (2000) described the Inkshed conferences (and the CASLL listserv that has replaced the newsletter as a primary forum and networking site) as having a "culture of informality, intimacy, interactivity, risk-taking, anti-hierarchy." These qualities express a set of "values and practices that [Inkshed] protects, such as its value for collaborative learning and collaborative scholarship, and its bias toward affirming . . . the needs and views of students rather than the demands of academic and corporate institutions" (p. 9). These values are at odds with the traditional academic culture that rewards research and publication; for example, they don't facilitate development of methodological expertise, or theory-building capacities, or competitive access to research grants. Canadians needed other forums to support these purposes, like international conferences, graduate programs, scholarly journals, and the organization (and conference) now called the Canadian Association for the Study of Discourse and Writing (CASDW). Some scholars began to make CASDW their primary Canadian site for intellectual exchange and support. (See chapter 3 on this shift.) Nonetheless, in the work of Canadian scholars like Schryer who are highly successful in these more traditional academic terms we will find evidence that these values are not lost, but can be traced in the deep structure of their research and theory, an enduring legacy of Jim Reither's epistemic newsletter.

CATHERINE SCHRYER AND THE COLLABORATIVE MULTIDISCIPLINARY RESEARCH ARTICLE

To illustrate Catherine Schryer's writings in this genre, I picked a set of four co-authored research articles reporting on a collaborative investigation of forensic report letters concerning child abuse. The co-authorship of these articles reflect the shifting membership and roles of a multidisciplinary research team working under the umbrella of Schryer's (2004) SSHRC grant entitled "Crossing Borders: Sites of Discursive Negotiation in Healthcare Practice." For this grant, Schryer and her longtime collaborators Lorelei Lingard and Marlee Spafford formed the original, "core" research team, amplified by other members as needed to include other fields, methods of data-gathering and analysis, students, and research assistants. This was the second research site studied under the "Crossing Borders" grant.

The selected articles, listed below, were published between 2009 and 2011:

> Mian, M., Schryer, C.F., Spafford, M.M., Joosten, J., & Lingard, L. (2009). Current practice in physical child abuse forensic reports: A preliminary exploration. *Child Abuse and Neglect*, 33(10), 679–683.
>
> Schryer, C.F., Afros, E., Mian, M., Spafford, M.M., & Lingard, L.A. (2009). The trial of the expert witness: Negotiating credibility in court documents in child abuse cases. *Written Communication*, 26(3), 215–246.
>
> Spafford, M.M., Schryer, C.F., Lingard, L., & Mian, M. (2010). Accessibility and order: Crossing borders in child abuse forensic reports. *Technical Communication Quarterly*, 19(2), 118–143.
>
> Schryer, C.F., Bell, S. Mian, M., Spafford, M.M., & Lingard, L.A. (2011). Professional citation practices in child maltreatment letters. *Written Communication*, 28(2), 147–71.

By the time of this research, Schryer was experienced in working and publishing with interdisciplinary research teams. This project followed successful completion of a previous three-year research grant with the same core team, which had focused on "the role of situated language practices in clinical education settings" for health care professionals (C. Schryer, CV). In 2007, having worked together more than five years, Schryer and several collaborators reflected on the complexities of such collaborative research (Lingard, Schryer, Spafford, & Campbell, 2007). Their description of this team and its work suggests how putting together members and research methods from such disparate fields (academic and professional) and perspectives (novice and expert, insider and outsider) enables extraordinary productivity and impact: "Three members have been constant . . . a professor of English who specializes in rhetoric [Schryer], a scientist trained in rhetoric who holds a faculty position in a department of paediatrics [Lingard], and a professor who is an optometrist with a doctorate in education [Spafford]." A fourth member, a social work researcher (Campbell), had recently been added. "Around these core members, the team has ebbed and flowed, reaching a maximum of nine members. . . . Because our research proceeds as a series of staggered case studies, clinical collaborators join and leave the team according to which case study is under way" (Lingard et al., p. 504). The resulting work "combines observational and interview methods with discourse analysis" and is situated in multiple domains of practice: the team has "ventured into inpatient and outpatient contexts, through clinical domains as diverse as paediatric medicine . . . optometry . . . and social work . . ." (p. 504) and published work addressed to diverse audiences of academics (especially scholars of writing and professional and technical communication), clinicians, and professional educators.

In the "Crossing Borders" project, Schryer's team collected data on practices of communication across professional boundaries from two research sites. The first study investigated discourse strategies used in referral letters by optometrists and corresponding consultant letters from ophthalmologists to jointly manage healthcare.[16] The second, documented in these four articles, focused on forensic report letters written by physicians and nurses to provide opinions on childcare abuse to the courts. In both cases, the team interviewed writers and readers and used linguistic and rhetorical methods to make fine-grained analyses of these texts, their functions, and effects. This work generated a cluster of articles that carve out specific topics or findings and modulate their emphases and purposes for different audiences. This modulation entails striking a different balance among possible functions: reporting results as information, conceptualizing their findings, setting them in theoretical frameworks, revising or inventing (genre) theories, drawing practical implications for practitioners and educators. Each article features a different proportion of data, theory, and practical implications fitted to its choice of goals and audience.

In this set, for example, the brief communication for the specialized journal *Child Abuse & Neglect* (Mian et al., 2009) provides purely descriptive data for professionals in a newly defined field (child abuse pediatrics) that has no previous literature on writing its forensic reports, laying ground for future work. A more theoretically oriented article in the group, "The trial of the expert witness," published in *Written Communication* (Schryer et al., 2009), details the methods—linguistic and rhetorical analysis, interviews of writers and readers—used to study a corpus of forensic reports and participants' accounts of them. The authors draw implications from their study at three different levels (professional practice, language theory, and professional education), but in this context (a research journal in writing studies) their emphasis is on specifying for genre theory the concept of "boundary objects" (drawn from Bowker & Star, 1999), which they introduce to explain communications like these letters that "traverse several communities of practice" (Schryer et al., p. 217). From the perspective of scholars of writing, professional communication, and genre theory, the study becomes an illustration of such a boundary object—the forensic letters—and the strategies used to achieve that function.

"Professional citations" (Schryer et al., 2011), also in *Written Communication*, focuses on linguistically detailed analysis of citation practices, albeit deeply embedded in theoretical frames for understanding them. The authors conceive "implications" here in terms of groups who can benefit from or be affected by their findings in practical ways: health care practitioners as writers who must deal with the complex rhetorical situation of writing letters regarding child abuse; by extension, the children and families who are subjects of the letters; and instructors of medical and professional communication. They give only a nod to writing scholars who study citation, noting they need to extend studies from academic texts to professional communication. In "Accessibility and order" (Spafford et al., 2010), published in *Technical Communication Quarterly*, the co-authors, using a rhetorical vocabulary, presents findings that would be of practical use to scholars and teachers of technical communication for students across domains of expertise. While incorporating theoretical concepts (emphasizing strategies of accessibility and order), they translate their findings into advice and recommendations for writers and teachers rather than thematizing a new contribution to genre theory.

If we step away from this set, we can see a pattern in the way Schryer's collaborative publications in this genre, in conjunction with her single-authored articles and chapters, participate in a larger research project with different levels of purpose—and corresponding audiences. On the one hand, collectively her writings layer study upon study to paint a rich picture of professional communication, focusing at different points on its textual features, its successful and unsuccessful strategies, and its processes of learning and methods of teaching, for the sake of understanding and improving practices of communication and education. Articles typically place new findings in the context of prior research by this team and others, explicitly building a cumulative knowledge base of use to practitioners and educators as well as scholars.

On another level, however, her project is to participate in building fundamental theories, specifically, genre theory. Typically, the longer articles in writing journals or chapters in scholarly collections are a primary venue for laying out the concepts that have been developed collaboratively with the team, step by step, study by study, and integrating them through summary, synthesis, and rationalization into a comprehensive, robust theory. Schryer and her colleagues have done this in the theory sections of many collaborative research articles, which tend to update the theory in concise summaries and then apply it or refine it based on the study at hand. For example, in "Professional citation practices," the authors summarized Schryer's "evolving" conceptualization of genre in 2011 as "stabilized-for-now or stabilized-enough constellations of regulated and regularized strategies that social agents use to negotiate their way through time and space" (Schryer et al., 2011, p. 149). This precisely worded definition references a sequence of previous writings where Schryer had formulated and refined concepts of "stabilized-for-now" genres (Schryer, 1993), "regulated versus regularized" strategies or resources (Schryer, Lingard, & Spafford, 2007), and the Bakhtinian idea of chronotope as situating negotiation in time and space (Schryer, 1999). Similarly, in "Regularized practices," the authors noted how "Schryer's endeavors in genre theory have worked toward" a particular view of genre in stages, refining a definition based on a series of studies (Schryer, Lingard, & Spafford, 2007, p. 30).

This approach is traceable from Schryer's earliest work, growing out of her dissertation study of literacy practices in a veterinary college (see Schryer, 1993) and laid out as a research model in her contribution to *Contextual Literacy*, co-edited with Laurence Steven (Schryer & Steven, eds., 1994). In her chapter, "A consultancy model of research for literacy and writing across the curriculum researchers," Schryer explained the principles and methods that would guide her future research: the interplay of emic (participant) and etic (researcher) perspectives; the development of a "shared vocabulary" with her subjects; the role of theory; and the first formulation of the dual purposes noted in these research articles—to serve both her own scholarly community and the practitioners of fields she studies (1994, pp. 128–36). Her chapter reflects the book's goal to explore and balance "contextual" and "critical" dimensions of literacy practices, teaching, and research. On the contextual side, she advocated studying literacy practices and texts in the contexts of their use (and learning) by disciplinary or professional groups. But her goal as an action researcher was not simply to support the development of contextual literacy—"the appropriate command of the ways of speaking and writing" as judged by the group (Schryer & Steven, 1994, p. 31), but to enable participants "to analyze the teaching and evaluation practices which constitute [critical] literacy" (Schryer, 1994, p. 128). This goal calls for a vocabulary shared by researchers and subjects for talking about their literacy practices: "Analytical constructs . . . must be familiar enough to be comprehensive and relevant, yet critical and distant enough that participants can use them to objectify their own practice and thus reflect on it" (Schryer, 1994, p. 134). This is the root from which genre theory (and its complements and supplements) develop over time in Schryer's sustained research project.

The most striking feature in this early statement of Schryer's principles is the ethical dimension that informs both her research goals (developing disciplinary knowledge and helping discourse communities achieve an effective and critical practice) and the dialogic method this requires: combining and playing against one another the outsider (etic, researcher) perspective and the insider (emic, participant) perspective. Her subsequent research both solidifies these commitments and develops in new directions. For example, as her team shifts focus from individual discourse communities to examining how fields talk to one another and to publics, her notion of the researcher's role evolves from that of consultant to a more nuanced concept of "knowledge broker" (Wenger, 1998) between discourse communities, embodied in "the acts of translation and transition that accompany our interdisciplinary work at the liminal edges of professional fields" (Lingard et al., 2007, p. 503).

In a recent theoretical chapter (2011), Schryer offers an account of her own journey as a genre researcher, which also serves as a history of the (largely Canadian) development of rhetorical genre studies (RGS), in part through its engagement with other theories (cf. Artemeva, 2006). In doing so, she expresses an understanding of RGS as itself a collaborative, multidisciplinary project. Here she recapitulates the conceptual innovations she and other RGS researchers have contributed (or adapted from other sources), and embeds these in an argument for the interdependence of theory and empirical method that we have seen practiced in her own articles. Her dialogic methodology has matured to posit a complementary relationship between "objective" methods (like discourse analysis) and methods that elicit the perceptions and lived experiences of discoursers themselves. This formulation is enriched by referencing it to Bourdieu's methodology of "social praxeology" (Bourdieu & Wacquant, 1992), which derives from a rich theory of practice and its symbolic resources for agency. That theoretical richness enables researchers of discourse in context to investigate and conceptualize complex, co-constructive relations between texts and contexts, between social structure (as sedimented in language and genre) and agents actively engaging their worlds (Schryer, Gladcova, Spafford, & Lingard, 2007; Schryer, 2011).

In Schryer's genre project, these and other dualities, traditionally oppositional, are reframed and investigated as constantly (re)negotiated relationships: between researchers and participants, theory and empirical methods, rhetorical genre theory and linguistic genre theories, discursive practice and discursive education. Schryer's team is acutely aware of how these concepts and negotiations apply reflexively to their own work, as suggested in their reflective study of the border crossing involved in their own multidisciplinary research and composing, negotiating not only among themselves but also "with the ideological and organizational forces structuring our scholarly worlds" (Lingard et al., 2007, p. 503). As Schryer acknowledges, the texts they write in the genre of the collaborative, multidisciplinary research article themselves serve as boundary objects, "because in each instance the findings which they articulate have been negotiated across these fields of practice. Furthermore, the writers themselves have functioned as 'brokers' articulating their own field concerns but also forming a community of practice in which expertise can be explored, challenged and negotiated" (Schryer, 2011, p. 45).

Sharon Hamilton and the Literacy Autobiography

Although she shared an American mentor (Janice Lauer) with Cathy Schryer, Sharon Hamilton is what microhistorians call an "outlier" in this group of scholars.[17] She made most of her contributions to literacy studies and undergraduate learning while working in the United States, and, of the four scholars, is least identified with Canadian writing studies and its communities of practice. In this respect, she is Jim Reither's counterpart as an expatriate: once having crossed the border, each became fully integrated into the scholarly scene of their adopted academic culture. But her roots are deeply Canadian, and her formative intellectual influences and mentors in language theory and pedagogy were British. In this she reflects Canada's heritage as a Commonwealth nation, as well as the international orientation of Canadian writing studies embodied in the dialogic conferences put on by Freedman, Pringle, and other Canadians, which made it possible for a provincial high school teacher to meet and converse with iconic British scholars.

However, these direct influences were also mediated in Hamilton's education by the American uptake of British views following the Dartmouth Conference in 1966, where educators like James Britton and John Dixon met American teachers of English and clashed over their opposing visions of language and pedagogy. This is often cited as a founding event in American composition, especially in histories that recuperate the role of English education in its twentieth century reinvention (Stock, 2012, especially Zebroski, 2012; Harris, 1997/2012; Rice, 2007). While James Britton may not have met Janet Emig before the Ottawa Conference in 1979, he and his colleagues had helped to decisively shape the tacit tradition of American composition studies that she articulated at the conference. The Canadians understood that: the conference was explicitly conceived and interpreted as a successor to the Dartmouth Conference that had first brought Americans into contact with this British scholarship (Freedman & Pringle, 1980, p. ix; Oster, 1979). Hamilton would have encountered their ideas before she went to London, as part of her intensive exposure to American rhetoric and composition at Lauer's Rhetoric Seminar in 1984. Years later, she contributed to a symposium on the Dartmouth Conference in *College English*. Referring to the conflicts played out at Darmouth between "a social-epistemic collaborative model" and a traditional pedagogy of knowledge-transmission, she wrote, "Educated in Canada, with doctoral studies in England, and currently teaching in the United States, I have become inevitably swept into the opposing currents of these positions" (Zebroski, Hamilton, Mayher, & Harris, 1992, p. 698). She went on to defend the British "growth" model against reductive interpretations and misunderstandings.

Earlier, however, when Hamilton met Rosen and Britton at the CCTE Conference one year after Ottawa, she was unfamiliar with this history or their radical view of literacy. Hamilton's hard-won Canadian schooling in English literature and English education was conservative in the British tradition. She had begun to rebel against this pedagogy in her teaching, based on her own intuitions about how children learn, but "unfortunately I did not have the theoretical background to give me confidence in my intuitions and to argue their validity, and so I wavered almost schizophrenically between traditional expectations of what goes on in English classrooms and my own views of what should go on . . . . When my intuitions were challenged, I succumbed to the traditional" (Hamilton, 1995, p. 84). So she was a highly receptive listener to the unconventional views of the British at the conference: "the door to a whole new world of understanding language, literature, and learning opened" for her during that week (p. 93).

It was Harold Rosen's closing address that "ignited the most explosive idea that I took away from that conference." When Hamilton questioned his criticism of the educational system as elitist, classist, racist, and sexist, he replied: "'You never judge a system by those who succeed in it. . . . You judge it by those it fails.'" It was a shocking concept, yet immediately compelling to her: "Visions of previously invisible students rushed through my head. . . . [I realized] I was perpetuating an elitist system of education that was setting up a large number of students for failure" (Hamilton, 1995, p. 94). Hamilton understood and identified with this radical vision of literacy because she was one of those invisible students. She had personally experienced the power of literacy to heal and transform a child who had been shaped by neglect and abuse into someone who seemed, to herself and others, unlovable and incapable of learning. Her autobiography portrays her lifelong struggle to transcend her own "miserable world" and its low expectations of her to shape a better self and a productive life (Hamilton, 1995, pp. 4–5). This process was enacted at every step through literate behaviors: being read to by her adoptive mother from her first day; reading fairy tales and Anne of Green Gables on her own; recording memories of her foster homes on a typewriter; relishing conversations about texts, language, and meanings with classmates and mentors in Manitoba and London.

Hamilton's writing, from her memory writing at age eight to her scholarly publications, is an objective correlate for these successive transformations, as she reveals in an article about how she re-learned to write while working on her doctorate (Hamilton, 1999). Her Canadian education had taught Hamilton a fail-safe method for producing academic papers that were thoroughly researched and organized into a "nicely coherent package of other people's ideas, marching to the rhythm of point-counterpoint" (Hamilton, 1999, p. 107). But when she turned in her first assignment in London, Harold Rosen responded: "'You can get by in academia with this third-person objective word-from-God North American dialect if you want to . . . but why on earth would you want to?'" He continued, "It's good; it's thorough; it's comprehensive . . . It's probably even publishable just as it is. . . . But I have no sense of why you are writing about this . . . Where are you in this text?'" (Hamilton, 1995, pp. 102, 107). Another tutor, Tony Burgess, told her that even the dissertation's literature review isn't *just* a literature review, but an invitation to readers to join her on an intellectual journey. She remembers her response: "What a challenge! What a lesson! Dissertation as a journey— as a story of an intellectual journey. I saw in an instant what all these lessons were leading to: the power of narrative to explore and explain. What a forceful set of lessons about writing, identity, and audience to take with me from my three years of doctoral work in England" (Hamilton, 1995, p. 113).

When Hamilton returned to the States with her doctorate, she wrote fluently in traditional academic genres, the kind that use the "North American dialect" Rosen had derided: case studies, reports, edited books. Only the literary flair of some of her titles ("Barking at Straw Dogma," or "Snakepit in Cyberspace") suggests that she remembered her tutors' lesson. She wrote in print, online, and audiovisual media for many audiences: educators, the public, composition teachers, assessment specialists. But it was not until 1995 that Hamilton finally brought herself, inspired by the "horrors and challenges" of her students' lives, to write her own story, in hopes it would help them "cross the chasm" from the lives they led to the lives they wanted (Hamilton, 1995, p. 4). In doing so, she entered (uniquely among the scholars in our study) into an intertext of narrative and memoir that goes back a long way in American composition, where it is linked to the pedagogical tradition often called dismissively "expressivist." As a theory of language and a pedagogy, that tradition is often rightly traced to the Dartmouth Conference and the British emphasis on personal development, especially in the work of James Britton and his colleagues, who introduced a concept and category of "expressive" writing into writing studies (Britton, Burgess, Martin, McLeod, & Rosen, 1975). But it has a larger context in the many theories in literary studies, cognitive psychology, developmental science, anthropology, feminist studies, and other fields that conceive narrative as a fundamental function of language.

In recent years, academics in American rhetoric and composition have begun not only to teach and assign autobiography, memoir, and other narrative genres (expanding these into visual, digital, and multimodal forms), but to write these genres themselves. Hamilton's piece "You Can Get By" appeared in an American collection of such academic narratives, called *The Personal Narrative* (Haroian-Guerin, 1999). Many of these writings reflect the unappreciated radical potential in such genres. *My Name's Not Susie* takes its place alongside Victor Villaneuva's *Bootstraps* and Keith Gilyard's *Voices of the Self* in taking up questions about class, gender, and race as they affect literacy and learning.

These examples represent a particular subgenre of the literacy autobiography, which is informed by studies of literature and language and blends memoir with critical analysis and theory. As Janice Lauer pointed out in her foreword to Hamilton's book, "Sharon the theorist is in the background, but "never far behind . . ."; she is "both scholar and subject, the teller and the tale" (Hamilton, 1995, p. xii). But another, much more inclusive context for Hamilton's narrative is the wealth of literacy autobiographies written by people from all works of life. Cynthia Selfe has assembled a large and growing digital archive of literacy narratives (DALN) collected from contributors of any background, in multiple formats and forms, along with sample compositions.

Hamilton's life story throws a new light on her own apparently conventional academic articles and books. They are not decontextualized or discontinuous with her personal life, but an expression of the identity she forged. Conceptually, they are extensions and applications of the theories and values by which she framed an understanding of literacy and learning. As she moved (like many US-writing scholar-administrators) into a broader sphere, from writing studies per se to promoting undergraduate learning at the institutional and cross-institutional level, national and international, we can trace a straight line from the Dartmouth Seminar and her British mentors to the two literacy practices she studied, implemented personally and institutionally (in a very rigorous way), and disseminated in her writing and consulting: e-portfolios and collaborative learning. The goals and philosophies of these two international educational movements, to which she made important contributions, have their roots not only in all that she learned as a writing scholar and educator, but in the deeply imprinted understanding of the power of literacy to rescue lives that she developed in her Canadian childhood.

In a book that documents and theorizes institutions' use of e-portfolios, which includes Hamilton's institutional case study of IUPUI's program, Darren Cambridge describes integrative learning in portfolios in terms of two kinds of selves, the "networked" and the "symphonic." Whereas "the *networked self* focuses on creating intentional connections" and forges new relationships by "crossing boundaries such as those between courses, disciplines, institutions, and groups," "the *symphonic self* focuses on achieving integrity of the whole. Through examining and articulating how the sum of its experiences and ideas has an overall coherence, the symphonic self articulates enduring commitments and systemic understanding" (Cambridge, 2009, pp. 41–42). *My Name's Not Susie* is Hamilton's portfolio, integrating what the Swedish National Agency for Education (Skolverket) calls "life-long" and "life-wide" learning (Chen, 2009, p. 29).

Hamilton's career is an early example of the outflow of Canadian talent across the border because of the dearth of doctoral programs and jobs in writing studies in Canadian institutions—a loss that continues as scholars like Daniel Richards move to the US for doctoral studies and stay there to work, some of them permanently. Hamilton's work, like that of many of these expatriates, entered into American rhetoric and composition without a Canadian identification. She reminds us to include that expatriate community in the overall picture of Canadian writing studies.

Hamilton's revelatory memoir also vividly brings to life certain figures, iconic in the literature of American composition and rhetoric, who have little or no presence in Canadian writing scholarship: the teacher in the schools; the nontraditional student, especially those the system fails before they ever get to college; even the writing program administrator, who is ubiquitous in Canada but invisible as a scholar or change agent. They remain peripheral to the scholarly enterprise instead of being integrated into it as both subjects of and participants in research, as in US rhetoric and composition.

Hamilton was a longtime teacher in Canadian schools at the time early scholars like Freedman, Pringle, Reither, and Richard Coe saw these teachers as a crucial audience for spreading the new ideas of the discipline. Each of them, and others, made substantial efforts to offer professional development to teachers in the schools and bring teachers from all sectors of education into the conversation as active participants (Maguire, 1995; R. Coe, interview, January, 9, 2014). Many, like Phyllis

Artiss, were inspired to undertake advanced study or become teacher-researchers when they discovered (as she did at the 1979 Ottawa Conference) "that there were other teachers in English departments in this country who shared my commitment to teaching writing and were willing to actually talk about it in public! What was even more astonishing was to learn that there were lots of professors of English in universities (mostly in the US) who wrote books and articles about teaching composition, got research grants to do this kind of work, and won awards for it" (*Inkshed*, December, 1991, p. 1).[18] As pointed out in chapter 3, citing Dan Richards, for many Canadians today this still comes as a revelation.

Hamilton herself identified as much with the students who, in an elite system, never make it to college or, as in her case, struggle mightily when they do. Those students became special to her in her American teaching. And her career as an writing program administrator, a "WPA" who became more broadly an institutional leader, is exemplary of a role that is absolutely central to the development of Canadian writing studies and its scholars but is not yet regarded, as in the US, as itself a research-dependent scholarly practice. Underlying the many published accounts of Canadian writing programs are administrators whose intellectual work makes such programs work against long odds. Williams's analysis in chapter 3 of writing centre instruction at the University of Toronto illustrates powerfully both the integrated intellectual and practical work of an administrator (in American terms, a WPA) in the person of Margaret Procter, and the invisibility or devaluation of these important intellectual contributions outside the local context, especially since the institutional situation makes publication very difficult to prioritize. (See also MacDonald, Procter, & Williams, forthcoming). Writing centres and their faculty across Canada occupy a liminal, often vulnerable position that reflects the continuing difficulty of institutionalizing writing studies as a discipline in the Canadian academy.

Conclusion

Randall Collins (1998) describes thinking, and the ideas it produces, as emergent from communication, "which is to say interaction among bodily humans." The process of communication that creates ideas also "creates the thinkers as nodes of the process" (p. 2). Intellectual creativity needs to be energized in face-to-face communication, whether in the heightened social rituals like conferences or in the daily talk of co-located circles of scholars at institutional hubs (p. 379). But Collins also recognizes the special role that writing plays in intellectual activity by extending it both synchronically and diachronically. Writings distribute ideas from the concentrated hubs to widening circles of thinkers and users at a distance, and, as we've seen, connect people who have been isolated from the intellectual community, often drawing them toward the hubs. Texts, which Collins describes as chained to lectures or in-person debates, also secure the "long-term life of the discipline" by extending its sense of community both "backwards and forwards in time" (p. 27). "Intellectual events in the present—lectures, debates, discussions—take place against an explicit backdrop of past texts . . . and [new ones] are directed toward unseen audiences." Any communication is "implicitly part of an ongoing chain, which will be further repeated, discussed, or augmented in the future" (p. 27).

By pairing scholars with genres and tracing their intertextual and interpersonal trajectories through multiple contexts, this chapter values and integrates texts as an overlay and supplement to the social networks revealed in instructional, mentoring, emulative, and collaborative relationships in all our chapters. While we tend to recognize the way discipline-based research publications accomplish disciplinarity, this chapter brings to our attention the role of less visible, underappreciated, and innovative genres in network dynamics, especially in a country whose potential scholars have such limited access to the energy and cultural capital generated at the hubs.

Notes

1. I was following up my proposal for such a study in a 2012 speech (Phelps, 2014), as one way of combating oversimplified assumptions on both sides of the border about relations between Canadian writing studies and US rhetoric and composition.

2. In this preliminary study, I constructed a database recording the distribution and number of "mentions" of Canadian scholars on our list in the indices of thirty-eight sources (as of May, 2014). "Mention" is defined as the appearance in an index of an author's name coupled with a page reference. Each separate page reference (including inclusive pages x–y) counted as a mention. I also added information about appearances in CompPile and some bibliographies. I continued to add sources and scholars discovered during our collaborative work, drawing on interviews, surveys, and readings. Most of the sources are at least nominally US-based publications, since I was focusing on Canadian

contributions to American rhetoric and composition/writing studies. However, the data is quite difficult to interpret from a simple count of mentions because of the diversity of the sources in terms of disciplinary framework, audiences addressed (national, international), and especially time of publication (dates of the sources, excepting CompPile, range from 1983 to 2012). It would require careful discrimination to observe differences in scholars' visibility by time periods or in different research communities. However, it is evident that some Canadian scholars have a robust rhetorical presence over time, communities, and sources.

3. I treated the four scholars in this chapter as "Canadian" for different reasons, case by case, as will be discussed: they include an American-born and educated scholar who emigrated to Canada and spent his career there in writing studies; his counterpart, a Canadian-born schoolteacher with a British PhD who emigrated to the US for a position in writing studies; and two Canadian-born scholars with US educational or job experience who made their careers in Canada.

4. The scholars in this study each appeared in my mentions table, meaning their publications had achieved recognition among American and/or international audiences. They were all successful in the most traditional terms (single-authored research publications in scholarly books or refereed journals). However, the writings that attracted me in each case deviate in some way from normative expectations (in the humanities and social sciences) and/or would be accorded less value as scholarship (e.g., in tenure and promotion reviews) than other publications by the same authors.

5. Biographical information is drawn from CVs provided by each scholar, Hamilton's (1995) autobiography, surveys and interviews conducted for the collaborative project (see chapters 1 and 2), and personal communications with each scholar. (Freedman, Reither, and Hamilton provided CVs covering their careers up to retirement; Schryer's included publications through 2013.) My analysis of the texts rests on a base of broader investigation, with sources including American, Canadian, and international literature in writing studies; organizational and conference materials; listserv archives; contacts with scholars in both countries; and, of course, the data gathered through our collaboration.

6. I attended the 1979 Ottawa Conference while finishing my dissertation.

7. Lauer's seminar, often called the Purdue (Rhetoric) Seminar, began in 1976 at the University of Detroit (co-led by W. Ross Winterowd), but it moved with Lauer to Purdue and ran there under her leadership until 1989. Intended for post-graduates who wanted a short, intensive, but comprehensive introduction to rhetoric and composition, the Seminar was team-taught by a guest faculty of composition theorists (Lauer, 1998, p. 503), and was an important means for scholars educated in literature or other fields to retool in writing studies (Ede, 2004, pp. 56–58). According to Lauer's records, about 5% (31) of

637 participants over 13 years were Canadian, including Schryer, Freedman, Hamilton, Graham Smart, and Ron Freese in our study (J. Lauer, personal communication, Sept. 24–25, 2013).

8. For a microhistorical study of the conference and its inscriptions as a Canadian contribution to the early development of writing studies as a discipline, see Phelps, 2016.

9. Both Britton and Andrew Wilkinson spoke at the 1979 Ottawa Conference and are represented in the inscriptions: Britton, in *Reinventing* and *Learning to Write*; Wilkinson, in *Learning to Write*.

10. I have been unable to discover how widely or how long *Teaching, Writing, Learning* was in use (I would guess, in Canadian undergraduate classrooms or in-service classes), but as a kind of textbook tied to a particular state of the field it was inevitably outdated within a few years.

11. Yalden, then-chair of Carleton's Department of Linguistics and Director of the ESL Program, was responsible for the ESL strand of the conference, which had its own program and speakers.

12. Carleton's 1992 Colloquium on Rethinking Genre was followed by an International Conference on Genre at Simon Fraser in 1998. Canada became a center for "North American rhetorical genre studies," distinguished by the work of scholars in our study like Artemeva, Coe, Smart, Paré, and Schryer, many of whom worked directly with Freedman. In 2012, Carleton hosted, "Genre 2012," a colloquium on "Rethinking Genre 20 Years Later." Today, genre research has a worldwide reach; researchers are currently planning the seventh international symposium on genre studies (SIGET) in Brazil, Sept. 2015. See GBX (http://genreacrossborders.org).

13. There is a little ambiguity between the Sept. and Oct. (untitled) newsletters, since they are both labeled issue 1. I will call the first one the "inaugural" issue or the "September" issue; the other, the October issue. In November, 1982, the newsletter was titled *W&R/T&P*, becoming *Inkshed* in Dec., 1983.

14. See Hunt, 2006; Horne, 2012. A lot of ink has been shed over inkshedding itself, much of it in the Inkshed newsletter and more recently on the CASLL listserv that has taken over many of the functions of the newsletter (and conference). Inkshedders disagree about how much you can change the practice and still have it be "inkshedding"; about its value in conferences and teaching, in contrast to spoken dialogue or more reflective writing; about whether it is rigorous; about the benefit in making one's spontaneous writing public; and so on. Given a flexible definition, many seem to use it for multiple purposes and settings. When Doug Brent, one of our interviewees, recently asked colleagues on the CASLL listserv about their use of inkshedding in the classroom, replies showed they are continually adapting it to new contexts (e.g., international students, graduate education) and technologies.

15. Besides Reither, names of this group cited in the inaugural newsletter include Chris Bullock (Alberta), Anne Greenwood (University of British Co-

lumbia.), Russ Hunt (St. Thomas University), David Reiter (Cariboo College), Susan Stevenson (University of British Columbia), and Kay Stewart (Grant MacEwan Community College) (Newsletter, September, 1982, p. 2).

16. See, e.g., Schryer, Gladcova, Spafford, & Lingard (2007); Spafford, Schryer, & Lingard (2008).

17. While this chapter is not a microhistory, it does draw on some microhistorical concepts, in particular the concept of the outlier or *exceptional normal*. From a microhistorical perspective, compared to Freedman, Reither, and Schryer, Hamilton qualifies as exceptional because she left Canada for her academic career and was never part of its writing studies community. Although many Canadian writing scholars have crossed borders for their graduate education, she is exceptional in earning a PhD in England rather than the US. Yet, within the broader scene of Canadian writing studies, Hamilton looks more "normal": Canadian writing scholarship reflects British influences and addresses Commonwealth audiences; Canadian scholars continue their exodus to jobs in the US. Thus, the exceptional normal helps characterize the normal not only by contrast, but by revising an oversimplified idea of what is normal. For an overview of microhistorical concepts from a writing scholar, see McComiskey, 2016; on the concept of the outlier or exceptional normal (attributed to Grendi, 1977), see Magnusson & Szijarto, 2013, p. 19, and Muir, 1991.

18. Artiss went on to attend the Purdue Seminar and get her PhD at the University of Texas, Austin.

References

Artemeva, N. (2006). Approaches to learning genres: A bibliographical essay. In N. Artemeva & A. Freedman (Eds.), *Rhetorical genre studies and beyond* (pp. 9–99). Winnipeg: Inkshed.

Bourdieu, P., & Wacquant, L. J. D. (1992). *An invitation to reflexive sociology*. Chicago: University of Chicago Press.

Bowker, G., & Star, L. (1999). *Sorting things out: Classification and its consequences*. Cambridge, MA: MIT Press.

Britton, J., Burgess, T., Martin, N., McLeod, A., & Rosen, H. (1975). *The development of writing abilities (11–18)*. MacMillan Education: Schools Council/NCTE.

Cambridge, D. (2009). Two faces of integrative learning online. In D. Cambridge, B. Cambridge, & K. B. Yancey (Eds.), *Electronic portfolios 2.0: Emergent research on implementation and impact* (pp. 41–49). Sterling, VA: Stylus.

Chen, H. (2009). Using eportfolios to support lifelong and lifewide learning. In D. Cambridge, B. Cambridge, & K. B. Yancey (Eds.), *Electronic portfolios 2.0: Emergent research on implementation and impact* (pp. 29–35). Sterling, VA: Stylus.

Collins, R. (1998). *The sociology of philosophies: A global theory of intellectual change*. Cambridge, MA: Belknap.

Ede, L. (2004). *Situating composition: Composition studies and the politics of location*. Carbondale: Southern Illinois University Press.

Freedman, A., & Medway, P. (Eds.). (1994a). *Learning and teaching genre*. Portsmouth: Boynton/Cook Heinemann.

Freedman, A., & Medway, P. (Eds.). (1994b). *Genre and the new rhetoric*. London: Taylor & Francis.

Freedman, A., & Pringle, I. (Eds.). (1980). *Reinventing the rhetorical tradition*. Conway, AK: L & S Books (CCTE).

Freedman, A., Pringle, I., & Yalden, J. (1983). *Learning to write: First language/second language: Selected papers from the 1979 CCTE conference, Ottawa, Canada*. London: Longman.

Grendi, E. (1977). Micri-analisi e storia sociale. *Quaderni Storici*, 35, 506–520.

Hamilton, S. J. (1995). *My name's not Susie: A life transformed by literacy*. Portsmouth, NH: Boynton/Cook Heinemann.

Hamilton, S. J. (1999). "You can get by...": A cross-cultural odyssey in search of voice and identity. In G. Haroian-Guerin (Ed.), *The personal narrative: Writing ourselves as teachers and scholars*. Portland, ME: Calendar Islands.

Haroian-Guerin, G. (Ed.). (1999). *The personal narrative: Writing ourselves as teachers and scholars*. Portland, ME: Calendar Islands.

Harris, J. (1997/2012). *A teaching subject: Composition since 1966* (new ed.). Logan, UT: Utah State University Press.

Horne, M. E. (2012). *Writing in a community of practice: Composing membership in Inkshed*. Winnipeg: Inkshed.

Hunt, R. A. (2004). What is inkshedding? Retrieved from http://www.stu.ca/~hunt/whatshed.htm

Hunt, R. A., & Reither, J. A. (1994). A workshop: Knowledge in the making in writing, English, and other content courses. In C. F. Schryer & L. Steven (Eds.), *Contextual literacy: Writing across the curriculum* (pp. 137–157). Winnipeg: Inkshed.

Inkshed Newsletter archives, 1982–2009. Available from http://www.inkshed.ca

Lauer, J. M. (1998). Disciplinary formation: the Summer Rhetoric Seminar. *Journal of Advanced Composition*, 18(3), 503–508.

Lingard, L., Schryer, C. F., Spafford, M., & Campbell, S. L. (2007). Negotiating the politics of identity in an interdisciplinary research team. *Qualitative Research*, 7(4), 501–519.

Magnusson, S. G., & Szijarto, I. M. (2013). *What is microhistory? Theory and practice*. London: Routledge.

Maguire, M. H. (Ed.). (1995). *Dialogue in a major key: Women scholars speak*. Urbana: NCTE.

Matsuda, P. (1999). Composition studies and ESL writing: A disciplinary division of labor. *College Composition and Communication*, 50(4), 699–721.

Matsuda, P. K., M Fruit, & T.L.B. Lamm (Eds.). (2006). *WPA, 3*(1/2). Special issue on second language writers and writing program administrators.

McComiskey, B. (2016). Introduction. In B. McComiskey (Ed.), *Microhistories of Composition* (pp. 3–38). Logan, UT: Utah State University Press.

Mian, M., Schryer, C. F., Spafford, M. M., Joosten, J., & Lingard, L. (2009). Current practice in physical child abuse forensic reports: A preliminary exploration. *Child Abuse and Neglect, 33*(10), 679–683.

Muir, E. (1991). Introduction: Observing trifles. In E. Muir & G. Ruggiero (Eds.), *Microhistory and the lost peoples of Europe* (pp. vii–xxviii). Baltimore: Johns Hopkins University Press.

Oster, J. (1979). Tulips, tagmemics, and the ghost of Dartmouth. *The English Quarterly, 12* (Fall), 23–32.

Phelps, L. W. (2014). The historical formation of academic identities: Rhetoric and composition, discourse and writing. Keynote address, Canadian Association for the Study of Discourse and Writing. Waterloo, ON. (2012). *Canadian Journal for Studies in Discourse and Writing, 25*(1), 3–25. Retrieved from http://journals.sfu.ca/cjsdw/index.php/cjsdw/article/view/37/22

Phelps, L. W. (2016). The 1979 Ottawa conference and its inscriptions: A Canadian moment in American rhetoric and composition. In B. McComiskey (Ed.), *Microhistories of composition* (pp. 58–89). Logan, UT: Utah State University Press.

Pringle, I., & Freedman, A. (Eds.). (1981). *Teaching, writing, learning.* Ottawa: CCTE.

Reither, J. A. (1981). Some ideas of Michael Polanyi and some implications for teaching writing. *Pre/Text, 2*(1–2), 33–43.

Reither, J. A. (1985). Writing and knowing: Toward redefining the writing process. *College English, 47*(6), 620–628.

Reither, J. A. (1985). Epistemic newslettering, or Inkshed as a mode of learning. *Inkshed, 4*(1), 1–3.

Reither, J. A., & Vipond, D. (1989). Writing as collaboration. *College English, 51*(8), 855–867.

Revel, J. (1996). Microanalysis and the construction of the social. In J. Revel & L. Hunt (Eds.), *Histories: French constructions of the past* (A. Goldhammer, Trans.) (pp. 492–502). New York: New Press.

Rice, J. (2007). *The rhetoric of cool: Composition studies and new media.* Carbondale: Southern Illinois University Press.

Schryer, C. F. (1993). Records as genre. *Written Communication, 10*(2), 200–234.

Schryer, C. (1994). A consultancy model of research for literacy and writing across the curriculum researchers. In C. F. Schryer & L. Steven (Eds.), *Contextual literacy: Writing across the curriculum* (pp. 128–136). Winnipeg: Inkshed.

Schryer, C. F. (1999). Genre time/space: Chronotopic strategies in the experimental article. *Journal of Advanced Composition, 19*(1), 81–89.

Schryer, C. F. (2002). Genre and power: A chronotopic analysis. In R. Coe, L. Lingard, & T. Teslenko (Eds.), *The rhetoric and ideology of genre* (pp. 73–102). Cresskill, NJ: Hampton Press.

Schryer, C. F. (2011). Investigating texts in their social contexts: The promise and peril of rhetorical genre studies. In D. Starke-Meyerring, A. Paré, N. Artemeva, M. Horne, & L. Yousoubova (Eds.), *Writing in knowledge societies* (pp. 31–52). Fort Collins, CO: WAC Clearinghouse/Parlor Press.

Schryer, C. F., Afros, E., Mian, M., Spafford, M. M., & Lingard, L. A. (2009). The trial of the expert witness: Negotiating credibility in court documents in child abuse cases. *Written Communication, 26*(3), 215–246.

Schryer, C. F., Bell, S., Mian, M., Spafford, M., & Lingard, L. A. (2011). Professional citation practices in child maltreatment letters. *Written Communication, 28*(2), 147–171.

Schryer, C. F., Gladkova, O., Spafford, M. M., & Lingard, L. (2007). Co-management in healthcare: Negotiating professional boundaries. *Discourse and Communication, 1*(4), 452–479.

Schryer, C. F., Lingard, L., & Spafford, M. (2007). Regularized practices: genres, improvisation, and identity formation. In M. Zachry & C. Thralls (Eds.), *Communicative practices in workplaces and the professions: Cultural perspectives on the regulation of discourse and organizations* (pp. 21–44). Amityville, NY: Baywood.

Schryer, C. F., & Steven, L. (Eds.). (1994). *Contextual literacy: Writing across the curriculum.* Winnipeg: Inkshed.

Schryer, C., & Steven, L. (1994). Introduction. *Contextual literacy: Writing across the curriculum* (pp. 1–10). Winnipeg: Inkshed.

Smith, T. S. (2000). Inkshed—"What kind of shed are you?": A micro-ethnography of the CASLL/Inkshed listserv and conference. *Inkshed 2000 live archive [unedited conference proceedings].* Retrieved from http://www.inkshed.ca/shed2000/tsethnog.htm.

Spafford, M. M., Schryer, C. F., & Lingard, L. (2008). The rhetoric of patient voice: Reported talk with patients in referral and consultation letters. *Communication and Medicine, 5*(2), 93–104.

Spafford, M. M., Schryer, C. F., Lingard, L., & Mian, M. (2010). Accessibility and order: Crossing borders in child abuse forensic reports. *Technical Communication Quarterly, 19*(2), 118–143.

Stock, P. L. (Ed.). (2012). *Composition's roots in English education.* Portsmouth, NH: Boynton Cook/Heinemann.

Wenger, E. (1998). *Communities of practice: Learning, meaning, and identity.* Cambridge: Cambridge University Press.

Wilkinson, A. M. (1978). Criteria of language development. *Educational Review, 30*(1), 23–33.

Wilkinson, A. M., & Wilkinson, M. E. (1978). The development of language in the middle years. *English in Education*, *12*(1), 42–52.

Zebroski, J. (2012). Hidden from history: English education and the multiple origins of contemporary composition studies, 1960–2000. In P. L. Stock (Ed.), *Composition's roots in English education* (pp. 26–50). Portsmouth, NH: Heinemann Boynton/Cook.

Zebroski, J. T., Hamilton, S. J., Mayher, J. S., & Harris, J. (1992). Symposium on "After Dartmouth: Growth and conflict." *College English*, *54*(6), 694–714.

5 A Case-Study Approach to Examining Cross-Border Networks

Jennifer Clary-Lemon

While using case study as a methodological approach has long been employed in writing studies to frame for researchers best practices of methods and methodological intention (see Lauer & Asher, 1988; Newkirk, 1992; Hayes et al., 1992), we have seen fit here to draw connections from a range of other methodological distances to the case study to foster what we call here *network sense* (see Mueller, forthcoming). Rather than create distances among ways of knowing or theories of knowledge, here we seek, as Johanek (2000, p. 88) has forwarded in *Composing Research: A Contextualist Paradigm for Rhetoric and Composition*, to view methods together in the spirit of *desire to know*. We do this, in part, to avoid "misguided arguments that only certain methods are sensitive to [the] same context—contexts we either ignore or construct artificially after our chosen method is comfortably in place" (p. 90). Thus the case-study approach taken here represents dwelling in a particular node to foster a link, or what Flusser calls an intersubjective (rather than hierarchical) "field of relations" (qtd. in Gochenour, 2011, p. 4) that, taken in and linked with other representative nodes of scale fostered in chapters 2 through 4, allows for a far richer view of interdependent cross-border interrelationships.

Perhaps nowhere is the case study as a method as inextricably linked with writing studies than in the examination of programmatic development. This is clearly detailed in *Composition Forum*'s eight-year run of the "Program Profile" feature of the journal, as well as an influx of program-based case studies about undergraduate writing majors that have appeared in well-known volumes like O'Neill, Crow and Burton's

(2002) *A Field of Dreams*, and Giberson and Moriarty's (2010) *What are We Becoming*. These areas have begun to converge within the large topic of the internationalization of writing studies, as collections such as Chris Thaiss et al.'s (2012) volume *Writing Programs Worldwide: Profiles of Academic Writing in Many Places* and David Martins' (2015) *Transnational Writing Program Administration* have begun to address. Yet documenting the Canadian "case" has a long-standing history. This is reflected in part by definitional work written by a range of scholars: the work of Nan Johnson (1987) in documenting composition in nineteenth-century Canadian colleges and universities in the mid-eighties; the 1988 work of R.S. Harris in documenting English studies at the University of Toronto; Henry Hubert's (1994) historical and contrastive work on textual studies in Canada throughout the nineties, the contemporary work of Roger and Heather Graves (2006) in providing detailed and rich research into writing instruction and location in Canadian universities.[1] Thus, despite being a nation unto itself, Canada has always been but a "case" in composition and often one portrayed as straining against an Americanized model.

And although emergent activity of note is beginning to be taken up—as "hubs" of Canadian writing studies activity in chapter 3 suggest—it seems that more often than not, it is the "case" that has become tradition in Canada, as is exemplified by Sheese et al.'s (2006) look into York's Centre for Academic Writing (now Writing Department, since 2012). Yet within the tradition of examining the Canadian context through these acts of definition, one particular twenty-year case study has emerged, that of the University of Winnipeg's department of Rhetoric, Writing, and Communications. Noted as a relative anomaly on the Canadian landscape in Graves' work in 1994 (See also Graves & Graves, 2012, 118), the Writing Program at the University of Winnipeg came into being in 1986, and as early as 1997 the department's earliest beginnings were overviewed and published in *WPA: Writing Program Administration* (Kearns & Turner, 1997). This was followed by updates on its movement toward independent status as a Centre in 1995 and again, as an independent department, in 2002 (Kearns & Turner, 2002). Programmatic development was later discussed in 2006 (Turner & Kearns, 2006) and then again in 2012 in *Writing Programs Worldwide* (Turner & Kearns, 2012; see also Kearns & Turner, 2016). According to Robert E. Stake (2005, p. 445), we may view the University of Winnipeg as an *intrinsic* case study, one undertaken because those writing about it had an intrinsic interest in both its particularities (i.e., that it stands uniquely alone as a writing program in Canada and as an independent department of rhetoric and writing studies) and its ordinariness (marking a trend in the discipline of creating independent programs and units away from traditional English departments). As this chapter seeks to provide a networked approach to case study, I argue that the thirty-year-old case of the University of Winnipeg, which now holds the status of an independent department with professorships in all ranks, is now an *instrumental* case study—that is, one that may be "examined mainly to provide insight into an issue or to redraw a generalization," in which "the case is of secondary interest . . . [because] it facilitates our understanding of something else" (Stake, 2005, p. 445). To that end, the University of Winnipeg as a case study holds instrumental value for facilitating our understanding of the "something else" of cross-border interdependencies among Canadian and American scholars, which I take up in discussing its inception (in examining the role of a synchronic mentor), its 2011 curricular consultation process, and its subsequent curricular redesign process in 2012–2014. Taken together, and considering survey participation of five of the department's faculty as taken up by prior chapters, these three glimpses into the case of the University of Winnipeg suggest that throughout the department's tenure, the interdependent nature of its development demonstrates a network dependent on what Lauer (2002, p. x) calls "heuristic thinking," formed by "open-ended but inventional acts" that have held true over time to its cross-border foundations.

Synchronic Mentoring and How Ideas Travel

While the tumultuous history of the beginnings of the Centre for Academic Writing in the late 1980s has been extensively covered by Kearns and Turner (1997), here I turn not to details of the movement from program to Centre and its attendant difficulties, but rather to a moment in time and an examination of the particular framework that gave rise to later programmatic and decision making curricular agreements (and disagreements). As Kearns and Turner (1997, p. 32) note, the inception of the Writing Program in 1986 was overseen "by a Director who reported to the English Department on curriculum and to the Dean of Arts and Science on more general program matters; he alone of the Program's faculty members held a professorial rank." While Kearns and Turner describe the tenor that such hierarchical administrative decision making might strike, as well as both self-study and internal and external reviews that resulted in the program-cum-centre, their piece, as a programmatic overview, omits specifics that might be deemed either inessential or damaging in uncovering nearly a decade of programmatic transformation. As a current member of the department faculty making sense of the case of my departmental home while looking cross-border interdependencies, however, different details introduced by Kearns and Turner become relevant. As they note, not only does the department share a narrated history similar to American writing programs, but it has also been filled, from inception, with "American influences"—notably, the Dean of Arts and Sciences, who first lobbied for the writing program, and the first Director of the program, brought in particularly to administer the program, were both American (1997, p. 41). Beyond this description, however, Kearns and Turner don't devote much space to examining how such "Americanness" travelled to Winnipeg, other than in setting up a writing program typical of others existing in the United States at the same time or looking at American models as guidelines in how to do so. Here I focus in on how ideas themselves cross-pollinate, by directing attention to the role of the American Director of the Centre in 1987, Roland Huff, and his appointment by the Dean of Arts and Sciences, Michael McIntyre.

The Writing Program came into being as a major initiative undertaken by McIntyre, who received his PhD in neuropsychology at the University of Minnesota and completed post-doctoral work at Cornell University before coming to the University of Winnipeg in 1975. Working in conjunction with the English department (among other faculties), McIntyre has suggested the inception of the program was influenced by American scholars working in the area of communications, English, and writing, notably Richard Larson (City University of New York), Alice Kersnowski (St. Mary's University, San Antonio), and Frank Kersnowski (Trinity University, San Antonio) (personal communication, June 22, 2015). Working with the English Department, McIntyre appointed Huff as Director of the program. Although Huff spent twenty years teaching in the English faculty at the University of Winnipeg and thus, his two-year tenure as Director of the Centre for Academic Writing was markedly short (1997, p. 32), the ways in which his Americanness situated those within the program in specific ways nonetheless had marked impact. Given his limited time overseeing the Centre and the irrecoverability of institutional memory, I don't wish to mark Huff in some way as either instigating particular movements or decrying others; however, I wish to note him for these purposes as what Mueller has deemed a *synchronic mentor* in some capacity to a fledgling program. Thus, rather than viewing Huff's mentorship as meaningful across a period of time (i.e., diachronic), instead I see his influence as meaningful for a variety of reasons *at a particular point in time*, that is, synchronic.

Huff received his PhD in English from Indiana University, served on the English faculty of Washington State University and the University of Texas at Austin, and directed undergraduate and graduate programs in rhetoric and composition at Eastern Washington University. While at UT Austin, Huff co-published pieces with James Kinneavy and Charles Kline in 1974 and published *The Contemporary Writing Curriculum* with Kline in 1987. Noted as a member of the "Developmental School" of rhetorical thinkers by Paul T. Meyers (1994, p. 225), a colleague at Washington State, he is listed in thinking next to such scholars as James Britton, Tony Burgess, Nancy Martin, Alex McLeod, Harold Rosen (collaborators on the instrumental book *The Development of Writing Abilities*), Janice M. Lauer, and James Moffett. Huff himself had English roots, and the classification of his work alongside other British thinkers that generally noted that writing was developed over a lifetime suggests that not only did Huff bring "Americanness" to Winnipeg, but also that he cross-pollinated the Commonwealth into his American studies (for a fuller discussion of similar "developmental" thinking inspired by Britton, see Phelps's discussion of Freedman and Pringle in chapter 4).

It is important to situate Huff not only as an American scholar but also as one who espoused a particular view of writing and writing instruction at the time. As per his own textbook written with Kline (1987, p. 23), Huff aimed to "resolve the dichotomy between expressive and transactional writing," using a process-based approach that drew heavily from both expressive (journal writing) and rhetorical (audience based) traditions. However, in his move into the Director position at the University of Winnipeg, it was clear that he also needed to conceptualize a response to the mandate that the institution be responsive to both student access and WAC and WID approaches (Kearns & Turner 1997, p. 34). This was done, in part, by the creation (incentivized by Huff and McIntyre) of a Writing Centre and a computing lab used for writing students, as well as a partnering of those initiatives with practicum components open to Education students. As I next discuss, Huff was also attuned to premises espoused by scholars such as Britton et al. and Moffett that had been used to conceptualize other, American WAC programs like that at Michigan Tech in the late 1970s.[2] In a synthesized approach to programmatic development appearing in *Language Connections: Writing and Reading Across the Curriculum*, a book edited by Toby Fulwiler, Randal Freisinger (1982, p. 3) suggests that these three premises (used to frame Michigan Tech's program) similarly work with developmental, expressive, and rhetorical approaches: "(1) writing promotes learning; (2) writing is a complex developmental process; and (3) the universe of discourse includes a broad range of writing functions and audiences." With these ideas in mind, I turn now to the ways in which such ideas travelled across borders into a framework during the program's naissance.

The Writing Program, overseen by Huff, hired its first batch of faculty with English MAs from local programs at the University of Manitoba in 1988. None were trained specifically in composition because that training was unavailable in Canada at the time, and remains so, to a large degree. As new faculty were hired, each was given twelve free books, chosen by Huff, to read as a way to understand both the new culture and vision of teaching writing in the program: Huff and Kline's (1987) *The Contemporary Writing Curriculum*; Fulwiler's (1986) *Teaching with Writing*; Carl Koch and James Brazil's (1978) *Strategies for Teaching the Composition Process*; Ken Macrorie's (1970) *Telling Writing*; Mina Shaughnessy's (1977) *Errors and Expectations*; Peter Elbow's (1973) *Writing Without Teachers*; Janet Emig's (1971) *The Composing Process of Twelfth Graders*; James Moffett's (1983) *The Universe of Discourse*; Art Young and Toby Fulwiler's (1986) *Writing Across the Disciplines: Research Into Practice*; James Kinneavy's (1971) *A Theory of Discourse*; Richard Young, Alton Becker and Kenneth Pike's (1970) *Rhetoric: Discovery and Change*; and Timothy Donovan and Ben W. McClelland's (1980) edited collection *Eight Approaches to Teaching Composition* (with contributions by Donald Murray, Paul Escholz, Stephen Judy, Janice Lauer, Kenneth Dowst, Harvey Wiener, Thomas Carnicelli, and Robert Weiss).

Any scholar in rhetoric and composition will recognize the formidable nature of this list, its inclusion of landmark works, and its reflection of the process movement (Koch and Brazil, 1978; Emig, 1971; Shaughnessy, 1977; Fulwiler, 1986), expressivism (Elbow, 1973; Macrorie, 1970), and rhetorical and discursive approaches to teaching writing (Young, Becker, and Pike, 1970; Kinneavy, 1971; Moffett, 1983; Lauer, 1980). Further, such ideas contained within the list clearly draw on the WID philosophy espoused by those at Michigan Tech (and reflected by Young and Fulwiler's (1986) volume as required reading): Emig's clear thesis that writing and learning are intertwined; the well-defined notion of writing as a process; and a focus on rhetorical awareness of genre and audience, or variety of discourses (see Kinneavy, 1971). Too, this list returns to those thinkers instrumental in the 1979 CCTE Conference: Emig, Kinneavy, Young, Britton, Murray (see Freedman & Pringle, 1980; Phelps this volume). While Writing Studies as a discipline may have diverged from and made more complex some of these core principles in the last thirty-odd years, nonetheless they were well-known and represented contemporary knowledge about writing in the late 1980s. Such a list, every volume authored by American scholars, represents not only a way of seeing writing at the time, but also represented a quick education in teaching writing for any new instructor—indeed, such a list might still offer more by the way of knowledge about writing than many Canadian teachers of writing receive in the present day. This knowledge was further nurtured by in-house workshops from visiting American scholars who visited in the early nineties, as Andrea Lunsford and Lillian Bridwell-Bowles did, as well as external programmatic review by well-known Canadians in the field, Judy Segal and Anthony Paré.

It is clear, at least from the reading list, that Huff looked to create a grounded model for teaching, and the *Writing Program Coursebook* (1990), the common curriculum created by instructors at the time, represents a process-based, expressivist-meets-rhetoricist curriculum that took students through a writing process; included information on theses and usage; and led students through narrative, issue analysis, proposals, problem-solution papers, and research. However, as is noted in *Inkshed* publications by Evans (1985); Besner, Huff, & McIntyre (1988); and Besner (1992), the common curriculum both strained at the edges of instituting that all instructors teach from the same course text as well as ran up against those values espoused by instructors trained in English literature (see Besner, 1992). The common curriculum was disbanded in 1993, and at least two of the instructors teaching in the writing program returned to the English department rather than continued on with the Centre; however, the program's roots in these synthesized views of writing had already been established.

To read these texts and professional development opportunities in terms of Huff's tenure as director of the program, which was notably brief, doesn't accurately depict his abilities as an administrator. Instead he may be read as an American influence on the moment and within a

Canadian network of scholars, one who ushered in not only an Americanized program model, but also American ideas about writing that shaped incoming Canadian faculty. As these faculty were encouraged to develop a curriculum to sustain the program in the late 1980s, they were doing so out of a foundation that resonates with heuristic thinking: thinking that is guided (in this case by landmark scholarly works from the American tradition of rhetoric and composition), yet open-ended enough to be adaptable to particular and local ends. Based in these roots, these early faculty were those who later argued for the program's increased status as a Centre, then as a Department with a developed undergraduate major, and who are now at the highest rank of the professoriate. Thus, ideas about writing have carried, yes, but have carried in such a way that reflects far more than one individual's actions. In the next section, I examine another such opportunity for cross-border transfer with the consideration of another American scholar's 2011 visit to the University of Winnipeg.

A Reflective Project: Institutional (Re) Invention

In 2006, I came to the University of Winnipeg as an Assistant Professor, having done my own graduate study in rhetoric and composition in American institutions as is the longstanding tradition in many Canadian programs with expertise in writing studies. As I struggled to understand my own place in the department, I also was faced with questions about my place in the discipline, in the country, and in the Canadian conception of the field. Thus I was drawn not only to prior published case studies of the University of Winnipeg, but also to figuring out what Canadian writing studies was coming to mean (see Clary-Lemon, 2009) and what departmental futures might look like, given the past twenty years of growing strength around writing and rhetoric at one particular institution. As I began to feel "at home," my questions became more pointed: how stable would the department remain, should contextual elements—changing program architecture, administrative transition at the university, generational change in faculty, or disciplinary developments in the field—alter over time?

Too, my research interests and professional activities had long been allied with the definitional work in the American field as I struggled to understand that there was no immediate transfer into the Canadian one. I was well-versed in the language of CIP codes and taxonomies of the National Research Council, thanks to participating in the CCCC-affiliated Master's Degree Consortium of Writing Program Specialists in 2007–2008, and thus grew familiar with the Visibility Project put forward by Louise Phelps and John Ackerman (2010) when Louise came to present to the group about the project in its earliest stages.[3] Yet I had no such grasp on the Canadian equivalent territory of the Social Science and Humanities Research Council (SSHRC) grants or listed fields for funding initiatives, which suffers from the same kinds of disciplinary invisibility on the Canadian landscape that rhet/comp suffers in the American one. To try to make sense of these, and other, institutionally-centered questions, in January of 2011, I located Louise, who was a Fulbright Specialist Program (FSP) Scholar at the time, and applied for a grant to have her travel to the University of Winnipeg for the purposes of institutional review, given her expertise. It should be noted that, like the National Research Council and the Survey of Earned Doctorates, the Fulbright Program does not list rhetoric, composition, or writing studies among its various "Primary Disciplines;" as such, I looked to apply for the grant under "Applied Linguistics/TEFL," through which applicants could name specific scholars to be connected with. Thus, it was through the FSP "named project request," in which interested applicants could examine a Specialist's Roster to find scholars whose expertise aligned with the project they had in mind, that I first contacted Louise with my interest via email, and later collaborated on the grant application which would see her spend six weeks in Winnipeg to examine "Writing Studies at the University of Winnipeg: Future Directions" in a curricular consultation.

Before I discuss outcomes of the Fulbright project and later processes of curricular redesign, I want to pause for a moment to examine Louise Phelps's role in terms of cross-border collaboration, idea transfer, scholarly networks, and heuristic thinking. I borrow the subheading of this section from her own work in *Composition as a Human Science* (Phelps, 1988, p. x), which should by anyone's estimation be considered a compelling and provocative *"reflective project* in the self-understanding of the discipline" in which she seeks to make sense of composition in terms of hermeneutical interpretation and application. It should be noted that, like the heyday of Huff's influence on the now-department, *Composition* turns to the time span of 1976–1986 to do its reflective work. Significantly, too, there is overlap between those scholars Huff was most drawn to, as reflected in the distributed book list, and those Phelps (1988) draws on to frame the disciplinary conversations taking place within the pages of *Composition*: in particular, Janice Lauer, James Kinneavy, and Janet Emig (p. xv). Similarly, Phelps's expertise in faculty work (see Denham et al., 1996) and institutional invention has drawn from and clarified inventional work from rhetorical theorists such as Corbett and Young, Becker, and Pike (Phelps, 2002, pp. 92–94). While I do not wish to suggest that she has much, if anything, in common with Huff, I do wish to note that Louise's visit to the University of Winnipeg in 2011, along with our Canadian-American partnership during the curricular consultation, may also be seen as continuing a particular tradition of American thinkers that have come to play a role in the department in a way that is far more complex than could be framed in a six-week visitation.

Similarly, such a moment in 2011 cannot be wholeheartedly separated out from future cross-border mentoring relationships and networks of ideas that have continued out from that particular place in time. Phelps's strong mentoring and supervisory role at Syracuse and her reliance on mapping as a metaphor and tool that has framed a variety of projects (see Wiley, Gleason, and Phelps, 1996, pp. 1–7; Phelps and Ackerman, 2010, p. 194) cannot be separated out from her similar mentoring role to Derek Mueller (co-author, this volume). Louise served as a reader in 2009 on his dissertation committee and the director of one of his graduate classes, "CCR712/Advanced Theory and Philosophy of Composition: Mapping the Future: Theory and Practice of 'Writing' the Discipline," which first emphasized mapping using *Composition in Four Keys*. The ways in which the documents she produced during the course of the Fulbright project influenced the writing of this chapter can similarly not be discounted. We also cannot ignore the ways in which Phelps's work has been forwarded in Canadian venues since 2011 that continue to take up place in meaningful ways: for example, Louise's keynote talk at the 2012 Canadian Association for the Study of Discourse and Writing, later published in the Canadian Journal for the Study of Discourse and Writing, resulted in her not only meeting with Andrea Williams of the University of Toronto (co-author, this volume) but also introducing Andrea to another of her Syracuse PhD students, Tanya Rodrigue. Both Williams and Rodrigue are now co-editing a special issue of *Across the Disciplines* on the role of TAs in WAC initiatives, another example of cross-border collaboration that has moved out from Louise's work at the University of Winnipeg.

Thus, the case of Winnipeg, viewed in terms of these circulations of people, texts, and historical moment, is one that clearly interweaves American and Canadian scholars and scholarship when examined beyond a timeline of programmatic development. A further demonstration of the ways in which these ideas mingled happened during Louise's visit to Winnipeg and is evidenced by the recommendations that emerged as a result of her research into a Canadian program. Louise visited the University from April 24 to June 4, 2011, conducting interviews with faculty, administration, and students; reading a body of work by faculty and by administration as well as by Canadian writing scholars; and interviewing a number of Canadian scholars at other institutions (Phelps, 2011, p. 2). Over the period of the six weeks of her curricular consultation, Louise regularly met with a coordinating committee of departmental faculty (of which I was a member), in which we discussed curricular growth and challenges among other immediate issues facing the department and the university. At Louise's suggestion, the committee began with reading—not only her own work on institutional invention and disciplinarity (see Phelps, 1996; 1988; 2008) but also each other's syllabi, assignments, and faculty publications—an open-ended design that was meant to cultivate a "hermeneutical appreciation" of one another's work. As the committee struggled to make sense of a curricular moment that questioned the alignment of first-year outcomes and upper-division courses in the undergraduate major in Rhetoric and Communications, we relied on American conversations about transfer, genre knowledge, and course outcomes. The coordinating committee relied on the *WPA Outcomes Statement* (Council of Writing Program Administrators, 2008) as a framing document for conversations, as well as read (and forwarded on to the departmental first-year subcommittee to consider) a variety of American texts: Linda Bergmann and Janet Zepernick's (2007) "Disciplinarity and Transfer;" Mary Jo Reiff and Anis Bawarshi's (2011) "Tracing Discursive Resources;" Doug Downs and Elizabeth Wardle's (2007) "Teaching about Writing, Righting Misconceptions;" Susan Jarratt et al.'s (2007) "Pedagogical Memory and the Transferability of Writing Knowledge;" Gerald Nelms and Ronda Dively's (2007) "Perceived Roadblocks to Transferring Knowledge from First-Year Composition to Writing-Intensive Major Courses;" Rounsaville, Goldberg, and Bawarshi's (2008) "From Incomes to Outcomes;" Wardle's (2009) "Mutt Genres" and "Understanding Transfer" (2007); and Tweedie, Courtney, and Wolff's (2010) "What Exactly Is This Major?" While not an exhaustive list, these readings clearly point to the ways in which the coordinating committee was attuned to American models and contemporary ideas about transfer while still interpellating those ideas from a localized standpoint drawing on distinctly Canadian contexts to understand such ideas' applications (see Turner & Kearns, 2012, 132).

At the end of her six-week stay, Louise's Fulbright report, *Liminal Practice in a Maturing Writing Department* (2011), made seven recommendations about curricular changes at the university. The report details the climate of the university under the then-president and his focus on civic engagement, upcoming generational change and its impact on the department in the next 5–10 years, and opportunities for program renewal. The report not only focused on local contexts and departmental history, but also curricular design: levels of curriculum, articulation between levels, and losses and gaps in current practices. The report also took up the feasibility of an MA program, a coordination of Canadian intellectual traditions represented by the Department's name—rhetoric, writing, and communications—and the process by which such revisioning might be done in a collegial and efficient fashion (pp. 4–5).

In what follows, I take up one of the final recommendations of the Fulbright report, which was to modify the groups of courses in the major: "In place of defined 'streams,' [of course groupings, to] lay out and make available on the web a number of exemplary student programs that demonstrate different 'paths' related to different interests and goals" (Phelps, 2011, p. 27). As with any set of recommendations, the time from receipt to implementation is one that is dependent on a variety of factors, whether they be resources, feasibility, or popularity. Given my emphasis on cross-border interdependencies in this case, however, I wish to focus in on the ways in which the department took up Louise's recommendation: the call to reconsider existing course groupings. In the next section, I consider how this process continued the tradition of interweaving and adapting American and Canadian models.

CURRICULAR REDESIGN: IDEAS IN ACTION

Following Louise's visit and distribution of her Fulbright report, faculty met at monthly departmental meetings to discuss its content, noting that the years to come would represent internal work and conversations that may have no immediate outcome but would be beneficial to all (especially current and future students). A first order of business was to investigate the current system of course groupings, which were created with the undergraduate major in 2003 and were not only confusing for students but also failed to reflect departmental and faculty strengths, in three out of four groupings placing a large emphasis on "communications," despite the fact that the department lacked—and continues to lack—faculty in this area. Figure 1 indicates the course groupings that were in place at this time, of which students are required to take at least one course from each group.

Group One: Rhetoric		Group Three: Specialized Communication	
RHET-3138(3)	Modern Rhetorical Theory	EDUC-4600(3)	Critical Literacy for Empowerment
RHET-3139(3)	Rhetorics of Visual Representation	RHET-2350(3)	Reading and Writing Online
RHET-3150(3)	Studies in the Rhetoric of Nonfiction	RHET-3154(3)	The New Journalism
RHET-3152(3)	Rhetoric and the World Wide Web	RHET-3310(3)	Communicating Science
RHET-3153(3)	Studies in the Rhetorics of Gender	RHET-3320(3)	Forms of Inquiry in Written Communication
RHET-3155(3)	Writing on the Environment	RHET-3329(3)	Writing for Scholarly Audiences
		RHET-3330(3)	Investigative Journalism
		RHET-3331(6)	Writing Partners Practicum
		RHET-3340(3)	Technical and Professional Communication
Group Two: Written and Oral Communication		Group Four: Media, Communication, and Society	
EDUC-2601(3)	Introduction to Information Technology for Educators	POL-3455(3)	Politics of the Mass Media in Canada
RHET-2145(3)	Theories and Practices of Oral Communication	RHET-2246(3)	Revolutions in Communication
		RHET-3151(3)	Critical Studies of Discourse
RHET-2246(3)	Revolutions in Communication	RHET-3321(3)	Composing Our Winnipeg: Rhetoric of/and the City
RHET-2505(1)	Tutoring Academic Writing		
RHET-2520(1)	Tutoring Second Language Learners	RHET-3331(6)	Writing Partners Practicum
RHET-3236(3)	Orality and Literacy	RHET-3420(3)	Rhetorics of Identity
RHET-3250(3)	Composition Studies	SOC-3214(3)	Mass Communication and Media
RHET-3255(3)	Narrative Thinking and Writing		

Figure 1: UW Course Groupings Created in 2003

Prior to Louise's visit, the department was having contentious conversations about regrouping courses, primarily because the favoured re-grouping centred around dividing courses into those focusing on "rhetoric," "writing," or "communications," looking something like Figure 2:

Rhetoric (9)	Writing Studies (12)	Communications (7)
2135 Rhetorical Criticism	2131 Professional Style & Editing	2137 Contemporary Communication Theories
3138 Modern Rhetorical Theory	2350 Reading and Writing Online	2145 Theories and Practices of Oral Communication
3139 Rhetorics of Visual Representation	2505/2515/2520 (Tutoring Courses)	
	2530 Rhetorical Grammar	2246 Revolutions in Communication
3150 Studies in the Rhetoric of Nonfiction	3154 The New Journalism	3236 Orality and Literacy
	3155 Writing on the Environment	3310 Communicating Science
3151 Critical Studies of Discourse	3250 Composition Studies	3330 Investigative Journalism
3152 Rhetoric and the WWW	3255 Narrative Thinking and Writing	3340 Strategies for Technical and Professional Communication
3153 Studies in the Rhetorics of Gender	3320 Forms of Inquiry in Written Communication	
3401 Rhetoric of the Public Sphere	3321 Composing Our Winnipeg	
3420 Rhetorics of Identity	3329 Writing in the Humanities and Social Sciences	
	3331 Writing Partnerships Practicum	

Figure 2: UW Courses Grouped in Disciplinary Terms

Although organizing courses this way made them seem more transparent for students, faculty were not happy with the ways titles of courses may or may not have placed them in the correct disciplinary category. Rather than a process that superficially rearranged courses to fit with perceived (but unarticulated) divisions between disciplinary terminology, the Fulbright report (Phelps, 2011, p. 23) suggested that the department employ a system of "backwards design"—that is to say, to employ American Educational consultants Grant Wiggins and Jay McTighe's (2005) concept that faculty engage in developing goals based on research and work backwards to design or redesign courses, curricula, and learning environments to meet them. Such heuristic—rather than algorithmic—thinking encouraged faculty to go back to the drawing board, so to speak, and to investigate in order to re-see what our current curriculum actually delivered to students.

In order to do that, the curriculum committee had to ask our faculty, regardless of the name of their courses, what they actually did, what they valued in terms of student learning, and what they expected students to know both before they entered their classroom and after students left. To a large extent, then, our questions were not about disciplinary territory of courses offered, but outcomes that, as a faculty, we agreed were important for students to have experienced before they earned a degree in our department. Thus, our language turned from that of disciplinary terminology to that of outcomes, activities, and traditions based in qualitative inquiry—specifically, surveys and mapping.

The curriculum committee turned to a model used by the University of Rhode Island in order to try and understand what departmental colleagues valued in the courses that they taught. In 2006—notably, before I had come to the University of Winnipeg—I had attended a panel at the American Conference on College Composition and Communication—CCCC—titled "Claiming Our Moment: Constructing a Writing Major," featuring presentations by Nedra Reynolds, Jeremiah Dyehouse, and Libby Miles at the University of Rhode Island (URI). I had held on to the materials they featured in their talk, which essentially allowed their audience to observe their departmental process in developing a writing major. While the University of Winnipeg's goals were different in 2011—a programmatic renewal rather than a curricular invention or overhaul—nonetheless, I offered up the materials from Rhode Island to the curriculum committee to use as framing documents for rethinking departmental curriculum. These materials primarily consisted of a developed list of outcomes and an Outcomes Tracking Map. Since the presentation in 2006, URI has made both their outcomes and outcomes tracking map available online.[4]

Viewing URI's outcomes for their majors in writing and rhetoric, one can see their close alignment with those from the *WPA Outcomes Statement* (Council of Writing Program Administrators, 2008, 2014), extended out in traces specific to their departmental curriculum—rhetorical knowledge, process and collaborative textual evaluation, craft, genre, editing, textual production and delivery, and reflective learning. While we recognized that the specifics of UW's Canadian program were not equivalent to the undergraduate program at URI, nonetheless, we began with URI's outcomes and adapted them to suit what we thought our departmental outcomes were for the BA in Rhetoric and Communication. While we had existing outcomes that were created with the major in 2003, they had not been adjusted, despite new courses emerging and old ones being retired. After discussions on the curriculum committee and with the faculty at large, we refined URI's outcomes to suit what we felt were appropriate outcomes for our degree program, arriving at four types of outcomes which drew on both URI's categories as well as our prior existing outcomes (underlined in Figure 3).

We both borrowed from our 2003 existing outcomes and modified categories from URI's template, adding an emphasis on discursive practices (reflecting faculty and curricular development in this area) and reducing emphasis on information technology and collaborative practices, which did not appear uniformly across offered courses. Once the curriculum committee brought these outcomes to the entire faculty for agreement, we needed to track how and whether the courses we offered actually emphasized the outcomes that we privileged.

RHETORICAL & DISCURIVE THEORIES	TEXTUAL PROCESS & PRODUCTION
• Identify rhetorical situations calling for a wide range of responses • Evaluate the appropriateness of rhetorical choices in discursive events • Demonstrate a command of different theories and methodologies • Apply different theories to a range of situations • Demonstrate familiarity with the histories of Rhetoric, Writing Studies, and/or Communications • Understand the relationships among Rhetoric, Writing Studies, Communications, and (if applicable) other disciplinary approaches	• Produce documents with other writers • Evaluate and respond to peer writing • Identify and evaluate options for text production and circulation • Use current technologies to produce and deliver texts • Demonstrate facility in communicative performance
EDITING & STYLE	**REFLECTIVE PRACTICES**
• Arrange the organization of texts **to conform to genre conventions** • Produce complex texts with correctness • Consider and apply stylistic options\ • Develop **a multi-staged, recursive writing process that employs revision as a means of invention**	• Synthesize and integrate insights across courses • Articulate an **informed reflection** on public and private identities • Demonstrate **judgment and adaptability in communicative decision-making grounded in theory and ethics**

Figure 3: Revised UW Outcomes Based on URI Model

The curriculum committee turned to a variety of sources of data in order to design and implement what we came to know as "outcomes tracking." We began with informal surveys to all faculty about first-year writing borrowed directly from the appendix of Nelms and Dively's (2007) piece on knowledge transfer in order to get a sense of what kinds of concepts, activities, assignments, and student preparation faculty were expecting out of first-year courses that aligned with outcomes for the undergraduate major. Then the curriculum committee again turned to URI's documents—this time, the Outcomes Tracking Map, which mapped each course in our curriculum with our agreed-upon outcomes, as well as whether or not a course "Introduced" (I), "Reinforced" (R), or "Emphasized" (E) a particular outcome. A small group of faculty on the curriculum committee first met to try to fill in the outcomes tracking map based on both the IRE terminology and on collected faculty syllabi for all courses. While it was a generative exercise based on the introductory tracking of outcomes and the discrepancies among even a small group of faculty, the curriculum committee realized that a) faculty have differing definitions of "introducing," "reinforcing," and "emphasizing" concepts and disciplinary knowledge and b) syllabi only revealed a scant amount of knowledge to an uninitiated faculty reader about what kinds of outcomes might be met by a particular course. As a result, the curriculum committee created a faculty survey using SurveyMonkey in order to more holistically complete the Outcomes Tracking Map; faculty were given explicit definitions of criteria for introducing, reinforcing, and emphasizing course material and then asked to complete the survey for every 2000-level and above course that they taught. The survey emphasized that one individual course could not fulfill all outcomes, and that it was perfectly fine to say that a course did not fulfill one or more outcomes. Our return rate on these surveys was ninety-seven percent, notably because our faculty is small and it is commonly known who teaches which course. After the surveys were in, the curriculum committee met to discuss the results. In cases that two instructors differed on either an outcome or its emphasis, the committee made collaborative decisions based on either compromise or the original Outcomes Tracking Map exercise which used faculty syllabi.

As a result of the survey, the curriculum committee was able to complete an Outcomes Tracking Map based on the input of the faculty (see Figure 4); this was also presented to faculty in monthly meetings.[5] By reading the IRE data, we were able to get a sense of where our curriculum was weak—for example, a lack of courses that "reinforced" particular outcomes at the 2000 level—as well as outcomes that perhaps we as a faculty believed we were more proficient in than we could actually collectively demonstrate—for example, in the outcome "use current technologies to produce and deliver texts." As well, it created a gap of introductory outcomes in "textual process and production" that faculty clearly believed our first-year course should fulfill. These notable "gaps" helped inform our first-year subcommittee; they also made the curriculum committee question what, exactly, students were currently getting in their courses, as well as what they "should" get in terms of course delivery in the future.

	2131	2135	2137	2145	2246	2350	2500	3132	3138	3139	3151	3152	3153	3154	3155	3236	3255	3329	3330	3320	3321	3329	3331	3340	3401	3420
RHETORICAL AND DISCURSIVE THEORIES																										
Identify rhetorical situations calling for a wide range of responses	I		I		I					E	R	E	E	E	E	E	E	E		E	E	E	E		E	E
Evaluate the appropriateness of rhetorical choices in discursive events	I		I	I								R	R	E	E	E	E	E		E	I	E	E	R*	E	E
Demonstrate a command of different lines of inquiry, theories and methodologies relevant to the fields of Rhetoric, Writing Studies, and Communications			I	I	I				E	E	R	R	E	R	E	E	E	E		E	E	E	E	R*	E	E
Apply different theories to a range of situations			I							E	E	R	E	R	E	I*	I*	E		R	E	E	E	R*	E	E
Demonstrate familiarity with the histories of Rhetoric, Writing Studies, and/or Communications			I		I				I	R	R	E	R	R	R	E	I*	E				E			R	
TEXTUAL PROCESS & PRODUCTION																										
Produce extended documents independently and with practical judgment and flexibility	R		R	R	R				R	R	E	E	R	E		E	E	E		E	E	E	E	R	R	E
Work collaboratively with peers and/or other writers on the production of a document	R	?	R	I					R	R	E		R			R	R	E		R	R	R	E	R	R	R
Evaluate and respond to peer writing	R		R													E	R	E		R	R	E	E	R	R	
Use current technologies to produce and deliver texts			I	I						R						E	R	R		I*	E	R	R	R	R	R
Demonstrate facility in communicative performance			I	I						E	E	E				E	I*	E		R	R	E	E	R	R	R
Develop a multi-staged, recursive writing process that employs revision as a means of invention	R													E		R		E					R	R		
EDITING & STYLE																										
Arrange the organization of texts to conform to or, if appropriate, depart from genre conventions	R	R		R	R				R	R	R	E	R	E		E	E	E		E	E	E	E	R*	R	E
Produce complex texts with correctness	R	R	R	R	R				R	E	E	E	R	E		E	E	E		R	R	E	E	R	R	R
Consider and apply stylistic options	E*	I	R						R	E	R	E	R	R		E	E	E		R	R	E	E	R	R	
REFLECTIVE PRACTICES																										
Synthesize and integrate insights across courses	I		I	I	I				R	R	R	E	E	E		E	I*	E		R	E	E	E	I*	E	E
Articulate an informed reflection on public and private identities	I	I	I		I				E		R	R	R	I		E	E	E		E	R	E	E	I*	E	E
Demonstrate judgment and adaptability in communicative decision-making grounded in theory and ethics			I						R	R	R	E	R	E		E	E	E		E	R	E	E	R	E	E

Figure 4: UW 2012 Outcomes Tracking Map

The major goal that was achieved in this process was a rethinking and reconsideration of how the department grouped its current courses in order for students to meet departmental outcomes for the Bachelor of Arts degree, which was a recommendation of the 2011 Fulbright Report. Prior to the heuristic process of employing backwards design, faculty were undecided about re-grouping courses based on disciplinary content, yet not happy with the current system. As a result of this outcomes-based process, the curriculum committee decided upon a three-group system that clarified for students what they needed to take in the degree, but also more genuinely reflected departmental outcomes and values (see Figure 5).

Textual Process and Production
RHET-2131(3) Professional Style and Editing
RHET- 2145(3) Theories and Practices of Oral Communication
RHET-2350(3) Reading and Writing Online
RHET-2500(3) Tutoring Writing
RHET-3155(3) Writing on the Environment
RHET-3255(3) Narrative Thinking and Writing
RHET-3310(3) Communicating Science
RHET-3321(3) Composing our Winnipeg: Rhetoric of/and the City
RHET-3329(3) Writing for Scholarly Audiences
RHET-3330(3) Investigative Journalism
RHET-3331(6) Writing Partnerships Practicum
RHET-3340(3) Technical and Professional Communication
Criticism and Analysis
RHET-2135(3) Rhetorical Criticism
RHET-3139(3) Rhetorics of Visual Representation
RHET-3150(3) Studies in the Rhetoric of Nonfiction
RHET-3151(3) Critical Studies of Discourse
RHET-3152(3) Rhetoric and the World Wide Web
RHET-3153(3) Studies in the Rhetorics of Gender
RHET-3154(3) The New Journalism
RHET-3420(3) Rhetorics of Identity
History and Theory
RHET-2137(3) Contemporary Communication Theories
RHET-2246(3) Revolutions in Communication
RHET-3132(3) Directed Readings in Rhetoric and Composition
RHET-3138(3) Modern Rhetorical Theory
RHET-3236(3) Orality and Literacy
RHET-3250(3) Composition Studies
RHET-3320(3) Forms of Inquiry in Written Communication
RHET-3401(3) Rhetoric in the Public Sphere

Figure 5: UW New Course Groupings, adopted 2014

Rather than four groups that invoked confusing representations of the department, the new system of three groups, Textual Process and Production, Criticism and Analysis, and History and Theory, draws upon content areas that faculty emphasize in the courses they teach. It doesn't privilege disciplinary terms such as rhetoric, writing, or communications, but is activity and content-based. Because the process was collaborative and inclusive of prior curricular development and processes, this new grouping system has had buy-in from all faculty in different ranks, was approved by University Senate in 2014, and was implemented in practice for student degrees in 2015.

The inclusion of the details of decision making in this case is twofold: first, it details for those Canadian and American scholars who may be struggling with program inception or redesign a concrete and inclusive strategy (though admittedly a slow process). Secondly, and more importantly for the purposes of this chapter, it represents an inside look at some of the ways in which "Americanness" still travels to the University of Winnipeg and how "Canadianness" travels out,[6] as well as the way in which outcomes tracking and curricular design still reflect the department's founding programmatic ideas about writing and rhetorical study: that writing is how students learn, that it is a complex process, and that it requires adaptability to a wide range of situations and audiences. Too, the outcomes exercise demonstrates the changing nature of a discipline that did not exist in Huff's time: a fledgling field realized, and with it, the necessity of pedagogical outcomes that emphasize field-specific histories and theories, research methods, and new technologies. Finally, as a response to the Fulbright project (itself a cross-border collaborative entity), the curricular regrouping process reveals the ways in which American ideas, program models, and processes of developing undergraduate majors are both *taken up* and *modified* within new environs elsewhere (as the URI "map" and specific definitions of IRE at Winnipeg demonstrate).

The moments taken up in continuing the case of the University of Winnipeg here—how founding ideas of the American field in the late 1970s and early 1980s shaped the program's philosophies about writing; the ways in which cross-border collaboration and scholarly networks emerged from the 2011 Fulbright consultation with Winnipeg as its home base; the ways in which Winnipeg's curricular redesign still very much depended on uptake and adaptation of URI's model and the *WPA Outcomes Statement*—suggest more than a case of intrinsic value of "what's happening with writing studies in Canada." Instead, these moments offer up a "close" view of the interior work of cross-border connections and relations, which provide for us an instrumental look at the networks of American and Canadian scholars that have formed over the course of a more than thirty-year history. To that end, too, this case suggests the importance of heuristic thinking across time: the ability to see cross-border relationships as collaborations and recursive connections of networks, links, and scholarly nodes of people, places, and ideas rather than a contrastive or oversimplified approach that rests on suggestions of discrete and separable boundaries between two interconnected nations.

NOTES

1. For a fuller list of definitional work of the Canadian writing landscape, see Clary-Lemon (2009, pp. 100–101).

2. See Young and Fulwiler (1986) for a complete discussion of the WAC program at Michigan Tech.

3. See Phelps and Ackerman (2010) for a full description of the Visibility Project.

4. See http://harrington.uri.edu/undergraduate-program/writing-rhetoric/undergraduate/learning-outcomes/ for University of Rhode Island's Writing and Rhetoric list of outcomes, and http://harrington.uri.edu/wp-content/uploads/2013/01/rhodemap-1.xls for the Outcomes Tracking Map.

5. Note that column blanks represent surveys about courses not completed by faculty members.

6. A version of this chapter section was delivered at the Writing Research Across Borders conference in February 2014 in Paris, France.

REFERENCES

Baseley, V., Freeman, J., McLeod Rogers, J., Nolan, B., Page, S., Schnitzer, D., Sumpter, E., & Taylor, C. (1990). *University of Winnipeg writing program coursebook*. Winnipeg, MB: The University of Winnipeg.

Bergmann, L. S., & Zepernick, J. (2007). Disciplinarity and transfer: Students' perceptions of learning to write. *WPA*, 31(1–2), 124–149.

Besner, N. (1992). Invention and its discontents: A polemical free-write. *Inkshed*, 11(2), 12–14.

Besner, N., Huff, R., & McIntyre, M. (1988). Writing program, University of Winnipeg. *Inkshed*, 7(2), 6–10.

Clary-Lemon, J. (2009). Shifting tradition: Writing research in Canada. *American Review of Canadian Studies*, 39(2), 94–111.

Corbett, E. (1971). *Classical rhetoric for the modern student*. New York, NY: Oxford Universsity Press.

Council of Writing Program Administrators. (2008). *WPA outcomes statement for first-year composition*. Retrieved from http://www.in.gov/che/files/WPA_Outcomes_Statement_for_First-Year_Composition.pdf

Council of Writing Program Administrators. (2014*). WPA outcomes statement for first-year composition v 3.0.* (2014). Retrieved from http://wpa-council.org/files/WPA%20Outcomes%20Statement%20Adopted%20Revisions%5B1%5D_0.pdf

Denham, R., Kramsch, C., Phelps, L.W., Rassias, J., Slevin, J., & Swaffar, J. (1996). Making faculty work visible: Reinterpreting professional service, teaching, and research in the fields of language and literature. Report of the MLA commission on professional service. *Profession*, 161–216.

Donovan, T., & McClelland, B. (Eds.). (1980). *Eight approaches to teaching composition*. Urbana, IL: NCTE.

Downs, D., & and Wardle, E. (2007). Teaching about writing, righting misconceptions: (Re) envisioning "first-year composition" as "introduction to writing studies." *CCC*, *58*(4), 552–584.

Elbow, P. (1973). *Writing without teachers*. New York, NY: Oxford University Press.

Emig, J. (1971). *The composing processes of twelfth graders*. Urbana, IL: NCTE.

Evans, M. (1985). Cohort report. *Inkshed 4* (3), 8.

Freedman, A., & Pringle, I. (1980*). Reinventing the rhetorical tradition*. Conway, AR: L&S Books.

Freisinger, Randall. (1982). Cross-disciplinary writing programs: Beginnings. In T. Fulwiler & A. Young (Eds.), *Language connections: Writing and reading across the curriculum* (pp. 3–13). Retrieved from http://wac.colostate.edu/books/language_connections

Fulwiler, T. (1986). *Teaching with writing*. Portsmouth, NH: Boynton/Cook, Heinemann.

Giberson, G., & Moriarty, T. (Eds.). (2010). *What we are becoming: Developments in undergraduate writing majors*. Logan, UT: Utah State University Press.

Gochenour, P. (2011). Nodalism. *DHQ: Digital Humanities Quarterly*, 5(3). Retrieved from http://digitalhumanities.org/dhq/vol/5/3/000105/000105.html

Graves, R. (1994). *Writing instruction in Canadian universities*. Winnipeg, MB: Inkshed Publications.

Graves, R., & Graves, H. (2012). Writing programs worldwide: One Canadian perspective. In C. Thaiss et al. (Eds), *Writing programs worldwide: Profiles of academic writing in many places* (pp. 117–127). Fort Collins, CO: WAC Clearinghouse

Graves, R., and Graves, H. (Eds). (2006). *Writing centres, Writing seminars, writing culture: Writing instruction in anglo-Canadian universities.* Winnipeg, MB: Inkshed Publications.

Harris, R.S. (1988). *English studies at Toronto: A history.* Toronto, ON: University of Toronto Press.

Hayes, J., et al. (1992). *Reading empirical research studies: The rhetoric of research.* Hillsdale, NJ: Lawrence Erlbaum Associates.

Hubert, H. (1994). A history of college rhetoric in the US and Canada: Different traditions. In S. Baardman, S. Straw, & L. Atkinson (Eds.), *Social reflections on writing: To reach and realize* (pp. 13–31). Winnipeg, MB: Literacy Publications.

Huff, R., & Kline, C. (1987). *The contemporary writing curriculum: Rehearsing, composing, and valuing.* New York, NY: Teachers College Press.

Huff, R., Kinneavy, J., & Kline, C. (1974). *Training English teachers for Texas community colleges.* Austin, TX: University of Texas.

Jarratt, S., et al. (2007). *Pedagogical memory and the transferability of writing knowledge: An interview-based study of UCI juniors and seniors.* Irvine, CA: University of California, Irvine. Retrieved from http://www.writing.uci.edu/researchdocs/pedmemory.pdf

Johanek, C. (2000). *Composing research: A contextualist paradigm for rhetoric and composition.* Logan, UT: Utah State University Press.

Johnson, N. (1987). English composition, rhetoric, and English studies at nineteenth-centuryCanadian colleges and universities. *English Quarterly, 20*(4), 296–304.

Kearns, J., & Turner, B. (1997). Negotiated independence: How a Canadian writing program became a centre. *WPA: Writing Program Administration, 21*(1), 31–43.

Kearns, J., & Turner, B. (2002). No longer discourse technicians: Redefining place and purpose in an independent Canadian writing program. In P. O' Neill, A. Crow, & L. Burton (Eds.), *A field of dreams: Independent writing programs and the future of composition studies* (pp. 90–103). Logan, UT: Utah State University Press.

Kearns, J., & Turner, B. (2016). An outsider's perspective: Curriculum design and strategies for sustainability in a Canadian IWP. In J. Everett and C. Hanganu-Bresch (Eds.), *A minefield of dreams: Triumphs and travails of independent writing programs.* Fort Collins, CO: The WAC Clearinghouse.

Kinneavy, J. (1971). *A theory of discourse.* New York: Norton.

Koch, C., & Brazil, J. (1978). *Strategies for teaching the composition process.* Urbana, IL: NCTE.

Lauer, J. (2002). Foreword. In J. Atwill, & J. M. Lauer (Eds.), *Perspectives on rhetorical invention* (pp. ix–x). Knoxville, TN: University of Tennessee Press.

Lauer, J.M., & Asher, J.W. (1988). *Composition research: Empirical designs.* New York, NY: Oxford Press.

Macrorie, K. (1970). *Telling writing*. Rochelle Park, NJ: Hayden.
Martins, D. (Ed.). (2015). *Transnational writing program administration*. Logan, UT: Utah State UP.
Moffett, J. (1983). *Teaching the universe of discourse*. Portsmouth, NH: Boynton Cook.
Mueller, D. (in press). *Network sense: Methods for visualizing a discipline*. Fort Collins, CO: WAC Clearinghouse.
Meyers, P. (1994). Slaying the hydra: Quality management of the multi-volume, multi-subject, multi-author, multi-rhetorical aim, competitive commercial proposal. In M. Steehouder, C. Jansen, P. van der Poort, & R. Verheijen (Eds.), *Quality of technical documentation* (pp. 211–227). Amsterdam, EU-12 & Atlanta, GA:: Rodopi.
Nelms, G., & Dively, R. (2007). Perceived roadblocks to transferring knowledge from first-year composition to writing-intensive major courses: A pilot study. *WPA: Writing Program Administration*, *31*(1–2), 214–240.
Newkirk, T. (1992). The narrative roots of the case study. In G. Kirsch & P. Sullivan (Eds.), *Methods and methodology in composition research*. Carbondale, IL: SIUP.
O' Neill, P., Crow, A., & Burton, L. (Eds). (2002). *A field of dreams: Independent writing programs and the future of composition studies*. Logan, UT: Utah State University Press.
Phelps, L. W. (1988). *Composition as a human science: Contributions to the self-understanding of a discipline*. New York, NY: Oxford University Press.
Phelps, L. W. (1996) Composition studies. In T. Enos (Ed.), *Encyclopedia of rhetoric and composition* (pp. 123–134). New York, NY: Garland.
Phelps, L. W. (2002). Institutional invention. In J. Atwill and J. Lauer (Eds.), *Perspectives on rhetorical invention* (pp. 64–95). Knoxville, TN: University of Tennessee Press.
Phelps, L. W. (April 2008). The symbolic construction of disciplinarity: Composing the "integrated" past, the fragmented present, and myths of future unity. Presentation at the Conference on College Composition and Communication.
Phelps, L. W. (2011). *Liminal practice in a maturing writing department*. (Unpublished Fulbright Project Report).
Phelps, L. W. (2014). The historical formation of academic identities: Rhetoric and composition, discourse and writing. *Canadian Journal for Studies in Discourse and Writing*, *25*(1), 3–25.
Phelps, L., & Ackerman, J. (2010). Making the case for disciplinarity in rhetoric, composition, and writing studies: The visibility project. *CCC*, *62*(1), 180–215.
Reiff, M., & Bawarshi, A. (2011). Tracing discursive resources: How students use prior genre knowledge to negotiate new writing contexts in first-year composition. *Written Communication*, *28*(3), 312–337.

Rounsaville, A., Goldberg, R., & Bawarshi, A. (2008). From incomes to outcomes: Prior genre knowledge, meta-cognition, and the question of transfer. *WPA: Writing Program Administration, 32*(1), 97–112.

Shaughnessy, M. (1977). *Errors and expectations: A guide for the teacher of basic writing*. New York, NY: Oxford University Press.

Sheese, R., Spencer, J., Rehner, J., Greenwald, T., & Rozendal, P. (2006). Faculty of arts centre for academic writing: York university, Toronto. In R. Graves, & H. Graves (Eds.), *Writing centres, Writing seminars, writing culture: Writing instruction in anglo-Canadian universities*, (pp. 256–272). Winnipeg, MB: Inkshed Publications.

Stake, R. (2005). Qualitative case studies. In N. Denzin, & Y. Lincoln, (Eds.), *The sage handbook of qualitative research* (pp. 443–466). 3rd ed. Thousand Oaks, CA: SAGE.

Thaiss, C., Bräuer, G., Carlino, P, Ganobcsik-Williams, L., & Sinha, A. (Eds.). (2012). *Writing programs worldwide: Profiles of academic writing in many places*. Fort Collins, CO: WAC Clearinghouse and Parlor Press.

Turner, B., & Kearns, J. (2006). Into the future: A prairie writing program extends its traditions. In R. Graves, & H. Graves (Eds.), *Writing centres, Writing seminars, writing culture: Writing instruction in Anglo-Canadian universities* (pp. 273–296). Winnipeg, MB: Inkshed Publications.

Turner, B., & Kearns, J. (2012). Department of rhetoric, writing and communications at the university of Winnipeg. In Thaiss, C., Bräuer, G., Carlino, P, Ganobcsik-Williams, L., & Sinha, A. (Eds.), *Writing programs worldwide: Profiles of academic writing in many places* (pp. 129–138). Fort Collins, CO: WAC Clearinghouse.

Tweedie, S., Courtney, J., and Wolff, W. (2010). "What exactly is the major?": Creating disciplinary identity through an introductory course. In G. Giberson & T. Moriarty (Eds.), *What we are becoming: Developments in undergraduate writing majors* (260–276). Logan, UT: Utah State University Press.

University of Rhode Island. (2013). Writing & rhetoric learning outcomes. Retrieved from http://harrington.uri.edu/undergraduate-program/writing-rhetoric/undergraduate/learning-outcomes/

Wardle, E. (2007). Understanding 'transfer' from FYC: Preliminary results of a longitudinal study. *WPA: Writing Program Administration*, 31(1–2), 65–85.

Wardle, E. (2009). Mutt genres and the goal of FYC: Can we help students write the genres of the university? *CCC, 60*(4), 765–789.

Wiggins, G., & McTighe, J. (2005). *Understanding by design*. Alexandria, VA: Assn. for Supervision & Curriculum Development.

Wiley, M., Gleason, B., & Phelps, L. (1996). *Composition in four keys: Inquiring into the field*. Mountain View, CA: Mayfield.

Young, A., & Fulwiler, T. (Eds.). (1986). *Writing across the disciplines: Research into practice*. Upper Montclair, NJ: Boynton/Cook.

Young, R., Becker, A., & Pike, K. (1970). *Rhetoric: Discovery and change*. New York, NY: Harcourt.

6 Conclusion

Derek Mueller, Andrea Williams, Louise Wetherbee Phelps, and Jennifer Clary-Lemon

SCHOLARLY IDENTITY

We didn't start out to study scholarly identity; rather, the concept emerged from our examination of scholarly networks and participants' identifications. In asking scholars (both in surveys and interviews) how they located themselves and their work, we soon realized that what had initially seemed a relatively straightforward category was in fact a complex and highly ambiguous concept. A multiscopic approach such as the one employed here is well-suited to an examination of scholarly identity, which we've shown operates at multiple and overlapping levels, including individual, institutional, national, and disciplinary. For example, for most scholars, questions of national and disciplinary identity were seldom straightforward and usually changed over time. The complexity and ambiguity that we found with respect to scholarly identity should not have surprised us for, as White (2010) has argued, academics are increasingly expected to "fashion themselves in particular ways" in the workplace "where there are many layers to consider" (1). If we look beyond the level of the individual and examine writing programs such as the University of Winnipeg's, we can also see how identity is complex: enabled and constrained by not only individual faculty members, but also local and national conditions as well as broader disciplinary norms, all of which change over time.

Like other concepts examined in this study, our understanding of identity has evolved as we traced the career trajectories of individual scholars within social networks. Rather than finding identity to be a singular and stable concept, whether pertaining to a person (how people see or imagine themselves), place (how people see or imagine their institution, for example), or entity (how people see or imagine the programs or departments, organizations, or disciplines to which they belong), we have found it to be multiple, layered, and fluid. Prior's (1998) study examined the layered or "laminated" identities of student writers and Roozen, Woodard, Kline, and Prior (2015) explored the complex identities of novice teachers, but this is the first study to explore the multiple and layered workings of mature scholarly identity. Besides discovering the laminated nature of mature scholarly identity, we found that it involves a degree of agency. Some of the ways that the scholars we studied shaped their scholarly identity included the institutions they enrolled in for graduate study, the conferences they attended, the organizations they served, the people with whom they collaborated, the audiences for whom they wrote, the venues where they published, and the disciplines they adopted or to which they acculturated. For example, Lingard described intentionally crafting a particular scholarly identity and place for her scholarship within medicine. Some scholars embraced plural or hybrid identities to suit their varied research interests, whereas others assumed different identities as a professional survival mechanism in a country with few tenure-track job opportunities in the field. Identities available to scholars were influenced (and constrained by) their social networks: mentors and collaborators seemed to have as much impact as funding and job opportunities on scholarly identity. In this way, we found scholarly identity to be something we both choose and that is chosen for us.

We found that scholarly identity is shaped intentionally as well as opportunistically through networks that connect us to other people, texts, institutions, organizations, and events, the latter of which speaks to the diachronic or historic dimension of scholarly identity. A key source of scholarly identity was disciplinary organizations, both Canadian ones like Inkshed/CASLL (the Canadian Association for the Study of Language and Learning) and the Canadian Association for the Study of Discourse and Writing, and in the United States the Conference on College Composition and Communication, which provided scholars with intellectual and social communities from which they derived vital support, particularly if it was in short supply at or absent from their home institution. For all of the scholars as well as the departmental major studied here (chapter 5), identity changed over time, contingent on factors such as scholars' evolving interests, roles, and career and life stage, and the professional and disciplinary organizations to which they belonged.

In short, identity is something that scholars both create and, over time, recreate, and that is created and recreated for them.

In addition to the importance of professional and disciplinary organizations in shaping identity, institutions proved to be a key source of identity for scholars. Institutional hubs or circles are dense local networks that comprise a critical mass of closely connected individual scholars, mostly within but sometimes also across institutions, as in the case of the Carleton-McGill university group. Such hubs may have at their centre a strong leader/mentor (such as Dale Jacobs of the University of Windsor) or a collaborative group (Carleton University) and provide scholars with not only an institutional home but also peer and/or cross-generational mentoring and networks. Institutional hubs such as Carleton have been critical to the development of the field in Canada by establishing graduate programs and bringing together in one location scholars with shared intellectual interests (in the case of Carleton, rhetorical genre studies and writing in a variety of professional and disciplinary contexts). Moreover, in connecting prominent scholars from the United States and the United Kingdom at conferences such as the ones organized by Aviva Freedman, Ian Pringle, and Peter Medway, hubs like Carleton University have contributed to the internationalization of the field and in this way also function as spokes, disseminating ideas in increasingly wider circles of networks through the actual events as well as through their textual traces (for example, conference proceedings). Whereas Carleton University exemplifies a research-oriented institutional hub with its graduate programs and many faculty publications, the University of Toronto exemplifies a hub with a teaching focus, namely, providing its many permanent writing faculty and even larger number of contract instructors (mostly in writing centres) with ongoing professional development opportunities. Although less recognized because the impact of such teaching-focused institutional hubs is primarily local and leaves few textual traces, they are nonetheless important to the field in Canada for they are where PhDs wishing to stay in or return to Canada will likely find jobs, and their members are increasingly participating in the discipline through conference activity and publications.

One of the most striking features of the Canadian hubs we studied was that, although they are composed of scholars with strong institutional ties, most are isolated from each other, forming closed rather than open networks. The prominence of closed networks in Canada is attributable to both geographical (the vast distances between universities) and institutional factors: the disparate locations of writing studies scholars in Canadian universities—dispersed across writing centres; WAC programs; departments of communication, education, English, language and linguistics, and psychology; faculties of engineering; and independent writing programs—make creating a common disciplinary identity difficult. The isolation of hubs is particularly pronounced when the hub is centered on a lone figure rather than a group of scholars. In such cases, we found that the isolated lead scholar tends to identify more closely with and direct his or her energy towards the American rather than to the Canadian field. Although it was cross-border networks linking Canadian hubs to the United States that laid the foundation for writing studies in Canada, the lack of connections across institutional hubs poses a serious threat to the field in Canada, particularly given that disciplines are funded nationally. In contrast, the vital hubs can usually be characterized as open networks where members are connected to other hubs both nationally and internationally. We found that many of the senior scholars we interviewed (such as Freedman, Graves, and Schryer) have played important roles within networks by connecting different groups, a position that Simmons (2015) found is tied to individual career success, despite whatever challenges people in open networks face:

> People in open networks have unique challenges and opportunities. Because they're part of multiple groups, they have unique relationships, experiences, and knowledge that other people in their groups don't. This is challenging in that it can lead to feeling like an outsider as a result of being misunderstood and under-appreciated because few people understand why you think the way you do. It is also challenging, because it requires assimilating different and conflicting perspectives into one worldview. (Simmons, paras. 24–25).

More open networks in Canada would help connect more scholars to nationally funded research projects and provide scholars who are otherwise isolated with much needed intellectual and social community. Even more importantly, linking the many closed institutional hubs would strengthen the discipline in Canada.

In addition to institutional hubs often being situated across vast distances from each other, individual writing studies scholars in Canada often have few, if any, disciplinary colleagues in their home institution so that cross- or multidisciplinary collaborative research with colleagues from different disciplinary and professional contexts is common. Yet this collaborative and multidisciplinary approach is a double-edged sword: although cross-disciplinary scholarship enriches the field by introducing new ideas and approaches, in an academy that recognizes and rewards distinct disciplines such scholarship isn't always recognized as writing studies.

Presence

The term "presence" came into our lexicon through Louise Phelps's original project for our collaboration and underwent a transformation as a result of what we learned through our joint study. In her 2012 address to the Canadian Association for the Study of Discourse and Writing (Phelps, 2014), she had argued the need to reconstruct Canadian scholars' conflicted and limited view of American writing studies (caught between dependence and resistance) in terms of a more pluralistic set of relations. Specifically, she suggested that revisionist histories should examine the flow of Canadian writing scholarship across the border into the US, where she conjectured that it had a "quiet presence" long unrecognized by historians on either side of the border as specifically Canadian. When we began our collaboration, she decided to take on this project.

Louise's conjecture was based on the fact that all of us knew of Canadian scholarship that was either published in the US or read by American scholars yet was seldom identified as Canadian, nor recognized as comprising a distinctively Canadian body of work. She set out to identify Canadian scholars who had achieved some visibility in the networks of US rhetoric and composition. To even recognize such scholars as Canadian required a list of Canadian writing scholars encompassing several generations, the joint construction of which was the first step in the larger project of this book (see chapter 2). As this list was being developed, recommendations from American scholars provided one informal source of evidence that a particular Canadian scholar was "known" in the networks of rhetoric and composition. Louise used our final list to conduct her initial project, in which she studied the incidence and number of "mentions" of scholars on the list in selected sources, primarily in the indices of works that aim to represent "the field" as a whole—encyclopedias, sourcebooks, edited volumes, and the like (see note 2, chapter 4).

In identifying scholars' visibility with such "mentions," Louise operationalized a concept of scholarly presence as a function of publication in traditional genres, reflecting a deeply engrained premise of the academic value system. But as our interview and survey data began to flow in, we became doubtful that this concept could account for our findings, and Louise set aside her original project for the hermeneutical study reported in chapter 4. In order to understand how and why this understanding of "presence" evolved into a much more complex concept through our collaborative study, we want to begin by analyzing its meaning at the source.

Although not a citation study, Louise's use of "mentions" to establish Canadian scholars' presence in US rhetoric and composition shared two widespread assumptions that underlie citation studies: 1) that a scholar's achievement or worth is measured by recognition amongst peers in scholarly networks and 2) that such recognition rests almost entirely on scholarly publications in the literature of the field. (See Clary-Lemon, 2009, p. 20, which focuses on publications to document Canadian "scholarship" in writing; and Mueller, 2012.) These assumptions represent academic norms expressed most overtly in the university policies that determine how a scholar will be assessed for promotion and tenure and what will "count" in that process. Through a sampling of such policies, it is possible to pull out the linked propositions that represent a traditional concept of "presence" and its role in assessing a scholar's worth. We focus here only on the parts of those policies that deal with "research" or "scholarship" (specifically, the "scholarship of discovery," in the terms of Boyer, 1997), as formulated for research universities, which are at the top of the hierarchy by which scholars are judged cross-institutionally.

In a random sampling of American university promotion and tenure policies posted online, we identified two clusters of terms and phrases corresponding to these two propositions.

The first cluster concerns *recognition by peers*, ranging in degrees from being "known" or "recognized" to earning a major reputation and having an "impact "on the field.

Cluster 1: Recognition by Peers
known or *well-known*
reputation
recognized, recognition, peer recognition: e.g.
• "*be recognized as authorities* . . . by external colleagues—national and/ or international"
• [pieces of scholarship that] "*warrant recognition*"
• "*recognition* as a scholar or writer with a *major reputation* in one's field"
• "earn a national or international *reputation*"
• "work that has been *widely perceived among peers* as outstanding"
• "accomplishment and *impact on a field*"
• "significant *contributions to the field*"

This notion of reputation is more or less explicitly comparative and competitive in US promotion and tenure policies. Duke University's guidelines state that scholars must "stand in competition with the foremost person of similar rank in similar fields," and a typical letter soliciting a scholarly review asks the reviewer to "compare X's development as a scholar with others in parallel stages of development." The second cluster specifies publication as the primary basis for such recognition.

Cluster 2: Publications
scholarly production
contributions to the literature
refereed publications
research and scholarly productivity as measured by quality and quantity of published articles, monographs, books, or creative work

But publications are valued very selectively. It is usually specified that publications must be of high quality, original, and make significant contributions to the field (features that can only be determined directly by internal and external reviewers). However, the channel of publication itself is a surrogate for direct review, by the same criterion applied to the scholars themselves—recognition, along with selectivity and refereed submissions. In some cases (for example, University of North Carolina-Greensboro's Department of English), what "counts" for tenure and promotion (to associate professor) is even more narrowly specified: "publication of a monograph with a nationally recognized university, independent, or commercial press that engages in rigorous professional review."

A random sampling of Canadian tenure and promotion criteria at the university level shows a similar approach to determining a scholar's impact that focuses on reputation as judged by knowledgeable peers and impact through publications. At the most traditional end of the spectrum, the University of Toronto describes scholarly impact in terms of "advancement of knowledge" with an emphasis on originality as well as "importance to the field." Similarly, the University of British Columbia explicitly refers to reputation in terms of the candidate achieving "wide recognition" and "distinction in their discipline," presumably earned through "sustained and productive scholarly activity," and the University of Waterloo expects faculty members to "be active participants in the evolution of their discipline," although it offers a broader concept of scholarship (including "the discovery of new knowledge," "the coordination, synthesis or integration of knowledge," and "new and useful applications" of knowledge). Notably, Waterloo was the only institutional policy we analyzed that mentioned the expectation that faculty seek external funding to support their scholarly work, likely because it is located in Kitchener-Waterloo, Ontario, a Canadian innovation hub where former giant, RIM (Research in Motion, the creator of the Blackberry) and other technology firms and tech start-ups are located.

A statement from Syracuse University's recently revised university-wide guidelines for promotion puts the two dimensions of presence together: "Scholarship, *as measured by peer recognition* of its *originality, impact on, and importance* to the development of the field(s) or relevant disciplines, is *demonstrated* most typically by *refereed publications*—in journals, books of high quality, or other influential venues." In summary, presence within scholarly networks is the sine qua non required for promotion and tenure, the universal standard of success in the academy. Recognition by peers is the *measure* of presence, and peer-reviewed, selective publication in the literature of the field persists as the primary *means* in most Canadian and American institutions by which presence is both achieved and demonstrated.

This summary refers to the most traditional academic norms and is simplified in several respects. It doesn't account for variations among fields, like the critical role of grants in the natural and social sciences and the professions in the United States (and in all fields in Canada), and it ignores for our purposes the alternate or secondary scholarly activities that are (variably, according to the institution) acknowledged as contributing to a scholar's record of achievement and its manifestation as presence.

More important, in the US these norms are evolving under the pressure of reform movements (see Boyer, 1990; Boyer, 1996) and changes in disciplines themselves. However, tradition is a powerful force conserving this understanding of presence, especially in the most elite institutions. Faculty perceptions of controlling norms may lag behind the reality that they are gradually becoming more flexible: a case in point is Syracuse University, which has recently published new guidelines for promotion that expand notions of what kind of activity "counts" as scholarly, what forms of communication and audiences are appropriate, and what kinds of "peers" can legitimately judge a scholar's work and reputation.[1]

What counts as contributions to knowledge in a field varies considerably by institution in Canada. The University of Toronto specifies that such knowledge must be communicated in traditional scholarly forms, namely, "through the publication of books, articles, papers, reviews, and other scholarly work" and that knowledge must be communicated to and judged by peers or professionals. York University and Ryerson University have broader criteria for how scholarship is communicated. For example, York University also includes public service and the production or performance of works of art alongside scholarly publications and Ryerson specifies that "scholarship, research, and creative activity" may take "a variety of different forms" and allows for disciplinary differences: "different disciplines may have differing criteria for how these activities are to be evaluated." Nonetheless, although less overtly competitive than the policies from the American institutions we analyzed, the Canadian polices also value recognition by peers, and most still place a premium on traditional publications. For a discipline in formation like writing studies, to be acknowledged by the academy as legitimate it is important to meet the most traditional standards of scholarship, as most of our scholars emphasized. For example, in Schryer's interview she endorsed these standards repeatedly, emphasizing the importance of a research agenda; methodological rigor; and the quality, quantity, and citation rate of publications for scholars in writing studies.

This close look at the concept of presence embodied in promotion and tenure guidelines yields a surprising insight. Of the two propositions, most faculty would identify "publication" as the more fundamental, the primary basis on which they are judged. But it is clear through our ministudy of the policies that what matters most is a scholar's recognition in scholarly networks: publication is not itself the measure of worth, but the means by which a scholar's presence is created and validated in a dynamic, competitive environment. As Collins, 1998 explains:

> The intellectual world is a massive conversation, circulating cultural capital in intermittent face-to-face rituals as well as in writing. What makes one an intellectual is one's attraction to this conversation; to participate in the talk at its "hot center," where the ideas have the greatest sacredness, and if possible to attach one's identity to such ideas so that one's ideas are circulated widely through the conversation, and one's personal reputation with it. (pp. 30–31)

Publication creates presence by attaching a scholar's identity to significant ideas and symbols, distributing them through authorized channels, and opening them to validation as impactful contributions to the field through their history in the literature, which includes the work's original acceptance for publication and, subsequently, published reviews, engagement by other scholars, and citation.

However, as some US reforms and Canadian variations among institutions imply, the same functions can be accomplished by less restrictive means, including alternate forms of communication and a broader base of communities that may be the object of communication and may provide expert judgments. The emphasis on selective genres and approved channels of publication has fossilized a set of practices that conflates the literature of a field with its scholarly conversations and obscures the genuine requirement of "presence" as a basis for valuing scholars.

Since the Canadian scholars we studied in this book (and, more generally, Canadian writing studies as a discipline) are subject to the norms represented in these two propositions, our findings don't refute them as important forces shaping scholars' choices and careers, whether they simply accept them as facts of academic life, advocate them as values, or resist their hegemony. But we do find many ways in which these propositions, especially taken together, and the concept of *presence* they embody, are inadequate to explain the kinds of contributions we observed our Canadian scholars making to writing studies in Canada and beyond.

The first proposition, in its emphasis on recognition, corresponds closely to our own focus on networks and the circulation of ideas through social relations as fundamental to disciplines. But we think that the dynamic meaning of this component of scholarly presence may be obscured through its linkage to publication, which tends to identify it with a static notion of texts as a cumulative repository of "knowledge" that advances the field. Instead, we suggest, the emphasis on being "known" to peers (over publication as an end in itself) actually captures, and ascribes value to, the degree of a scholar's active engagement with the social networks through which ideas flow and debates are conducted. In a competitive framework, what faculties seem to be seeking in candidates for promotion and tenure is centrality in those networks, which, Collins (1998) argues, have only a limited attention space for scholars to shine at the "hot center," where a few significant issues and debates dominate the conversation at the "inner core" (p. 43). This kind of prominence in the conversations of a field is associated with "productivity," which, although identified with numbers of texts produced and published, is actually better understood as the constant generation of symbols and ideas that engage other scholars.

Undeniably, this conception of presence dominates judgments of scholars in the academic rewards system, which are in essence a network's verdict on a scholar's identity as defined by participation in its conversations. Publications are a medium of that conversation, but they also build on (and are surrogates for) an even more basic stream of intellectual exchanges, the face-to-face interchanges that Collins (1998) calls "interaction rituals," for example, conferences and symposia. We argue that, by relying entirely on publications, highly restricted by type and venue, to document participation in and impact on a field, the traditional way of defining presence falls short in several ways.

First, this concept of presence, in its emphasis on visibility in national and international networks, overlooks the local. What is accomplished by a scholar locally and known directly only to those present in an institutional or regional setting can have indirect effects that are, nevertheless, significant and widespread. One example in the US field of rhetoric and composition is the influence of Theodore Baird, whose unique first-year writing course ("English 1–2") was taught to generations of students at Amherst College. According to Varnum (1996), the course involved fifty instructors and six thousand students over thirty years (p. 1). Baird's influence on composition pedagogy was relatively unknown until Varnum (1996) published an archival study of his approach and the teaching tradition it generated among his students who entered the field of composition—for example, William E. Coles. Jr.—and those students' students, in turn, for example David Bartholomae and Joseph Harris. (See Horner, 1994, on Coles's and Bartholomae's shared teaching tradition.) Typically, this impact occurs through embodied others, as they absorb ideas or attitudes and practices and then, as they travel, spread these as seeds in other locations. The impact is quiet, long-term, and often hard to recognize; even though it is felt and impactful—"present"—it may not be widely identified with the scholar who is its source.

Yet, as Derek observed, these scholars in their presence are both emplaced and distributed. In our study, Margaret Procter of the University of Toronto and Dale Jacobs of the University of Windsor exemplified institutional presence that through mentoring and curriculum development connected scholars to the larger field. In establishing writing programs with related, permanent faculty positions, securing funding for contract instructors to attend conferences, and organizing professional development sessions, Procter's institution-focused activities ensured that Canada's largest university would become an active contributor to the field. Unlike Procter's institutional presence, which has strengthened Canadian disciplinary networks, Jacobs's presence at the University of Windsor has contributed to cross-border networks as a result of the many MA students of his who have done doctoral studies in the United States, some of whom have remained (like Dan Richards) and others of whom eventually returned to Canada (like Jay Dolmage).

These examples bring attention to a variety of scholarly roles, besides authorship, whose impact is not accounted for in the traditional definition of presence. We've already pointed to two: the graduate mentor who encourages and prepares future scholars and the teacher-administrator who shapes programs, their teachers, students, and institutions. Other examples are the catalyst, like Aviva Freedman through collaborations, mentorship, and events she organized; and the external consultant, like Louise Phelps at the University of Winnipeg, or reviewer—both roles that have been played by Roger Graves, Anthony Paré, and other Canadian scholars we interviewed. In these roles, ideas are communicated through genres like edited conference volumes and consulting reports and, most significantly, by people who, through personal contact with particular scholars or exposure to scholarly ideas and networks they facilitate, become conduits for ideas and energy, with far-reaching consequences. Many of the scholars we studied exemplify other roles, such as editor, publisher, and organizational leader, which have contributed to forming and sustaining the organizational base for the discipline in Canada.

The examples we've given demonstrate that scholars' ideas and identities are projected into the networks of a discipline along two routes: embodied and textual. The embodied route, in which scholars' influence travels through others' bodies and minds, through direct encounters and through the events and relationships they enable or mediate, is hardly accounted for in a concept of presence tied entirely to publication. It is also harder to "recognize" in terms of a "national or international reputation," so it is indeed a quiet presence that has to be traced back to its source from others' activities and productivity.

Along the textual route, we discovered in our study that the second proposition, which limits texts that "count" to refereed publications in authorized channels, fails to explain the range of kinds of communication by which people accomplish scholarship, influence others' scholarship, and generate presence, from local to national and international. We came to believe that researchers need to examine and appreciate the function of a much larger, diverse range of genres that enter into scholarly discourse, carry ideas and put them into dialogue, shape the discipline itself as a community, and project the identity of scholars who write them. Louise's refigured project (chapter 4) took up this purpose, focusing on scholars' writings in four genres that diverge in different ways from the traditional publication genres used to determine presence in the academic reward system.

As we pursued our interviews, gathered survey data, read CVs and scholars' writings, and read materials from Canadian organizations, we became especially interested in "humble genres" like the organizational newsletter (*Inkshed*) produced by James Reither (chapter 4) and curriculum documents or maps, as exemplified in the University of Winnipeg's curriculum revision (chapter 5), which are circulated but not necessarily published in the traditional sense. Many of these are also what we call "ephemeral" genres, having an inherently limited lifetime reflecting their function and their relation to particular events or moments in time. Documents in these genres are often replaced by updated versions or sequels or not archived at all. Other examples of ephemeral genres include the edited collection that disseminates materials from a conference (Freedman and Pringle, 1980); a research volume that updates the state of affairs at a given moment (Graves, 1994, on writing instruction in Canadian universities; Clary-Lemon's 2009 inventory of Canadian scholarship; or Artemeva's 2006 bibliographical essay on genre); and editions periodically updating a research-based textbook (the third edition of Giltrow, Gooding, Burgoyne, and Sawatsky's *Academic Writing: An Introduction*, 2014). These become historical as time passes. Today, many ephemeral genres, such as blogs and listserv exchanges, are born digital or are digitalized, where they become linked to myriad other documents. Because our study was skewed to established scholars, it only minimally represents the newest, tech-savvy generation, whose networks, habits of communication, and online presence through digital genres and digital distribution of ideas and symbols have hardly been scratched in this study.

A final lesson emerged from this re-examination of presence. An unexamined assumption of the traditional concept of presence is that what defines a "contribution to the discipline" is advancement of its knowledge base through active participation in its central disputes and major research projects. From this perspective, the discipline has a hierarchical organization, essentially a star system, in which scholars compete for attention, influence, and hence reputation. The two propositions that govern academic valuations of scholars accurately capture this vital aspect of scholarship as it is actually practiced. However, that conception doesn't capture some of the important features of disciplines as distributed social networks—in particular, the need for scholars to create, extend, and sustain the networks themselves. That work includes achieving a critical mass of nodes for sustainability, reproducing the network with new members, keeping them in communication, and providing an organizational base (for example, journals and presses) to keep them afloat. We would argue that many of the roles we identified other than author, and genres other than traditional publications, are absolutely essential for networks to form and thrive, never more so than when a new discipline is developing. These kinds of contributions are vital to our study of Canadian writing studies as an emerging field.

Interdependencies

We formulated the concept of *cross-border interdependencies* early on in our joint project as an alternative to prevailing ideas about Canadian writing studies in its historical relationship to American rhetoric and composition, posing a false choice between mere dependence and total autonomy. The concept of cross-border interdependencies has remained a robust, central feature of our study, but it has also become more complex and multi-dimensional in its application. Briefly, the borders crossed have become international and more than geographical, and the meaning of *interdependencies* has come to exceed our original notion of a two-way relationship between Canadian writing studies and US rhetoric and composition through their respective social networks.

Our project set out to push back on the common impression, dating from the rise of Canadian writing studies during the 1980s, that it is derivative from and dependent on US rhetoric and composition, without reverting to the opposing claims of its autonomy and difference (reflecting the long history in the Canadian academy of rejecting American composition as a teaching model and discipline). In our original application of the concept, we thought of it mostly in terms of a two-way flow of people, ideas, and publications between the Canadian and US communities, imagining and visualizing the relationship especially in embodied terms: mentorship and sponsorship; co-presence in graduate programs, conferences, seminars, and workplaces; and movement of individuals back and forth across a permeable border. This understanding was amply supported by our data, but it was quickly complicated by the discovery from surveys and interviews that the interdependencies of Canadian writing scholars and of the discipline, internally and externally, are far more complex. First, we found that from the very beginning Canadian scholarship about writing had multinational sources and connections, as evidenced in the 1979 Ottawa Conference (see chapter 4), particularly between Canada and the Commonwealth nations. These international relationships have continued to broaden as writing studies itself spread to more countries and took form as an international, interdisciplinary field, recently formalized as the International Society for the Advancement of Writing Research or ISAWR. (See CompPile International Writing Studies-Comp FAQ for a list of other international organizations relating to multidisciplinary studies of writing and rhetoric.) For example, North American rhetorical genre studies grew up in dialogue with its linguistically oriented counterparts in Great Britain and Australia (Schryer, 2011) and now engages with genre scholars worldwide (Bawarshi and Rieff, 2010). We also documented shifting orientations of some scholars from national to transnational, global audiences, collaborators, and publication channels as international writing studies developed (see chapter 3).

Beyond these geographically defined interdependencies, we discerned in the work of Canadian writing scholars a broader pattern of border crossing in various contexts not defined by geography. This insight led us to redefine interdependencies broadly as a kind of reciprocity between people, ideas, and social institutions across different types of borders—geographical, disciplinary (both inter- and intra-disciplinary), academic, professional. Witness, for example, the cross-disciplinary work of scholars like Schryer, Lingard, Artemeva, Paré, and Giltrow, or the Canadian focus on relations between academic learning and learning in the workplace (Dias, Freedman, Medway, and Paré, 1999).

Ultimately, we came to see intellectual interdependencies as a general feature of networked disciplinarity, supporting our original hypothesis that ideas arise and flow through intellectual networks that connect scholars, not only to one another, but to widening networks of human and non-human actors. This idea has been developed in depth by Valsiner and van der Veer (2000) and van der Veer and Yasnitsky (2011), who argue that to understand how ideas develop one must examine them in relation to social networks and in their cultural-historical context. In an article on the work of Vygotsky and his "circle," van der Veer and Yasnitsky (2011) explain how one might pursue a cultural-historical approach at four levels of analysis:

> We fully endorse the proposal to consider the "interdependency of ideas" in their historical development that in a most general sense encompasses the four levels of (1) individual knowledge construction by a scholar, (2) interpersonal communication between individuals [as] scholars occupying specific social positions, (3) pursuing their interests in accordance with disciplinary agendas of specific fields of knowledge and branches of science, and, finally, (4) positioned within the framework of a specific society and its multiple institutions (Valsiner and van der Veer, 2000). (van der Veer and Yasnitsky, 2011, p. 489)

The above citation is from Valsiner and van der Veer's earlier book, *The Social Mind: Construction of the Idea* (2000), in which the authors "try to make sense of a threefold relation:—social institutions, scientists, nature—of the object of the given science" (p. 10). Intellectual interdependencies arise when individuals construct or transform knowledge (reflecting their uniqueness as historical, situated persons) and aim it at particular persons through a dialogic communication process (Valsiner and van der Veer, pp. 10–13). While fully crediting the creativity of scientists (individually and in collaboration), Valsiner and van der Veer conclude from their studies that intellectual interdependency is not just a function of the individual scholar and his or her circle: it involves layered networks of participants: "not just scientists but also their grandmothers, their doctoral students, research assistants, or other laypersons, social institutions (universities, research institutes, popular media, governmental and private agencies), and scientific institutional categories called 'disciplines'" (p. 20). This conclusion leads Valsiner and van der Veer to propose the four-level analysis referred to above, in order to capture the dialogic construction of knowledge as it appears at each level and understand how different forces at different levels influence or constrain scholarly work. Dialogues at these levels include:

1. intrapersonal dialogue (internal "voices" in a Bakhtinian sense) and interpersonal dialogue with texts or persons, through which the individual scholar interacts with other scholars

2. "extrapersonal dialogues" among scholars who "are in some intellectual 'kinship relation' with each other," based on their respective social roles and the differential power these entail

3. dialogues at a meta-level, in which scholars relate their work and their discipline to other disciplines, based on their disciplines' relative social-institutional positions

4. dialogues between "the sciences" (any scholarly discipline) and "society"—other social actors, stakeholders, and institutions. (pp. 34–36)

The method of four-level analysis suggested by Valsiner and van der Veer seems particularly well-adapted to analyzing the kinds of interdependencies studied in this book, and serves as a complement to the networked methods we have practiced here.

Networked Methods

After enacting the *networked methodological approach* we articulated in the introduction, here we revisit the four definitional properties of networks introduced by Spinuzzi (2008)—heterogeneity, multiply linked, transformative, and black boxed (pp. 198–99)—focusing in particular on a deepened sense of the usefulness of this approach, greater intricacy in our use of explicitly network-based terms and concepts, and noted aspects of innovation as well as limitations for other research. That is, as we reflect upon the contributions and limitations of this methodology, posing again the central research question on the nature of Canada-US interdependencies for writing studies, we consider some of the ways it enacts and extends Spinuzzi's definitional concepts, acting upon them or performing them in the context of this study. Toward this end, the etymology of *methods* as a Greek blend of *meta-* (above, beyond) and *-hodos* (ways, paths) is pertinent because our networked methodological approach names an intentional, coordinated research design throughout that we were, as four collaborators, both setting out on distinctive pathways and orchestrating across these for complementarity and convergence. In revisiting Spinuzzi's definitional properties of networks, we also note the distinctive contribution made by our approach for its purposeful and self-conscious attention to patterned phenomena across multiple scales and at multiple scopes, or what we discuss in the following section as a *multi-scale/multi-scopic* quality of the study.

To extend and further contextualize the applicability of Spinuzzi's definitional bases for networks, we consider the networked methodological approach enacted across this study to be *heterogeneous* insofar as the methods we selected were chosen for the ways they were complementary and also distinctive; that is, for the ways they were *not the same*. Heterogeneity conveys about these methods that their mixing proved generative, that as a progressive series of studies, we were able to reinterpret images and ideas and thereby weave more thickly the relationships among the methods. Had we undertaken the studies independently, the set of methods would have been comparably more discrete and segmented. While the study focused on an assortment of related phenomena, systematic inquiries at one scale (e.g., the survey) elicited and refined emerging questions at another scale (e.g., curricular and programmatic case study). We consider these generative properties of the method-set to extend beyond the study as we've carried it out (to due and reasonable limits); that is, heterogeneity in a networked methodological approach acknowledges the epistemological value *among purposefully mixed methods*, seeking to connect and integrate phases of the study while simultaneously priming edges for yet further extension, self-consciously noting that the methods selected and featured here, while adequate, also position possibilities for studies that would update, extend, and expand upon this work.

A networked methodological approach is *multiply linked* for the ways we have, as a team of four researchers, oscillated between autonomy and close collaboration at all phases of the project's development, making explicit connections between the narrowed scope of differing phases of the study and returns to the broader research question—a locus—to which each of the phases responds. Spinuzzi (2008) writes that heterogeneity "is achieved through weaving and splicing," processes that are also reflected in the networked methodological approach due to the ways we solidified and strengthened dimensions of the study (weaved) while branching out exploringly and provisionally in others (spliced). One example of a splice can be found in the gradual narrowing, near the end of the second chapter, from the emplaced and distributed geographies of career networks generally, to the specific case of Dale Jacobs, which splits from the survey- and map-based studies only to resurface with greater detail in the chapter drawing upon interviews. Weaving, in this approach, is evident in the internal referentiality from each chapter to other chapters. This inward referentiality attests to multiple links that were both planned and also serendipitously discovered as we developed and circulated sections for input from each other. The multiply linked quality of a networked methodological approach presumes a coordinated reconciliation of myriad heterogeneous movements (i.e., multiple methods that mix, branch, and weave), which were a function of revising the research design iteratively and as was informed by discoveries as the study unfolded.

The networked methodological approach has also been *transformative* both in the sense of discordance among "represent[ations] and rerepresent[ations]," as Spinuzzi (2008) characterizes this quality (p. 199), and also in the sense of emergent insights and new, expanded terminology for studying complex and distributed disciplinary activity, particularly across international contexts. In this first sense of transformation, we noticed as we worked that accounts generated via specific methods became clearer as we sought coherent names for their internal logics. For example, Mueller's person-geolocation emphasis is similar to Clary-Lemon's focus on person-locale, and yet these respective studies of locations need a slightly different vocabulary to differentiate the very different scopes. Similarly, whereas Williams's interviews accord with interpersonal relationships, thereby bearing resemblance to the zoomed-in analysis of career geographies as well as to the series of case studies theorized by Phelps, each of these sections became more nuanced and refined in relationship to the accounts that came before and after it *(tolerance for small volatilities internal to the study)*. A networked methodological approach is internally transformative, as methods-driven accounts lend shape and focus to the other in-progress accounts. But we also consider this suite of methods outwardly transformative for its modeling an adaptive study whose coordinations, both during data-gathering phases and while planning and drafting, drew upon and extended ideas and insights initiated elsewhere in the study. This highlights the second sense of a networked methodological approach as transformative, for example, in our deliberate choice to adopt *interdependence* as a conceptual frame as opposed to polarity models that have pitted Canada and US disciplinary emergence as disparate, distinct, and in some instances disharmonious (particularly around the sponsorship of first-year writing requirements). As such, the transformative quality of a networked methodological approach addresses the study's capacity for change, refinement, and differentiation while the project was developing.

Finally, the networked methodological approach underscored throughout this study is *black-boxed*, woven through with positive qualities that accumulated over time and in negotiation, compromise, and consensus as segments of the study crystallized. Our working together to develop the survey questions, for instance, recalls a gradual and tacit dimension of the approach whose inner workings are obscured here and nowhere recorded with the precision that would make them accessible to readers. According to Spinuzzi (2008), networks are black-boxed in that they operate with a "quintessentially woven" quality that can downplay or altogether obscure the depth and dimension of "historically developing activities." We consider this black-boxed quality of a networked methodological approach as an occasion to acknowledge a gradual receding from view many of the exploratory build-ups, negotiations, reconciliations, and compromises that characterize past studies of professionalized US-Canada relationships and activities.

While, in effect, we have drawn upon Spinuzzi's definitional work as a basis for our methodologizing networks, and while these four qualities have provided our networked methodological approach with a useful heuristic, this study's performance of a networked methodological approach has contributed a multi-scale, multi-scopic method that we consider to be promising for comparable studies of continuing disciplinary emergence and formation, particularly across international contexts.

FUTURE DIRECTIONS FOR RESEARCH AND ACTION

We maintain that an additive strength of a networked methodological approach to Spinuzzi's (2008) definitional framework of networks is its multi-scale, multi-scopic consideration in thinking through research. Our project, which emphasizes nodal relationships of person-geolocation, person-person, person-text, and person-locale has allowed us to underscore both the local, narrow view, and a broadened, "wide" perspective in a coordinated way around a similar object of study—cross-border interdependencies. We maintain that such an approach is particularly well suited to study both diffuse texts (Brummett, 1994, p. 80) and diffuse knowledge problems valued in humanistic disciplines (Peck MacDonald; 1994, p.22). Relations of geography, people, genres, and institutional locations are routed in both textually and embodied ways; to that end, we argue that this approach is well suited to examine, as Lefebvre (1974/1991) contends,

> not texts but texture. We already know that a texture is made up of a usually rather large space covered by networks or webs; monuments constitute the strong points, nexuses, or anchors of such webs. The actions of social practice are expressible but not explicable through discourse; they are, precisely, acted—and not read (p. 222).

In tracing identities, roles, and rituals of nationally-bound considerations of how disciplinarity has been constructed through distant and close methods, a multi-scaled, multi-scopic approach to examining the texture of interdependent constructions of a discipline is one that offers far more than any one method or one view alone can encompass. To that end, we suggest that this approach is particularly well-suited to future research that:

- involves layered networks of participants and materialities (as augmented by the work of Valsiner and van der Veer, 2000; see also Latour, 1993);
- unites research methods and scopes across a sustained researchable question with a focus on scale, demonstrating the range of how combined methods provide complementary data to answer the question;
- focuses on interconnections between methods by attention to both historic and developmental incongruities (splicing) and po-

litical and rhetorical circulation (weaving) (see Spinuzzi, 2008, pp. 198–99);
- engages multiple researchers in mapping social actions across place, genres, and people, particularly in relationship to intellectual genealogies (see Crane, *Invisible Colleges*, 1972; Wagner, *The New Invisible Colleges*, 2008; Miller, Licastro & Belli, "The roots of an academic genealogy," 2016).

Further, we see our work as a product of intentional research design that may benefit other scholars working within the frame of networks that may help move beyond dyadic relationship models (i.e., person-person) to see how texture operates within and among various sites and actors. To some degree, we see this work as a fitting complement to edited collections that either have sought to engage with the field in geolocative-professional ways concerning one site (i.e., Rice and O'Gorman, 2008) or seek to engage in uniting multiply-sited and international traditions of writing practices (Bazerman, Krut, Lunsford, McLeod, Null, Rogers & Stansell, 2010). We see our work similarly complementary to works-in-progress that call to locate the field in terms of institutional practices (i.e., Strain and Potter, *MA Programs at Work*, 2016) or locales that invoke embodied ways of knowing *about* (i.e., Boyle and Rice, *Inventing Texas, 2016*). In taking on a self-reflective networked methodological approach, however, what we offer to augment current scholarship taking on emplaced research is also a call to researchers to work collaboratively around their research questions and methods in order to facilitate the kind of knowledge that emerges as research tools and data are shared, taken up in new ways, and applied differently depending on scale.

Finally, we see our work as a particularly valuable heuristic for those in the field interested in focused research activities around writing and disciplinarity in both established hubs (as in archival looks into and microhistories of one institution or department) and emergent sites (new writing centers, partnerships, and collaborations). We also see value for those who seek to examine surfacing practices, events, and ephemera that uniquely situate developing notions of writing studies at specific provincial, state, national, or international levels, or that might unite one-time approaches or projects toward a more cohesive understanding of visible and invisible relationships among them—to help, as Latour (1993) suggests, bring networks out of hiding (pp. 139).

As we noted in our introduction, visibility and agency have been key themes in the formation of Canadian writing studies. An important and unanticipated outcome of this project has been fostering a greater sense of connection between and among participants in this project and ourselves; through interviews in particular, we have facilitated and in some cases established relationships across scholarly sites in Canada and the US by undertaking a multi-scaled, multi-scopic approach to examining cross-border interdependencies. Yet we recognize that one project, limited in scope, reveals much about what still needs to be done; we therefore offer suggestions, above and beyond what we have said about future directions in terms of networked methods, for both follow-up studies and actions to strengthen disciplinary networks in Canadian writing studies.

First, our study suggests the need to revisit nationally oriented disciplinary histories in both Canada and the United States, which mostly overlook the cross-border connections that have informed our discipline, including the contributions of Canadian scholars to the American and international fields as well as the contributions of scholars from the United States and elsewhere to the Canadian field. In rethinking our disciplinary history in Canada, the distributed nature of scholars in different types of roles (both faculty and staff) and locations means that future studies would do well to take as broad a view of the field as possible. In studying Canadian scholarly networks, we found that scholarship which from the perspective of the American and international fields would be considered part of writing studies is seen as peripheral or outright excluded from writing studies in Canada as a result of the Canadian field's closed networks. Examples include scholarship in English Education (including that of Mary Maguire, Marian Crowhurst, and Frank Smith); psychology/cognitive studies (Marlene Scardamalia and Carl Bereiter, along with the many departments and centres that address cognition, language and literacy, and curriculum); linguistics/ELL (formerly called ESL or English as a second language, which was recognized in early Canadian work, like the 1979 Ottawa conference); communication studies; and rhetoric. Canadian scholarship in many of these fields is published in international writing studies volumes, yet few of these scholars have a presence in the disciplinary networks we examined. Identifying relevant scholarship in these and other related fields that share common interests and methods with ours would enrich the Canadian discipline and also help us forge strategic alliances that could strengthen the discipline in Canada.

Secondly, although our study focused on disciplinary networks relating to Canadian writing studies, our methods might be fruitfully applied both to other disciplines and other national contexts. For example, studying scholarly networks in other countries where writing studies or other fields are also in formation could help identify strategies to strengthen disciplinary identity in national academies in Canada and elsewhere.

Third, in mapping cross-border networks between Canadian and American scholars, this project has enhanced our understanding of Canadian disciplinary networks in writing studies as a whole. A logical follow-up project would be to examine how specific ideas (for example, the concept of genre or the concern with agency) have travelled through disciplinary networks and have been developed and elaborated in Canadian scholarship. Tracing the circulation of key ideas would enrich our understanding of scholarly networks as well as disciplinary formation. An important related project would involve examining how digital culture is changing scholarly networks by altering the media through which ideas circulate and relationships develop. For instance, in reflecting on our study, we wonder, would it have been different had more of the scholars we interviewed been younger and graduate students? To what extent are face-to-face relations and co-presence in workplaces still important, compared to relations facilitated by technology? How are digital and social media changing the speed of idea diffusion and the circulation of research and writing? Understanding the role of digital media in scholarly networks and identity formation would be a particularly important project in the context of Canadian writing studies where scholars are so widely distributed both geographically and in terms of institutional location.

Given the dispersed and decentred nature of writing studies scholars in Canada, a further suggestion for future study would be to conduct a current inventory of writing studies faculty positions in Canada, perhaps starting with but not limited to permanent positions. Knowing where scholars are located—in terms of region, province, and city as well as unit and institution (e.g., writing centre, writing or communication department), along with the nature of their appointment and role (e.g., staff or faculty, teaching- or research-stream, WPA, etc.), would enhance our understanding of the disciplinary status of writing studies in Canada. The linguistic and cultural divide between English and French Canada means that our discipline is almost entirely separate from and ignorant of the scholarship of our Francophone colleagues, a gap that future studies would also do well to fill. Lastly, an important related study would involve tracking Canadians from the field who are studying or working in the United States. Such data would not only be useful for future disciplinary histories, but also help suggest strategies for building the discipline in Canada.

A sense of disciplinary belonging was important for the scholars we studied who forged connections through texts (through both reading and publishing), organizations and events (such as seminars and conferences), and relationships (such as peer and cross-generational mentoring and collaborations). Conversely, for individuals and institutions alike, we found that isolation inhibits disciplinary identity. While Canadian scholars present their work in scholarly fora—national and international conferences, well-read and circulated journals in rhetoric and composition—they often do so without a sense of connection to how other Canadian colleagues' receive or circulate this work. Similarly, while hubs and centers of activity do important disciplinary work such as hosting disciplinary conferences and journals, they don't necessarily do this in ways that strengthen disciplinary connections within Canada. For example, the University of Winnipeg's hosting of the Western States Rhetoric and Literacy Conference in 2012 and housing and editing of the journal, *Composition Studies*, from 2010–2013 strengthened the institution's connection to the American discipline, but not to other Canadian scholars, institutions or organizations.

One of the first tasks must therefore be to connect institutional hubs or circles and thereby change what are mostly closed circles to open ones. A key way to do this would be to create an alliance of societies (an idea first proposed by Phelps, 2014) that would link the currently fragmented writing studies and rhetoric organizations in Canada (such as the Canadian Association for the Study of Discourse and Writing, The Canadian Society for the Study of Rhetoric, the Canadian Writing Centres Association, and Inkshed/the Canadian Association for the Study of Language and Learning) under a common umbrella group. Such an alliance could also help bridge the gap between writing studies scholarship relating to postsecondary contexts and that addressing K–12. According to Phelps, such an alliance would work best if representatives from each organizations could act as liaisons and participate in each other's conferences. Members would be encouraged to serve as evaluators on tenure and promotion files from Canadian institutions and thereby help strengthen disciplinary identity.

A central alliance could also use and improve Canadian funding structures. Unlike in the United States, scholars in many Canadian institutions are expected to secure research funding from the federal government. However, without a specific category for writing studies, securing grant funding will continue to be difficult for both graduate students and faculty and result in some scholars leaving writing studies for disciplines where they can better access research dollars and full-time academic appointments. Nonetheless, the SSHRC Connection Program, which seeks to "support the building of reciprocal relationships among social sciences and humanities researchers, and between social sciences and humanities researchers and those in a position to either co-create or use research knowledge" (2016), has been used to fund large-scale, multi-institutional research projects such as WAUC (Writing Across the Undergraduate Curriculum). We see potential in this program to facilitate connections between and among work being done, for example, at the University of Winnipeg, Carleton University, the University of Alberta, and the University of Toronto, York University, and Brock University. We also see potential in using embodied networks to strengthen Canadian writing studies as a discipline by having scholars act as SSHRC external assessors on writing studies projects and by listing other Canadian writing studies scholars as assessors when applying for funding.

In addition to the issue of research funding, the Canadian field needs to think critically about its textual representation. Many scholars struggled to find a wide enough audience for their work in Canadian publications. Artemeva mentioned the need for Canadian writing studies organizations such as CASDW and CASLL to develop higher international or even North American profiles to extend the reach of their journals. This view was shared by scholars like Brent who have felt compelled to publish in American rather than Canadian journals: "With the exception of Inkshed . . . everything I've published has been in the American journals and that's got a lot to do with reputation and the ability to have your writing noticed" (D. Brent, interview, December 12, 2013). The two journals primarily connected to the Canadian field are all but limping along: *CJSDW/Technostyle* has had long lapses in publication, and is currently unavailable through the CASDW website or from its prior hosted site at the University of the Fraser Valley, and the *CASLL/Inkshed Newsletter* was last issued in May 2015. Given the growing interest in and support for a wide range of approaches and topics that categorize Canadian scholarship in the field and its growing hubs of scholarly interest, it is time to establish a Canadian journal in writing studies that capitalizes on available talent on both editorial and institutional levels. A scholarly hub that would devote time, funding, and faculty expertise to such an endeavour would be an effective way to circulate and connect such disparate programs, people, and centres at a distance, and energize the Canadian field.

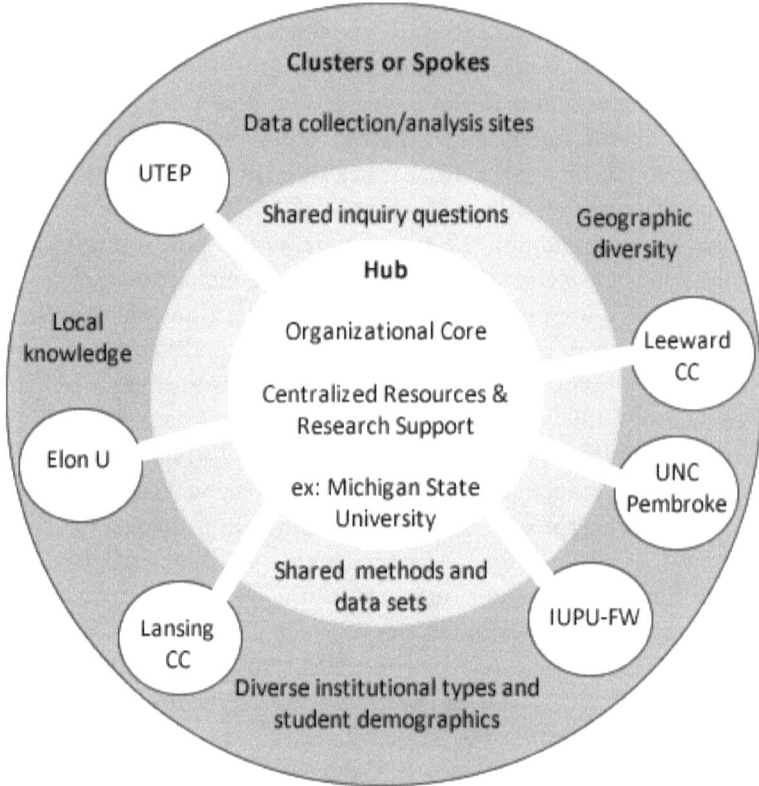

Figure 17. Hub and cluster model.

A potential model for networking Canadian writing scholars is the "hub and cluster" approach adopted by the Revisualizing Composition research group, centered at Michigan State University (Brunk-Chavez, Pigg, Grabill, Rosinski, & Moore, unpublished ms.): "In this research model, the 'hub' acts as a centralized location, or core, for organizing interactions and materials, while the 'clusters' or 'spokes' engage in various kinds of data collection and analysis, depending upon expertise, availability, and location" (p. 7). Their project enabled "local, contextualized, and yet systematic research" intended to develop and communicate to multiple stakeholders a broader understanding of "how writing is practiced and learned across geographical, institutional, and cultural contexts" (p. 3). In the Revisualizing Composition project, six diverse institutions (from high-research institutions to community colleges) joined with Michigan State (the hub) to produce collaboratively a large body of data about student writing. At the hub, a Research I institution, scholars had access to expert help with programming and statistics, as well as the resources to sustain the project, its records, and data over time while making these resources available to scholars at the distributed institutions. At the same time, individual researchers at each institution could make use of this scholarly network and its resources to conduct research adapted to their own institutions and purposes. Figure 1 shows this hub and spoke model, which could be instantiated in Canada around the hubs we discovered, particularly those with established graduate programs such as Carleton University.

We also see potential for building and shaping new programs in Canadian graduate studies. While establishing new programs is always challenging, recent successes suggest that programmatic development is possible: Brock's new Honours BA in Writing, Rhetoric, and Discourse; Ryerson's Master's in professional communication; and Carleton's Master's and PhD in Applied Linguistics and Discourse Studies are just a few examples. In fostering hubs of activity that work collaboratively across the region, we see potential in figuring out how to combine resources at separate institutions in order to jointly develop MA and PhD programs in writing studies across a range of provinces (for example, a combined "Western and Central Provinces" PhD inclusive of expertise in British Columbia, Alberta, Manitoba, and Ontario). However, even if additional Canadian doctoral programs are not established, an alliance of Canadian writing societies could develop a mentoring program that would enable Canadian students studying in the United States to stay connected to the Canadian field, an idea first suggested by Phelps (2014) and corroborated by some of the more junior scholars we interviewed. Using social media to connect with graduate students studying abroad and resurrecting the Canadian Caucus of the 4 C's (an ideal venue for face-to-face meetings with the many Canadians studying and working in the United States) are two ways to connect students not only with potential mentors but also with their peers. Although modest, we believe these strategies could strength Canadian disciplinary networks and the discipline as a whole and could potentially apply to other fields and other countries.

References

Artemeva, N. (2006). Approaches to learning genres: A bibliographical essay. In N. Artemeva and A. Freedman (Eds.), *Rhetorical genre studies and beyond* (pp. 9–99). Winnipeg, MB: Inkshed.

Bawarshi, A., and M.J. Rieff. (2010). *Genre: An introduction to history, theory, research, and pedagogy*. West Lafayette, IN: Parlor Press/WAC Clearinghouse.

Bazerman, C., Krut, R., Lunsford, K., McLeod, S., Null, S., Rogers, P. & Stansell, A. (Eds.). (2010). *Traditions of writing research*. New York: Routledge.

Boyer, Ernest. (1990). *Scholarship reconsidered: Priorities of the professoriate*. Princeton, NJ: Carnegie Foundation for the Advancement of Teaching.

Boyer, Ernest. (1996). The scholarship of engagement. *Journal of Public Outreach*, 1(1), 11–20.

Boyle, C., & Rice, J. E. (2016). CFP: Inventing Texas. Retrieved from http://caseyboyle.net/inventing-texas/

Brummett, B. (1994). *Rhetoric and popular culture*. New York: St. Martins.

Brunk-Chavez, B., Pigg, S., Grail, J., Rosinski, P., & Moore, J. (2013). Building, maintaining, communicating and publishing through a research network: Behind the scenes of the Revisualizing Composition Research Network. Unpublished manuscript.

Clary-Lemon, J. (2009). Shifting traditions: Writing research in Canada. *American Review of Canadian Studies*, 39(2), 94–111.

Collins, Randall. (1998). *The sociology of philosophies: A global theory of intellectual change*. Cambridge, MA: Belknap.

Crane, D. (1972). *Invisible colleges: Diffusion of knowledge in scientific communities*. Chicago: University of Chicago Press.

Dias, P., Freedman, A., Medway, P., & Paré, A. (1999). *Worlds apart: Acting and writing in academic and workplace contexts*. Mahwah, NJ: Erlbaum.

Freedman, A., & Pringle, I. (Eds.). (1980). *Reinventing the rhetorical tradition*. Conway, AK: L & S Books (CCTE).

Giltrow, J., Gooding, R., Burgoyne, D., & Sawatsky, M. (2014). *Academic writing: An introduction* (3rd ed.). Toronto: Broadview.

Graves, R. (1994). *Writing instruction in Canadian universities*. Winnipeg, MB: Inkshed.

Horner, B. (1992). Resisting traditions in composing composition. *Journal of Advanced Composition*, 14(2), 495–519.

Latour, B. (1993). *We have never been modern*. Cambridge, MA: Harvard University Press.

Lefebvre, H. (1991). *The production of space.* (D. Nicholson-Smith, Trans.). Oxford: Blackwell. (Original work published 1974).

Macdonald, S. P. (1994). *Professional academic writing in the humanities and social sciences.* Carbondale: Southern Illinois University Press.

Miller, B., Licastro, A., & Belli, J. (2016, January 1). *The roots of an academic genealogy: Composing the Writing Studies Tree.* Retrieved January 26, 2016, from http://kairos.technorhetoric.net/20.2/topoi/miller-et-al/acknowledgements.html

Mueller, D. (2012). Grasping composition by its long tail: What graphs can tell us about the field's changing shape. *CCC, 64*(1), 195–223.

Phelps, L. W. (2014). The historical formation of academic identities: Rhetoric and composition, discourse and writing. Keynote address, Canadian Association for the Study of Discourse and Writing. Waterloo, ON. (2012). *Canadian Journal for Studies in Discourse and Writing*, 25(1), 3–25. Retrieved from http://journals.sfu.ca/cjsdw/index.php/cjsdw/article/view/37/22

Prior, P. A. (1998). *Writing/Disciplinarity: A sociohistoric account of literate activity in the academy.* Mahwah, NJ: Erlbaum.

Rice, J., & O'Gorman, M. (2008). *New media/New methods.* West Lafayette, IN: Parlor Press.

Roozen, K., Prior, P., Woodard, R., & Kline, S. (2015). The transformative potential of laminating trajectories of pedagogical practice: Three teachers' developing practices and identities. In T. Lillis, K. Harrington, M. Lea, and S. Mitchell (Eds.), *Working with academic literacies: Research, theory, and design* (pp. 205–216). Fort Collins, CO: WAC Clearinghouse/Parlor Press.

Schryer, C. (2011). Investigating texts in their social contexts: The promise and perils of rhetorical genre studies. In D. Starke-Meyerring, A. Pare, N. Artemeva, M. Horne, & L. Yousoubova (Eds.), *Writing in knowledge societies* (pp. 31–52). Fort Collins, CO: WAC Clearinghouse/Parlor Press.

Simmons, M. (2015). The no. 1 predictor of career success according to network science. *Forbes.* Retrieved from http://bit.ly/2iPXdZu.

Social Science and Humanities Research Council. (2016). Connection program. Retrieved from http://www.sshrc-crsh.gc.ca/funding-financement/umbrella_programs-programme_cadre/connection-connexion-eng.aspx

Spinuzzi, C. (2008). *Network: Theorizing knowledge work in telecommunications.* New York: Cambridge University Press.

Strain, M., & Potter, R (2016). *MBA programs at work.* Manuscript in preparation.

Valsiner, J., & van der Veer, R. (2000). *The social mind: Construction of the idea.* Cambridge, UK: Cambridge University Press.

Van der Veer, R., & Yasnitsky, A. (2011). Vygotsky in English: What still needs to be done. *Integrative Psychological and Behavioral Science, 45,* 475–493.

Varnum, R. (1996). *Fencing with words: A history of writing instruction at Amherst College during the era of Theodore Baird (1938–1966)*. Urbana, IL: National Council of Teachers of English.

Wagner, C. (2008). *The new invisible college: Science for development*. Washington, DC: Brookings Institution Press.

White, J. (2010). Authoring the self: Scholarly identity in performative times. *Creative approaches to research, 3*(1), 1–2.

7 Afterword

Andrea A. Lunsford

What a delightful and instructive walk down memory lane it has been to read the essays that comprise this volume, which deserves a wide and deep reading by those in the field of writing studies today.

Flash back with me to the fall of 1976. I was working on my dissertation at Ohio State (a study of basic writing, directed by Edward P. J. Corbett and inspired by Mina Shaughnessy and Geneva Smitherman) and deeply into job market machinations. It was not a good year for English in general, and rhetoric and writing studies was a relatively new kid on the block. But to my surprise, I garnered a number of MLA interviews and steamed off to New York to try my luck. A child of the south who had not been west of the Mississippi River, I was especially excited by a job at the University of British Columbia—all the way to the west coast and in Canada to boot. That interview turned out to be a meeting with one person, the then Chair of the Department, Robert Jordan, whom I sat next to on a bar stool while he asked me questions. "So much for that!" To my surprise, I received an offer for the position, and so after finishing my degree, I packed up and headed out on what for me was a great adventure: I thought often of Huck "lighting out for the territories."

Over the summer I read as much about Canadian history as I could, pored over maps of Canada and BC, and began what would become a lifelong love affair with northwest coast art, especially that produced by the Haida people.

During my first year or two, I had a crash course in writing and rhetoric in Canada, which was not generally recognized as a field of study. Thanks to Rick Coe, I got some good guidance, though he left to go to Simon Fraser very soon after my arrival. I learned that in the course most students were required to take, writing was assigned but not taught; the focus was primarily on literature. But the students were wonderful: I still remember a young man from the prairies who started out his essay on Hamlet with "Shakespeare is to drama what Labatt is to beer." And the Chinese student who told me that my class was "the best he had taken at UBC," then let me know that he meant it was the best 101 class he had taken (it was his sixth try at passing the course . . .) This student, and many, many like him, were bright and eager to learn: they worked hard and succeeded. And while I enjoyed most of my colleagues and made lasting friends with many, I still remember an older colleague railing against the high percentage of Asian students: "My people [Scots-Irish] had to work for generations before we could go to University; they should do the same."

Still, as this volume details, this was the late seventies, and there were stirrings of interest in bringing everyone into the university as well as in writing and rhetoric across Canada. So I began to make connections with scholars at other Universities, and when Aviva Freedman and Ian Pringle advertised their 1979 Learning to Write conference, I was at the head of the line to register. Later, Janet Emig, who gave a magnificent keynote, said that the conference was "the single most electric professional meeting" she ever attended, and I think most people there felt the same way. We listened to Howard Rosen, Jimmy Britton, Emig—and lots of others—and came away ready to light a candle in our own backyards.

Over the ten years I was at UBC, I developed undergraduate and graduate courses in rhetoric and writing—and I discovered and refined my decades-long interest in collaboration and collaborative writing. Most of the inspiration came from the undergraduate students I taught in a year-long seminar: we worked in groups for the entire year and in the annual evaluations, students *always* identified this collaborative experience as the most effective and meaningful part of the course. Along the way I met and taught wonderful students, including Doug Brent, Will Garrett-Petts, Judy Segal, Susan Stevenson, Amanda Goldrick-Jones, and others—and I was able to lure Nan Johnson north to join us in our work.

In the following years I got to know Pat Diaz and Anthony Pare, Russell Hunt and Jim Reither, Phyllis Artiss, and of course the indomitable Aviva Freedman and her colleagues at Carleton. The first Inkshed conference, held in 1984 in Fredericton, introduced me to many other scholar/teachers of writing studies, and I continued to attend that groundbreaking conference for years. (I also began following the efforts at the University of Winnipeg to establish a writing program/writing centre there.) By the time I left UBC to join the faculty at Ohio State (1986–87), I felt deeply interconnected with this Canadian community of scholars, a community that influenced me and shaped the path of my research for the rest of my career. (And at Ohio State I got to work with other fabulous Canadian students, including Roger and Heather Graves, Andrea Williams, and Tania Smith.)

So I have savored every page of this book, from the detailed overview provided by the introduction to Mueller's amazingly instructive mappings, Williams's exploration of the work and careers of fourteen border-crossing scholars, Phelps's eloquent pairing of four scholars and four genres, and Clary-Lemon's insightful case study of Winnipeg's resilient and resourceful writing program/department. I especially admire the way the authors of this volume begin by taking the long view, looking at interconnections, intersections, and interdisciplinarities from afar and then moving, very carefully, ever closer to individual scholars and their careers, and then broadening out again in the last chapter to look at institutional setting. Taken together, these essays provide a close encounter with writing studies in the context of Canadian culture, a provocative encounter that will surely inspire other collaborative cross-discipline and cross-border efforts to map, explore, and chart out field of study.

The focus on scholarly identity is particularly instructive: throughout the volume, such identity emerges as "multiple, layered, and fluid (244). And, as the authors show, this identity changes over time, through its networked associations. The metaphor of the network permeates the book, emerging as a powerful image of how careers begin, develop, and expand through local, professional, disciplinary, and cross-border connections. But some of these networks are closed:

> The prominence of closed networks in Canada is attributable to both geographical (the vast distances between universities) and institutional factors: the disparate locations of writing studies scholars in Canadian universities—dispersed across writing centres, WAC programs, and departments of communication, education, English, language and linguistics, and psychology, to faculties of engineering and independent

writing programs—make creating a common disciplinary identity difficult. (213)

Isolated networks, along with the loose and disparate nature of writing studies in Canada (where scholars may be attached to many different programs, schools, or departments) can make the field less visible and thus less able to build a "core" identity. Yet writing studies has a growing presence in Canada—as well as what Louise Phelps calls a "quiet" but persistent presence south of the border.

The networks so thoroughly examined here reveal deep connections that the authors identify as *intellectual interdependencies*, a term they originally used to characterize relationships between Canadian and US writing studies scholars. As their work proceeded, however, these researchers found that such interdependencies reach far beyond the borders of the US and Canada. Indeed, one of the most exciting findings of this study to me is the degree to which such interdependencies are now clearly international, global in scope. And while the authors of this volume conclude on a cautious note in terms of the need to solidify the writing/rhetoric presence throughout Canada and in terms of all the work that still needs to be done to make that possible—I finished the book feeling quite encouraged. Thanks to the networking of writing/rhetoric associations and specifically to Chuck Bazerman and the Writing and Research across Borders conferences, we now have a loose but worldwide network of writing scholars and writing organizations. I heard about this study, in fact, at the 2014 WRAB conference outside Paris—and many of us from North America will no doubt be gathering at the next WRAB conference, in Bogota in February 2017. In addition, the cross-border collaborations with European scholars are growing exponentially, as are connections with scholars in Africa, Mexico, Australia, and elsewhere. Such interconnections and interdependencies are greatly enhanced and enabled by digital technologies that will help us convene virtually to further collaborative research.

Finally, the development and growth of new programs, centres, institutes, and departments that focus on writing and rhetorical studies suggest that our discipline is in productive flux, expanding its bases, hubs, and locations. At the same time, traditional disciplines are fragmenting and fracturing, leading to new possibilities and alliances. In such a time, stepping back to take a very close look at where we have been and are located and at the networks that bring us together or sometimes separate us seems prescient indeed. *Exploring Cross-Border*

Interdependencies in Canadian Writing Studies provides just such a judicious, insightful stepping back, along with a vision for the future and a clear, articulated method for ongoing research. I look forward to following the work of this group for years to come—as a devoted and self-proclaimed honorary Canadian!

Index

Page numbers followed by *f* indicate figures and those followed by *t* indicate tables.

4Cs. *see* Conference on College Composition and Communication (4Cs/CCCC)

A
Academic Writing: An Introduction (Giltrow, Gooding, Burgoyne & Sawatsky), 161
Ackerman, John, 46–47, 70, 131
Across the Disciplines (Williams & Rodrigue), 132
Actor-Network Theory (ANT), 7
Aereality: On the World from Above (Fox), 20
Alred, Gerald, 63
American scholarship, 2–3, 52, 126–130, 142
Artemeva, Natasha, 58, 62, 71, 173
Artiss, Phyllis, 113–114, 180
Association for Teachers of Technical Writing (ATTW), 54–55, 56
autobiography. *see* literacy autobiography

B
backwards design, 136–141
Baird, Theodore, 158
Bartholomae, David, 51, 158
Bawarshi, Anis, 133
Bazerman, Chuck, 17, 182
Becker, Alton, 128
Bell, Stephanie, 76
Bereiter, Carl, 75
Bergmann, Linda, 133
black-boxed networked methods, 9, 11–12, 167
Bootstraps (Villaneuva), 112
Bourdieu, P., 108
Brazil, James, 128
Brent, Doug, 3, 52–53, 58–59, 70, 76, 173, 180
Bridwell-Bowles, Lillian, 129
British scholarship, 109–111, 127
Britton, James, 61, 91, 92, 109, 111, 127, 180
Brooke, Robert, 43
Burgess, Tony, 91, 111, 127
Burkean principle of identification and division, 65
Burton, L., 123

C
Cambridge, Darren, 113
Canada: late arrival of disciplinarity in, 12–13; physical geography of, 21–22
Canadian Association for Teachers of Technical Writing (CATTW), 10, 59–60
Canadian Association for the Study of Discourse and Writing (CASDW) conference, 3, 13, 59–60, 102, 149
Canadian Association for the Study of Language and Learning

185

186 *Index*

(CASLL), 58. *see also* Inkshed/
   CASSL
Canadian Council of Teachers of
   English, 93, 109
Canadian Institutes for Health
   Research, 13
*Canadian Journal for Studies in
   Discourse and Writing* (CJSDW),
   30–31, 173
Canadian Special Interest Group,
   56
career footprint, 35
Carleton Colloquium on Rethinking Genre conference, 87
Carleton University, 85–87
Carleton-McGill group, 61–64,
   77, 150
Carnegie Mellon seminar, 56
CASDW. *see* Canadian Association
   for the Study of Discourse and
   Writing (CASDW) conference
case-study of cross-border networks: curricular redesign and,
   134–143; institutional reinvention and, 130–134; intrinsic vs.
   instrumental, 123–125; synchronic mentoring and, 125–130
CASLL (Canadian Association
   for the Study of Language and
   Learning). *see* Canadian Association for the Study of Language
   and Learning (CASLL)
CATTW. *see* Canadian Association
   for Teachers of Technical Writing
   (CATTW)
CCCC. *see* Conference on College
   Composition and Communication (4Cs/CCCC)
Centre for Academic Writing
   (York), 124, 125–127
Child Abuse & Neglect (Mian et
   al.), 104
child abuse research, 102–105

citation practices, 105
City University of New York
   (CUNY), 3
CJSDW. *see Canadian Journal for
   Studies in Discourse and Writing*
   (CJSDW)
Clary-Lemon, Jennifer, 1–18,
   22–23, 56, 123–143, 148–176,
   181
Coe, Richard, 51–52, 56, 72, 76,
   179
co-edited conference volumes,
   85–87, 92–97
Coles, William E., Jr., 158
collaborative multidisciplinary
   research articles, 89–90, 102–108
College English, 88, 109
Collins, Randall, 4, 82, 114–115,
   157, 158
*The Composing Process of Twelfth
   Graders* (Emig), 128
*Composing Research: A Contextualist
   Paradigm for Rhetoric and Composition* (Johanek), 123
composition, 64–65, 158. *see also*
   writing studies
Composition as a Human Science
   (Phelps), 131–132
Composition Forum, 123
Composition in Four Keys (Wiley,
   Gleason & Phelps), 132
Composition Studies, 172
Conference on College Composition and Communication (4Cs/
   CCCC): Canadians at, 98; as
   disciplinary gateway, 50–56; on
   Fulbright collaboration, 2–3, 4;
   supporting scholarly identity,
   149; on Writing Studies Tree, 3
conferences: 4Cs, 50–56; CASDW,
   59–60; as disciplinary gateways/
   hubs, 50–60; edited collections
   based on, 87; Inkshed/CASSL,

56–59; interpersonal interactions and, 82; involvement with, 28–29; vital role of, 77
Congress of the Humanities and Social Sciences, 60
The Contemporary Writing Curriculum (Huff & Kline), 127, 128
Contextual Literacy (Schyrer & Steven), 89, 97, 106
contrastive differentiation, 22–23
Corbett, Edward P. J., 51, 179
Cross-Border Collaboration in Charting a Department's Future, 2–3
cross-border networks: case-study approach to, 123–125; curricular redesign and, 134–143; development of, 1–6; institutional reinvention and, 130–134; role of, 12–18; synchronic mentoring and, 125–130
Crossing Borders: Sites of Discursive Negotiation in Healthcare Practice, 103
Crow, A., 123
CUNY. *see* City University of New York (CUNY)
curricular redesign, 134–143, 135f, 138f, 140f–141f
curriculum vitae (CV), 32–33, 33f

D
Dartmouth Conference (1966), 109, 111
Deen, Nazru, 95–96
definitional scholarship, of essences/differentiation/shapefinding, 22–23
Dewey, John, 76
diachronic career paths, 36–37, 37f, 39f
dialogic construction of knowledge, 164

Dialogue in a Major Key, 96
Dias, Pat, 62, 180
digital culture, 171
DiPardo, Anne, 17
Disciplinarity and Transfer (Bergmann & Zepernick), 133
disciplinary gateways, 50–60
disciplinary identity: changing/evolving, 71–77; cross-border relations and, 16–17; in decentralization of writing studies, 14–15; intellectual interdependencies in, 163; late arrival in Canada, 12–14; local conditions influencing, 15; sense of belonging in, 172
discourse and writing, 3. *see also* writing studies
disidentification, 65–66
Dively, Ronda, 133, 138
Dixon, John, 91, 109
Doctoral Consortium in Rhetoric and Composition, 34
Dolmage, Jay, 41f, 42–43, 53–54, 66–67
Donovan, Timothy, 128
Downs, Doug, 133
Duke University, 154
Dyehouse, Jeremiah, 136

E
Eight Approaches to Teaching Composition (Donovan & McClelland), 128
Elbow, Peter, 128
embodied route, of scholars' influence, 160
Emig, Janet, 61, 76, 94, 97, 109, 128, 129, 180
ephemeral genres, 160–161
Epistemic Newsletter; or, Inkshed as a Mode of Learning (Reither), 101

epistemic newsletters, 87–89, 97–102
Errors and Expectations (Shaughnessy), 128
essences, 22–23
expressivism, 65, 111
extrapersonal dialogues, 164

F
Faigley, Lester, 98
A Field of Dreams (O'Neill, Crow & Burton), 123–124
fixed essences, 22–23
Fleckenstein, K., 17
Flower, Linda, 52
Fourth International Conference on the Teaching of English, 95–96
Fox, Janna, 62
Fox, William I., 20
Freedman, Aviva, 50, 58, 61–63, 85–87, 89, 92–97, 159, 180
Freisinger, Randal, 128
From Incomes to Outcomes (Rounsaville, Goldberg & Bawarshi), 133
Fulbright Report, 130–134, 141–142
Fulbright Specialist Scholar, 1–18, 131
Fulwiler, Toby, 128
funding, for research, 12–13, 173

G
Garrett-Petts, 180
genre: conferences on, 87, 96, 117; relationship to presence, 11, 84, 152–161; scholar-genre pairing, 11, 83–85
Genre in the New Rhetoric (Freedman & Medway), 96
genre studies. see rhetorical genre studies

genre theory, 96, 104–108
genres, academic: ephemeral, 160–161; humble, 89, 115, 160; narrative, 112; undervalued by traditional norms, 84-85, 115–116, 159–161
geography: associated with career activity, 31–32, 32f, 32t; of Canadian publishing activity, 26–27, 26f–27f; physical and social, 21–22
geoJSON, 36–37, 37f
geolocative survey data, 34–43, 35f–39f, 41f
Giberson, G., 124
Giltrow, Janet, 63
Gilyard, Keith, 112
Gleason, B., 132
Gochenour, P. H., 8
Goldrick-Jones, Amanda, 180
graduate studies, 175
Graves, Donald, 61
Graves, Heather, 75, 124, 181
Graves, Roger, 52, 55, 57, 58, 74–75, 124, 159, 181
Grogan, Jared, 41f, 42–43

H
Hairston, Maxine, 98
Hamilton, Sharon J., 90–91, 108–114
Harris, Joseph, 158
Harris, R. S., 124
Hedge, Stephanie, 41f, 42–43
hermeneutical inquiry, 84–85, 87
heterogeneous networks, 8, 165
heuristic thinking, 125
Horne, M. E., 56
hub and cluster model, 174–175, 174f
Hubert, Henry, 124
hubs. *see* institutional hubs
Huff, Roland, 126–130, 131

humble genres, 89, 115, 160
Hunt, Russell, 56, 59, 88, 97–98, 102, 180

I
indexical aereality, 21, 34, 43
Inkshed Press, 30–31, 101
Inkshed/CASSL: as disciplinary gateway, 56–59; founding/vital role of, 88–89; lapses in publication, 173; supporting scholarly identity, 149
inkshedding, 56, 58, 65, 97
institutional hubs: alliance of, 172; Carleton-McGill group, 61–64; as closed networks, 150–151; fostering interpersonal interactions, 82; introduction to, 60–61; support of evolving identities, 77–78; supporting scholarly identity, 150; University of Toronto group, 67–69; University of Windsor group, 64–67
intellectual interdependencies, 163–164
interaction rituals, 158
interactive maps, of career activity, 38–41, 39f, 41f
interdependencies, 161–164, 182
International Society for the Advancement of Writing Research (ISAWR), 162
interviews on scholarly networks: conferences as gateways, 50–60; institutional context shaping identity, 60–69; introduction to, 46–50; role of scholarly communities, 77–78; shifting scholarly identities, 69–77
intrapersonal dialogues, 164

J
Jacobs, Dale, 41–43, 41f, 54, 55, 64–67, 159, 166

Jarratt, Susan, 133
Johanek, C., 9–10, 123
Johnson, Nan, 51–52, 56, 59, 124, 180
Johnson-Eilola, Johndan, 63
Jordan, Robert, 179

K
Kearns, J., 125–126
Kersnowski, Alice, 126
Kersnowski, Frank, 126
Keywords in Writing Studies (Swarts), 7
Kiernan, Julie, 41f, 42–43
Kinneavy, James, 98, 127, 128
Kirsch, Gesa, 17
Kline, Charles, 127
Kline, S., 149
Koch, Carl, 128

L
Language Connections: Writing and Reading Across the Curriculum, 128
Larson, Richard, 126
Latour, B., 168
Lauer, Janice, 56, 75, 79, 89, 91, 93, 108, 112, 116-117, 123, 125, 127, 128, 132
Law, John, 17
Learning and Teaching Genre (Freedman & Medway), 96
Learning to Write conference, 87, 88, 92, 180
Learning to Write: First Language/Second Language (Pringle, Freedman, & Yalden), 95
Lefebvre, H., 168
Lewiecki-Wilson, Cynthia, 54
Liminal Practice in a Maturing Writing Department (Phelps), 134
Lingard, Lorelei, 71–74, 89–90, 103, 149

190 *Index*

listservs, 29–30, 100–102, 161. *see also* Inkshed/CASSL
literacy autobiography, 90–91, 108–114
Lunsford, Andrea, 42, 51–52, 56, 58, 129, 179–183

M
MacDonald, B., 13
Macrorie, Ken, 128
Maguire, Mary, 95–96
mapping career activity: diachronic, 36–37, 37f; mentorship networks and, 40–43; online interactive versions, 38–40, 39f; from survey data, 34–35, 35f; synchronic, 35–36, 36f; two logics for, 38, 38f
Martin, Nancy, 127
Martins, David, 124
Master's Degree Consortium of Writing Studies Specialists, 34, 131
McClelland, Ben W., 128
McGill University, 61–63
McIntyre, Michael, 126
McLeod, Alex, 127
McTighe, Jay, 136
medical education research, 71–74
Medway, Pete, 62, 96
Mehler, Josh, 41f, 42–43
mentorship networks: importance of, 52; institutional, 62, 67; mapping of, 40–43; synchronic, 125–130
meta-level dialogues, 164
Meyers, Paul T., 127
Michigan State University, 174–175
Microanalysis and the Construction of the Social (Revel), 81–115
Miles, Libby, 136
Miller, Ben, 3

Miller, Carolyn, 62
Miller, Susan, 51
Moffett, James, 127, 128
Moriarity, T., 124
Morris, Janine, 41f, 42–43
Mueller, Derek, 1–18, 20–43, 46, 127, 132, 148–176, 181
multiply linked networks, 8–9, 165–166
multi-scaled data, 9–10, 17, 165
Mutt Genres (Wardle), 133
My Name's Not Susie (Hamilton), 91, 112, 113

N
National Research Council, 131
Natural Sciences and Engineering Council of Canada, 13
Nelms, Gerald, 133, 138
Network (Spinuzzi), 8–9
network sense, 123
networked methodological approach: to Canadian-US writing studies, 6–12; features of, 164–167; as multi-scale/multi-scopic, 168–169
networked self, 113
networks: characteristics of, 8–10; community support for, 77–78; cross-disciplinary, 68; environmental influences on, 15–16; intellectual interdependencies in, 163; interviews on scholarly. *see* interviews on scholarly networks; mentorship, 40–43; role of cross-border, 12–18
New Critical methods, 86
newsletters, epistemic, 87–89, 97–102
Nodalism (Gochenour), 8
Nold, Ellen, 51

O
O'Hara, J. Martin, 95

Ohio State University, 179–181
O'Neill, P., 123
Ong, Walter, 76
Ontario Institute for Studies in Education, 68
organizational newsletters, 87–89, 97–102, 160
organizations, involvement with, 28
Outcomes Tracking Map, 138–139, 140f
outcomes-based process, 136–142

P
Papper, C., 17
Paré, Anthony, 52, 53, 56, 57, 59, 62, 63, 70–71, 129, 159, 180
Paziuk, Greg, 41f, 42–43
Pedagogical Memory and the Transferability of Writing Knowledge (Jarratt et al.), 133
Perceived Roadblocks to Transferring Knowledge from First-Year Composition to Writing-Intensive Major Courses (Nelms & Dively), 133
Perl, Sondra, 3
The Personal Narrative (Haroian-Guerin), 112
Phelps, Louise Wetherbee, 1–18, 46–47, 61, 70, 81–115, 131–134, 148–176, 166, 172–173, 175, 181, 182
Pike, Kenneth, 128
Porter, James, 63
Porter, Tara, 34
presence, scholarly, 152–161
Present Tense online journal, 30–31
Pre/Text journal, 88
Pringle, Ian, 62, 86–87, 92–97, 180
Prior, P. A., 149
Procter, Margaret, 13, 67–69, 114, 159

promotion and tenure, 152–161
psychology, writing studies and, 76
publishing activity: geography of, 26–27, 26f–27f; involvement with, 30–31; scholarly presence and, 153–158
Purdue Seminar. see Summer Rhetoric Seminar (Rhetoric Seminar/Purdue Seminar)
Purdue University, 63

R
Rapley, T. J., 49
recognition by peers, 153–154
Reiff, Mary Jo, 133
Reinventing the Rhetorical Tradition (Freedman & Pringle), 87, 92, 93
Reither, James, 56, 59, 87–89, 97–102, 160, 180
reputation, 154–155
research: collaborative multidisciplinary, 89–90, 102–108; diversity, 17; funding for, 12–13, 173; future directions for, 168–176
"Rethinking Genre" Colloquium, 96
Revel, Jacques, 81–115
Revisualizing Composition project, 175
Reynolds, Nedra, 136
rhetoric, 2, 3, 70, 71–74. see also writing studies
Rhetoric, Writing, and Communications department (University of Winnipeg): curricular redesign and, 134–143, 135f, 138f, 140f–141f; institutional reinvention and, 130–134; instrumental case study of, 124–125; synchronic mentoring at, 125–130
Rhetoric: Discovery and Change (Young, Becker & Pike), 128

Rhetoric Seminar. *see* Summer Rhetoric Seminar (Rhetoric Seminar/Purdue Seminar)
rhetorical genre studies: development of, 107–108; Canadian/ North American, 2, 48, 62–64, 69, 96, 117; linked to international genre studies community, 62–64, 69, 77, 117, 162; scholars in, 62-63, 86–90, 117
rhetorician-in-residence model, 70
Richards, Daniel, 41f, 42–43, 53, 54–55, 66–67, 113, 114
Rickly, R., 17
Ridolfo, Jim, 34
Ritchie, Joy, 43
Rodrigue, Tanya, 132
Ronald, Kate, 43, 67
Roozen, K., 149
Rosen, Harold, 109, 110, 111, 127, 180
Ryerson University, 156

S
Scardamalia, Marlene, 75
scholar-genre pairing: co-edited conference volumes, 85–87, 92–97; collaborative multidisciplinary research articles, 89–90, 102–108; goals/methods, 83–85; introduction to, 81–83; literacy autobiography, 90–91, 108–114; organizational newsletters, 87–89, 97–102
scholarly communities. *see also* institutional hubs: changing, 69–77; role of, 77–78
scholarly identity: facets of, 148–152; interdependencies, 161–164; networked methods, 164–167; as presence, 152–161

Schryer, Catherine, 57, 59–60, 63, 67–69, 71, 89–90, 95, 97, 102–108, 156
Segal, Judy, 52, 129, 180
Selfe, Cynthia, 112
shape-finding, definitional scholarship of, 22–23
Shaughnessy, Mina, 128, 179
Sheese, Ron, 75–77, 124
Shifting Tradition: Writing Research in Canada (Clary-Lemon), 22
Simmons, M., 151
Smart, Graham, 58, 62–63, 71
Smith, Tania, 52, 56–57, 102, 181
Smitherman, Geneva, 179
The Social Mind: Construction of the Idea (Valsiner & van der Veer), 163
Social Network Analysis (SNA), 6–7
social praxeology, 108
Social Sciences and Humanities Research Council (SSHRC), 13, 75, 131, 173
The Sociology of Philosophies (Randall), 4
Spafford, Marlee, 103
Sperling, Melanie, 17
Spinuzzi, C., 8–9, 17, 164–167
splicing, of networks, 8–9, 166
St. Thomas University, 87–88
Stake, Robert E., 124–125
Steven, Laurence, 106
Stevenson, Susan, 180
Strategies for Teaching the Composition Process (Koch & Brazil), 128
Straw, Stan, 56
Street, Brian, 77
Summer Rhetoric Seminar (Rhetoric Seminar/Purdue Seminar), 56, 75, 79, 89, 91, 93, 109, 116–117, 118

survey, of Canadian scholars: on geographic reach of publishing activity, 26–27, 26f–27f; locations associated with career, 31–32, 32f, 32t; mapping of locations, 34–43, 35f–39f, 41f; on membership in organizations/conferences/listservs/publishing, 28–31; questions for, 24–26
Survey of Earned Doctorates, 131
Swarts, J., 7
Swedish National Agency for Education, 113
symphonic self, 113
synchronic career paths, 35–36, 36f, 39f
synchronic mentoring, 125–130
Syracuse University, 155–156

T
Teaching, Writing, Learning (Pringle & Freedman), 95
Teaching about Writing, Righting Misconceptions (Downs & Wardle), 133
Teaching with Writing (Fulwiler), 128
Technical Communication Quarterly, 105
Technostyle, 62, 173
Telling Writing (Macrorie), 128
territoire (institutional context) and terroire (identity), 60–69
textual route, of scholars' influence, 160
Thaiss, Chris, 34, 124
A Theory of Discourse (Kinneavy), 128
Tirrell, Jeremy, 34
Tracing Discursive Resources (Reiff & Bawarshi), 133
transformative networks, 9, 166–167

transnational networks, 3–12
Transnational Writing Program Administration (Martins), 124
Turner, B., 125–126

U
Understanding Transfer (Wardle), 133
The Universe of Discourse (Moffett), 128
University of Alberta, 55
University of British Columbia (UBC), 51, 155, 179–181
University of Rhode Island, 136–137
University of Toronto, 60, 155, 156
University of Toronto group, 67–69, 77, 150
University of Waterloo, 155
University of Windsor, 41–42, 77
University of Windsor group, 64–67
University of Winnipeg, 1, 124–125. *see also* Rhetoric, Writing, and Communications department (University of Winnipeg)
university research funding, 12–13, 173

V
Valsiner, J., 163–164
van der Veer, R., 163–164
Varnum, R., 158
Villanueva, Victor, 112
Visibility Project, 1, 131
Voices of the Self (Gilyard), 112

W
Wardle, Elizabeth, 133
weaving, of networks, 8, 166
Western States Rhetoric and Literacy Conference (2012), 172

What Are We Becoming (Giberson & Moriarity), 124
What Exactly Is This Major? (Tweedie, Courtney & Wolff), 133
White, J., 149
Wiggins, Grant, 136
Wiley, M., 132
Wilkinson, Andrew, 61, 92–93
Williams, A. L., 13
Williams, Andrea, 1–18, 46–79, 114, 132, 148–176, 181
Winterowd, Ross, 56
Woodard, R., 149
WPA: Writing Program Administration (Kearns & Turner), 124
WRAB. *see* Writing Research across Borders (WRAB) international conference
Writing Across the Disciplines: Research Into Practice (Young & Fulwiler), 128
Writing Across the Undergraduate Curriculum (WAUC), 173
Writing and Knowing: Toward Redefining the Writing Process (Reither), 88
writing centres, 67–69
writing pedagogy, 92, 95, 109–111, 129
Writing Program Coursebook, 129
Writing Programs Worldwide: Profiles of Academic Writing in Many Places (Thaiss et al.), 124
Writing Research across Borders (WRAB) international conference, 3, 4, 182
writing studies: Canadian attitude towards, 57; Canadian journal in, 173–174; Canadian-US interdependence, 3–6; community support for, 77–78; disciplinary status of, 171; environmental influences on, 15–16; funding barriers, 12–13, 173; geographical factors in, 14; graduate studies in, 175; hub and cluster model, 174–175, 174f; lack of visibility, 12; marginalization of, 13; networked methodological approach to, 6–12; range of roles/identities in, 74–77; as supplemental, 70–71
Writing Studies Tree, 3
Writing Without Teachers (Elbow), 128
Written Communication (Schryer et al.), 103, 105
Wyoming Conference, 56, 88, 98

Y
Yalden, Janice, 95
Yasnitsky, A, 163
York University, 75, 124, 156
Young, Art, 128
Young, Richard, 128

Z
Zebroski, James, 92
Zepernick, Janet, 133

About the Authors

Jennifer Clary-Lemon is Associate Professor in Rhetoric, Writing, and Communications at the University of Winnipeg, and past editor of the journal *Composition Studies*. Her research interests include writing and location, disciplinarity, critical discourse studies, and research methodologies. Her recent publications may be found in *Discourse and Society*, *The American Review of Canadian Studies*, *Composition Forum*, *Oral History Forum d'histoire orale*, *enculturation*, and *College Composition and Communication*.

Andrea Abernethy Lunsford is the Louise Hewlett Nixon Professor of English, Emerita, at Stanford University. The Director of Stanford's Program in Writing and Rhetoric from 2000 to 2013, she has designed and taught courses in writing history and theory, rhetoric, literacy studies, and women's writing and is the editor, author or co-author of twenty two books, including *Essays on Classical Rhetoric and Modern Discourse; Singular Texts/Plural Authors; Reclaiming Rhetorica; Everything's an Argument; The Everyday Writer; Writing Matters; The Sage Handbook of Rhetorical Studies; Writing Together;* and *Everyone's an Author*. A long-time member of the Bread Loaf School of English faculty, she is currently at work on *The Norton Anthology of Rhetoric and Writing*.

Derek Mueller is Associate Professor of Written Communication and Director of the First-year Writing Program at Eastern Michigan University, where he regularly teaches courses in visual rhetorics, writing pedagogy, and research methods. His research attends to questions concerning networked writing practices, rhetorical aspects of computational methods (e.g., data mining and visualization), and discipliniographies or field narratives related to rhetoric and composition/writing studies. Mueller's work has been published in *Kairos, Enculturation, Comput-*

ers and Composition, *Present Tense*, *Composition Forum*, and *JAC*. For more, visit derekmueller.net.

Louise Wetherbee Phelps is Emeritus Professor of Writing and Rhetoric at Syracuse University, where she was founding director of an independent writing department with a PhD in Composition and Cultural Rhetoric. Currently she teaches at Old Dominion University in the English Department's interdisciplinary doctoral program and consults for writing programs and departments of English and writing/rhetoric. Her publications include *Composition as a Human Science,* two co-edited volumes, and numerous essays and chapters on topics in rhetoric & composition/writing studies including disciplinarity, doctoral education, writing program administration, and Canadian writing studies. In the profession, she led the Visibility Project to gain recognition for the discipline and recently originated a cross-generational initiative at CCCC.

Andrea Williams is Associate Professor of Writing Instruction in the Faculty of Arts & Science at the University of Toronto where she leads a Writing-Across-the-Curriculum Program, WIT. She is vice-president of the Canadian Association for the Study of Discourse and Writing (CASDW) and her research interests include writing across the curriculum, writing assessment, and faculty and TA development. She recently coedited a special issue of *Across the Disciplines* on the role of Teaching Assistants in Writing-Across-the-Curriculum and she has also published in *Teaching and Learning Inquiry* and the *Journal of Chemical Education* and coauthored a book chapter in *A Minefield of Dreams: Triumphs and Travails of Independent Writing Programs.*

www.ingramcontent.com/pod-product-compliance
Lightning Source LLC
Chambersburg PA
CBHW032214230426
43672CB00011B/2557